TOGETHER *with* GOD

365
SERIES

TOGETHER *with* GOD
STORIES OF
FAITH

DAVE BRANON
EDITOR

Discovery House.
from Our Daily Bread Ministries

TOGETHER *with* GOD

Who does not love a good story?

Sometimes when I am standing in front of my class at Cornerstone University, where I teach as an adjunct professor, I will sense that I am losing my students' attention during a stellar lecture on coordinating conjunctions. So, I simply pause for a second and say something like, "The other day when I was at McDonald's . . ." Suddenly, every eye is on me, and I have these young adults' attention because they think they are about to hear a story.

And we all know how the whole atmosphere changes during the Sunday morning service when the pastor starts in on one of his tales. It's story time, and everyone is instantly invigorated and attentive.

Ever since *Our Daily Bread* came into existence back in 1956, one of the components that helped people remain interested in what we as writers have had to say was the stories we told. Of course, the real backbone of this devotional book is the biblical truth that underlies every article—without that, nothing we say would matter any more than a click-bait article on the internet.

But the stories are important because they help the reader see that *Our Daily Bread* is addressing real-life issues and using actual people as examples on the way to conveying the timeless truths and the eternal realities of God's Word.

In this collection of *Our Daily Bread* articles, there are primarily three types of stories included to help us understand things like the gospel of salvation, living for Jesus in a sometimes ungodly world, and dedicating our lives to honoring and glorifying our heavenly Father.

One type of story is what we might call the "God's special agent" story—stories about people like missionaries, pastors, and others who have been called and equipped by God for specific ministries. Another type of story we could designate the "daily living" story—stories that happen to regular people like you and me—Christians trying to make a difference in the real world as we seek to live for God. And there are Bible stories—perhaps a retelling of an incident we have all read about in God's Book.

As we read these stories, we are reminded again how God works in our lives—whether missionaries in a faraway land, regular churchgoers in the throes of regular day-to-day living, or the heroes of the faith enshrined in Scripture.

The articles in *Together with God: Stories of Faith* are meant to encourage you, challenge you, surprise you, and comfort you as you make your way through the story of your own life. They are stories that demonstrate how faith in action makes a huge difference in how we live. We are excited that you are joining us for this yearlong storytime, and we pray that this book will encourage you each day as you see how God's story intertwines with yours.

Dave Branon, editor and *Our Daily Bread* writer

A Lesson in Patience

PSALM 37:1–9

Be still before the LORD and wait patiently for him; do not fret when people succeed in their ways, when they carry out their wicked schemes.

PSALM 37:7

It may take only a year for a construction crew to put up a tall building, but God takes a century to grow a sturdy oak. So too, the Lord may seem to be working slowly to accomplish His purposes in our lives, but His grand designs take time.

The great New England preacher Phillips Brooks (1835–1893) was noted for his poise and quiet manner. At times, however, even he suffered moments of frustration and irritability. One day a friend saw him pacing the floor like a caged lion. "What's the trouble, Dr. Brooks?" asked the friend. "The trouble is that I am in a hurry," said Brooks, "but God isn't." Haven't we often felt the same?

Jonathan Goforth (1859–1936), a missionary to China, was convinced that the city of Changte should be his field of spiritual labor. But his faith was severely tested as he was mobbed and threatened when visiting the city. Finally, after six frustrating years, Goforth was granted permission to begin his work. Within three days of reaching Changte he had received no less than thirty-five offers of land, among them the very site he had chosen earlier as the most ideal spot for the mission.

Wait patiently for the Lord (Psalm 37:7). If you do, you'll find that He will give you what's best—in His time!

HENRY BOSCH

God is never in a hurry, but He is always on time.

Mary's Bible

PSALM 119:97–104

I delight in your commands because I love them.
PSALM 119:47

When Mary Jones was ten years old, she began saving money for something special she wanted to buy. She babysat, tended neighbors' gardens, and sold eggs from her own chickens. By the time she was sixteen, she had accumulated enough money to get what she so desperately wanted.

Was it a new car? A fresh wardrobe? A new cell phone? No, Mary Jones was sixteen in the year 1800, and what she had been saving for was a Bible. But there was no place to buy one in the tiny Welsh village where she lived, so she walked to Bala—twenty-five miles away. There Rev. Thomas Charles had one Bible left to sell, and after some convincing, Mary talked him into selling it to her.

Because of Mary's hunger for the Bible, Rev. Charles and others began discussing the need of making the Scriptures more readily available. The British and Foreign Bible Society was started, and during the next one hundred years it distributed more than two hundred million copies of God's Word worldwide. To Mary, nothing was more important than the Bible, and her persistence paid huge spiritual dividends.

Do we treasure God's Word as much? How often do we even walk across the room to pick up the Bible and read it?

Lord, help us to cherish your Word.

DAVE BRANON

Many people store the Bible on the shelf instead of in their heart.

I See You

PSALM 121

The LORD will watch over your coming and going both now and forevermore.
PSALM 121:8

When Xavier was two, he darted into one aisle after another in a small shoe store. Hiding behind stacks of shoeboxes, he giggled when my husband, Alan, said, "I see you."

Moments later, I saw Alan dash frantically from aisle to aisle, calling Xavier's name. We raced to the front of the store. Our child, still laughing, ran toward the open door leading to a busy street. Within seconds, Alan scooped him up. We embraced as I thanked God, sobbed, and kissed Xavier's chubby cheeks.

A year before I became pregnant with Xavier, I'd lost our first child during the pregnancy. When God blessed us with our son, I became a fearful parent. Our shoe store experience proved I wouldn't always be able to see or protect our child. But I discovered peace as I learned to turn to my only sure source of help—God—when I struggled with worry and fear.

Our heavenly Father never takes His eyes off His children (Psalm 121:1–4). While we can't prevent trials, heartache, or loss, we can live with confident faith, relying on an ever-present Helper and Protector who watches over us (vv. 5–8).

We may encounter days when we feel lost and helpless. We may also feel powerless when we can't shield loved ones. But we can trust that our all-knowing God never loses sight of us—His precious and beloved children.

XOCHITL DIXON

God always keeps His eye on His children.

Listeners and Doers

JAMES 1:22–27

*Religion that God our Father accepts as pure and faultless is this:
to look after orphans and widows in their distress and to keep oneself
from being polluted by the world.*

JAMES 1:27

The phone rang in the night for my husband, a minister. One of the prayer warriors in our church, a woman in her seventies who lived alone, was being taken to the hospital. She was so ill that she was no longer eating or drinking, nor could she see or walk. Not knowing if she would live or die, we asked God for His help and mercy, feeling particularly concerned for her welfare. The church sprang into action with a round-the-clock schedule of visitors who not only ministered to her but showed Christian love to the other patients, visitors, and medical staff.

James's letter to the early Jewish Christians encouraged the church to care for the needy. James wanted the believers to go beyond just listening to the Word of God and to put their beliefs into action (1:22–25). By citing the need to care for orphans and widows (v. 27), he named a vulnerable group, for in the ancient world the family would have been responsible for their care.

How do we respond to those who are at risk in our church and community? Do we see caring for the widows and orphans as a vital part of the exercise of our faith? May God open our eyes to the opportunities to serve people in need everywhere.

AMY BOUCHER PYE

True faith demands not only our words, but our actions.

An Athlete Dying Young

ISAIAH 55:6–11

"For my thoughts are not your thoughts, neither are your ways my ways,"
declares the LORD.

ISAIAH 55:8

No one ever played college basketball like Pete Maravich. He was a ball-handling wizard and a scoring machine who broke nearly every major college scoring record. Ten years as an NBA star and millions of dollars later, he retired—unhappy and empty.

But that's not the end of the story. In 1983, Pete surrendered his life to Christ. For the next four years, his driving passion was to share with others the wonderful joy he had found in Jesus. Then, early in 1988, he died suddenly of heart failure. He was only forty years old. Why did God take him so soon?

Why didn't He allow Pete to continue leading people to Christ with his hard-hitting testimony? Perhaps Pete's autopsy report holds the answer. Doctors discovered that Pete had a congenital heart problem that should have prevented him from playing basketball. Suddenly, we could get just a glimpse of God's marvelous ways. He didn't take Pete early; He preserved his life until he had accepted Christ and made his testimony known.

When death claims a believer who is still in the prime of life, we wonder why. That's natural. But our wondering should never lead to abandoning the reality of God's goodness or wisdom. He remains trustworthy. His ways are higher, and so much better, than our ways.

DAVE BRANON

**The more clearly we see God's sovereignty, the less perplexed
we are by man's calamities.**

The Secret of Strength

HEBREWS 11:32–40

That is why, for Christ's sake, I delight in weaknesses, in insults, in hardships, in persecutions, in difficulties. For when I am weak, then I am strong.

2 CORINTHIANS 12:10

If there's anything we tend to despise, it's weakness. Strength, on the other hand, is regarded as praiseworthy. But the apostle Paul made a puzzling statement: "When I am weak, then I am strong" (2 Corinthians 12:10).

How could he say that? He discovered that when his own strength gave out and his personal resources of energy and wisdom were depleted, he had to rely completely on God's inexhaustible grace. When he did that, his experience was like that of a traveler in the desert who tosses aside his bone-dry canteen because he has come to an oasis with an abundant supply of crystal-pure water.

Hudson Taylor (1832–1905), founder of the China Inland Mission (now OMF International), knew the secret of strength through weakness. Complimented once by a friend on the impact of the mission, Hudson answered, "It seemed to me that God looked over the whole world to find a man who was weak enough to do His work, and when He at last found me, He said, 'He is weak enough—he'll do.' All God's giants have been weak men who did great things for God because they reckoned on His being with them."

Have we learned the secret of abandoning our utterly inadequate self-sufficiency in order to draw on the resources of God's unlimited power?

VERNON GROUNDS

To experience God's strength, we must recognize our weakness.

Single Satisfaction

COLOSSIANS 2:6-10

In Christ you have been brought to fullness. He is the head over every power and authority.

COLOSSIANS 2:10

A friend of mine, Elizabeth-Ann, was single and radiantly contented. "But how is that possible?" she was often asked. To answer this question, she wrote a book titled *Complete As One*, which is based on Colossians 2:10. She recalls being challenged years ago by a comment about a friend: "You know what I appreciate about June [another friend]? She's so satisfied with Christ."

That phrase, "satisfied with Christ," left a profound impact on Elizabeth-Ann. She was twenty-one at the time and had been converted three years earlier. Her friends were getting engaged and married, and she was happy for them. But she was hearing comments like, "Have you seen how radiant Mary is?" and "I've never seen John so happy." This set her to thinking: These friends are Christians. Certainly it is appropriate for them to radiate happiness, but why do they have to get a spouse before they experience the joy and fulfillment Christians should have? So she began praying, "Lord, I don't want to marry until I have learned to be satisfied with you."

Elizabeth-Ann remained single, yet she believes that God has answered her prayer. She is rooted and built up in Christ. And that's the key to completeness—whether married or single.

JOANIE YODER

For lasting satisfaction, put God's will first.

Don't Run Alone

EXODUS 17:8–13

Since we are surrounded by such a great cloud of witnesses, let us throw off everything that hinders and the sin that so easily entangles. And let us run with perseverance the race marked out for us.

HEBREWS 12:1

My husband Jack was on mile 25 out of 26 when his strength failed him. This was his first marathon, and he was running alone. After stopping for a drink of water at an aid station, he felt exhausted and sat down on the grass beside the course. He had resigned himself to quitting the race when two middle-aged schoolteachers from Kentucky came by. Although they were strangers, they noticed Jack and asked if he wanted to run with them. Suddenly, he found his strength restored. Jack stood and accompanied by the two women he finished the race.

Those women who encouraged Jack remind me of Aaron and Hur, two friends who helped Moses, the leader of the Israelites, at a key point (Exodus 17:8–13). The Israelites were under attack. In battle, they were winning only as long as Moses held his staff up (v. 11). So when Moses's strength began to fail, Aaron and Hur held up his arms for him until sunset (v. 12).

Following God is not a solo endeavor. Companions can help us persevere through difficulty as we do what God has called us to do.

God, thank you for relationships that encourage me to continue following you. Help me to be a source of strength for others, as well.

AMY PETERSON

Who can I encourage to persevere through difficulty today?

When People Pray

ACTS 4:13–31

After they prayed, the place where they were meeting was shaken. And they were all filled with the Holy Spirit and spoke the word of God boldly.

ACTS 4:31

Peter and John were in danger. The religious leaders in Jerusalem opposing the gospel had warned them to cease their missionary efforts (Acts 4:18). When the apostles reported this to the other believers, they immediately held a prayer meeting.

What happened next is thrilling. The believers first praised God. Then they asked for boldness that they might continue the work. The results were dramatic. The house shook, and the believers were filled with the Spirit. They boldly witnessed (vv. 31, 33) and enjoyed spiritual unity (v. 32). They gave unselfishly to those in need (vv. 32, 34–37).

I have never felt a building shake at a prayer meeting, but I have seen God's power at work. When I've tried to help repair a broken marriage or a divided church, I've asked those involved to pray. Sometimes they refused. Other times they mumbled carefully worded prayers. The meeting failed.

But occasionally someone would pray in earnest. Almost immediately the atmosphere would change. Confession and forgiveness soon replaced charges and countercharges.

When we pray sincerely, praising God and presenting Him with petitions that seek His glory, great things happen. But first we must pray from the heart.

HERB VANDER LUGT

Our intercession may be the key to God's intervention.

It Takes Two

1 CORINTHIANS 12:12–27

God has placed the parts in the body, every one of them,
just as he wanted them to be.

1 CORINTHIANS 12:18

While visiting Christian workers in the country of Romania, Charlie VanderMeer, longtime host of the radio program *Children's Bible Hour* (now called *Keys for Kids*) went to an orphanage where people with physical and mental disabilities lived together.

Misha, a young man of twenty-four, broadcasted music and Christian programs into the orphanage buildings. Although he was paralyzed below the waist, he got around just fine. A friend, who has Down syndrome and cannot hear or speak, carried him on his shoulders.

Charlie could tell by the smile on the face of the man who carried Misha that this is his mission in life. According to a worker, when Misha had to be gone for a few weeks, his friend didn't know what to do.

What a picture of members of the body of Christ relying on one another! Each of us is a little like Misha. We are partially equipped to do the work of the Lord, but we need the "legs" of our fellow believers to carry us along.

This example of Misha and his friend reminds us that none of us can do the entire job alone. God designed us to rely on each other as we serve Him. So let's look for ways to help others, and as we do, we can learn to appreciate how much we can do together.

DAVE BRANON

Teamwork divides the effort and multiplies the effect.

The Journey Begins

2 PETER 1:5-11

If anyone is in Christ, the new creation has come:
The old has gone, the new is here!

2 CORINTHIANS 5:17

On January 11, 1933, a nine-year-old boy prayed to ask Jesus to be the Savior of his life. His mother wrote these words in a memory book: "Clair made a start today."

Clair—my dad—has walked with Christ for nearly nine decades. He always marked the day when he made his decision to follow Christ as the beginning of his journey. Growing spiritually is a lifelong process—not a one-time event. So how does a new believer feed his faith and continue to grow? These are some things I observed in my dad's life over the years.

He read the Scriptures regularly to increase his understanding of God, and he made prayer a daily part of his life (1 Chronicles 16:11; 1 Thessalonians 5:17). Bible reading and prayer help us grow closer to God and withstand temptation (Psalm 119:11; Matthew 26:41; Ephesians 6:11; 2 Timothy 3:16–17; 1 Peter 2:2). The Holy Spirit began to develop the "fruit of the Spirit" in him as he surrendered his life in faith and obedience (Galatians 5:22–23). We display God's love through our witness and service.

My dad's spiritual journey has always been an inspiration to many, and so should ours be. What a privilege to have a relationship in which we can "grow in the grace and knowledge of our Lord and Savior Jesus Christ"! (2 Peter 3:18).

CINDY HESS KASPER

Salvation is the miracle of a moment; growth is the labor of a lifetime.

Rewards of Faithfulness

MATTHEW 25:14–23

A faithful person will be richly blessed,
but one eager to get rich will not go unpunished.

PROVERBS 28:20

Missionary Jack Shiflett was speaking to one of his supporting churches. He spoke to them of spending eleven years in Spain and about presenting Jesus to people who didn't think they needed the gospel.

But then Jack told his listeners that he and his wife Cheryl finally began to see their ministry bear fruit. At least seventeen people accepted Jesus as Savior. To emphasize his appreciation for the faithfulness of the church where he was speaking, Shiflett said, "After eight years, we came to you and reported that we had led one person to Jesus Christ. And you sent us back."

The people at the church had recognized that the hallmark of servant-hood is faithfulness, not results. Results, they knew, rested in God's hands through the work of the Holy Spirit.

The Shifletts were faithful to the task and finally saw the harvest. Their example is encouraging, for we often go without results for even longer periods of time. And the example of the church in sticking with them is just as vital.

Perhaps you've been faithful at a task for a long time—seemingly without results. Stick with it, and leave the results with God. He'll send the rewards.

DAVE BRANON

God is more concerned with reliability than with results.

A Majority of One

2 CHRONICLES 32:1–8

"With him is only the arm of flesh, but with us is the LORD our God to help us and to fight our battles." And the people gained confidence from what Hezekiah the king of Judah said.

2 CHRONICLES 32:8

When Sennacherib, king of Assyria, invaded Judah, Hezekiah knew that the city of Jerusalem would come under attack, so he went into action to defend the city. He built up the broken wall and raised up another outside of it. He also "made large numbers of weapons and shields" and "appointed military officers over the people" (2 Chronicles 32:5–6).

But it would take more than that to save the city from the onslaught of the powerful armies of Sennacherib. So Hezekiah called the people together to encourage them. In the face of their seemingly hopeless situation, he declared, "There is a greater power with us than with him" (v. 7).

How could he say this? He gives the answer in the very next verse: "With [Sennacherib] is only an arm of flesh, but with us is the LORD our God to help us and to fight our battles." That was their hope. Sennacherib had power, men, and prestige—"an arm of flesh"—but the inhabitants of Jerusalem had the Lord!

Is there some "enemy" pressing in on you today? Do you feel as though the opposition is about to crush and destroy you? Does everything seem hopeless? Take heart, child of God! With the Lord on your side, you are never outnumbered.

RICHARD DEHAAN

One plus God is always a majority.

An Open Hand

ACTS 20:22–35

"In everything I did, I showed you that by this kind of hard work we must help the weak, remembering the words the Lord Jesus himself said: 'It is more blessed to give than to receive.'"

ACTS 20:35

In 1891, Biddy Mason was laid to rest in an unmarked grave in Los Angeles. That wasn't unusual for a woman born into slavery, but it was remarkable for someone as accomplished as Biddy. After winning her freedom in a court battle in 1856, she combined her nursing skills with wise business sense to make a small fortune. Observing the plight of immigrants and prisoners, she reached out to them so often that people began lining up at her house for help. In 1872, just sixteen years out of slavery, she and her son-in-law financed the founding of the First African Methodist Episcopal Church.

Biddy embodied Paul's words: "I showed you that by this kind of hard work we must help the weak, remembering the words the Lord Jesus himself said: 'It is more blessed to give than to receive'" (Acts 20:35). Paul came from privilege, not slavery, yet he chose a life that would lead to his imprisonment so he could serve Christ and others.

In 1988, benefactors unveiled a tombstone for Biddy Mason. In attendance were the mayor of Los Angeles and nearly 3,000 members of the little church she began over a century earlier. Biddy once said, "The open hand is blessed, for it gives in abundance even as it receives." The hand that gave so generously received a rich legacy.

TIM GUSTAFSON

The open hand is blessed, for it gives in abundance even as it receives.
—Biddy Mason

Our Best Defense

PSALM 31:1–8

*Turn your ear to me, come quickly to my rescue; be my rock of refuge,
a strong fortress to save me.*

PSALM 31:2

In late January 1956, during the tense days of the Montgomery Boycott, civil rights leader Dr. Martin Luther King Jr. could not sleep. A threatening phone call had terrified him. So he prayed, "I am here taking a stand for what I believe is right. But now I am afraid. The people are looking to me for leadership, and if I stand before them without strength and courage, they too will falter. I am at the end of my powers. . . . I can't face it alone."

King later wrote, "At that moment I experienced the presence of the Divine as I never experienced Him before. It seemed as though I could hear the quiet assurance of an inner voice saying, 'Stand up for righteousness, stand up for truth; and God will be at your side forever.' Almost at once my fears began to go. My uncertainty disappeared. I was ready to face anything."

The rest is history. Dr. King was a man who trusted God to help him show people of all colors that they could be free of the damage done by prejudice.

If we face opposition when we're trying to do what's right, we too must cry out to the Lord. He alone is our "rock of refuge, a strong fortress" (Psalm 31:2). He is our reliable source of strength and protection.

DAVID EGNER

When others speak ill of you, live so no one will believe them.

What Are You Known For?

HEBREWS 11:23–38

He regarded disgrace for the sake of Christ as of greater value than the treasures of Egypt, because he was looking ahead to his reward.
HEBREWS 11:26

A memorial stone stands in the grounds of a former Japanese prison camp in China where a man died in 1945. It reads, "Eric Liddell was born in Tianjin of Scottish parents in 1902. His career reached its peak with his gold medal victory in the 400-meter event at the 1924 Olympic Games. He returned to China to work in Tianjin as a teacher. . . . His whole life was spent encouraging young people to make their best contributions to the betterment of mankind."

In the eyes of many, Eric's greatest achievement was on the sports field. But he is also remembered for his contribution to the youth of Tianjin in China, the country where he was born and that he loved. He lived and served by faith.

What will we be remembered for? Our academic achievements, job position, or financial success may get us recognized by others. But it is the quiet work we do in the lives of people that will live long after we are gone.

Moses is remembered in the faith chapter of the Bible, Hebrews 11, as someone who chose to align himself with the people of God instead of enjoying the treasures of Egypt (v. 26). He, like Eric, served God's people by faith.

C. P. HIA

Faithfulness to God is true success.

A Coat in His Name

MARK 10:13-16

*"Whoever welcomes one of these little children in my name welcomes me;
and whoever welcomes me does not welcome me but the one who sent me."*

MARK 9:37

It was a bitterly cold morning at the inner city church. Among the 130 or so worshipers, the pastor took special notice of Ken, a young boy who arrived for Sunday school wearing just a sleeveless T-shirt, jeans, and tennis shoes with no socks.

After the worship service and a special luncheon, the pastor's wife took the six-year-old to the church's clothing closet to pick out a coat. Then the pastor and his wife drove him and his older brother John home. As they got out, John said, "Thank you for giving my brother a coat." The two boys became Sunday school regulars, and the pastor had a chance to visit with their mom and explain the gospel.

Are there any children in your world who need help with some basic necessities—a coat, a meal, a ride home? We might be tempted to say the problem is too big—that we can't help everyone, but that misses the point. Jesus placed great value on the life of a child. He said to His disciples, "Let the little children come to me, and do not hinder them; for the kingdom of God belongs to such as these" (Mark 10:14). He also told them, "Whoever welcomes one of these little children in my name welcomes me" (9:37).

A coat, a cup, a kind word. Given in Jesus's name, these are the tools of true ministry. Are we using them for God's glory?

DAVE BRANON

We show our love for Christ by what we do with what we have.

God Had Other Plans

1 PETER 1:1–9

*In their hearts humans plan their course,
but the LORD establishes their steps.*

PROVERBS 16:9

My friend Linda grew up planning to become a medical missionary. She loved the Lord and wanted to serve Him as a doctor by taking the gospel to sick people in parts of the world where medical care was hard to find. But God had other plans. Linda indeed became a medical missionary but not the way she expected.

At age fourteen, Linda developed a chronic health problem that required her to be hospitalized for major surgery several times a year. She survived bacterial meningitis that left her in a coma for two weeks and blind for six months. She once celebrated two birthdays in a row in the hospital—without going home in between. She had several experiences when she was not expected to live. Yet Linda was the most vibrant, grateful, and cheerful person you will ever meet. She once told me that her mission field, as she hoped and planned, was the hospital. But instead of serving God as a doctor, she served Him as a patient. No matter how sick she was, the light of the Lord radiated from her.

Linda exemplified the teaching of the apostle Peter. Despite her trials, she rejoiced, and the genuineness of her faith brought "praise, glory, and honor" to Jesus Christ (1 Peter 1:6–7).

JULIE ACKERMAN LINK

Write your plans in pencil and remember that God has the eraser.

Kossi's Courage

2 KINGS 23:12-14, 21-25

"You shall have no other gods before me. . . . You shall not bow down to them or worship them; for I, the LORD your God, am a jealous God."
EXODUS 20:3, 5

As he awaited his baptism in Togo's Mono River, Kossi stooped to pick up a worn wooden carving. His family had worshiped the object for generations. Now they watched as he tossed the grotesque figure into a fire prepared for the occasion. No longer would their choicest chickens be sacrificed to this god.

In the West, most Christians think of idols as metaphors for what they put in place of God. In some places in Togo, West Africa, idols represent literal gods that must be appeased with sacrifice. Idol burning and baptism make a courageous statement about a new believer's allegiance to the one true God.

As an eight-year-old, King Josiah came to power in an idol-worshiping, sex-obsessed culture. His father and grandfather had been two of the worst kings in all of Judah's sordid history. Then the high priest discovered the book of the law. When the young king heard its words, he took them to heart (2 Kings 22:8–13). Josiah destroyed the pagan altars and burned the vile items dedicated to the goddess Asherah (chapter 23). In place of these practices, he celebrated the Passover (23:21–23).

Whenever we look for answers apart from God—consciously or subconsciously—we pursue a false god. It would be wise to ask ourselves: What idols, literal or figurative, do we need to throw on the fire?

TIM GUSTAFSON

Dear children, keep yourselves from idols.
—1 John 5:21

Why Me?

RUTH 2:1–11

Why have I found such favor in your eyes?
RUTH 2:10

Ruth was a foreigner. She was a widow. She was poor. In many parts of the world today she would be considered a nobody—someone whose future doesn't hold any hope.

However, Ruth found favor in the eyes of a relative of her deceased husband, a rich man and the owner of the fields where she chose to ask for permission to glean grain. In response to his kindness, Ruth asked, "What have I done to deserve such kindness? . . . I am only a foreigner" (Ruth 2:10 NLT).

Boaz, the good man who showed Ruth such compassion, answered her truthfully. He had heard about her good deeds toward her mother-in-law, Naomi, and how she chose to leave her country and follow Naomi's God. Boaz prayed that God, "under whose wings" (2:12) she had come for refuge, would bless her (1:16; 2:11–12; see Psalm 91:4). As her guardian-redeemer (Ruth 3:9), when Boaz married Ruth he became her protector and part of the answer to his prayer.

Like Ruth, we were foreigners and far from God. We may wonder why God would choose to love us when we are so undeserving. The answer is not in us, but in Him. "God showed his great love for us by sending Christ to die for us while we were still sinners" (Romans 5:8 NLT). Christ has become our Redeemer. When we come to Him in salvation, we are under His protective wings.

KEILA OCHOA

Gratefulness is the heart's response to God's undeserved love.

Singing with Valma

PHILIPPIANS 1:21–26

I am torn between the two: I desire to depart and be with Christ, which is better by far; but it is more necessary for you that I remain in the body.
PHILIPPIANS 1:23–24

An elderly woman named Valma sat on her bed in a Jamaican infirmary and smiled as some teenagers stopped to visit with her. The hot, sticky, midday air came into her little group home unabated, but she didn't complain. Instead, she began wracking her mind for a song to sing. Then a huge smile appeared, and she sang, "I am running, skipping, jumping, praising the Lord!" As she sang, she swung her arms back and forth as if she were running. Tears came to those around her, for Valma had no legs. She was singing because, she said, "Jesus loves me—and in heaven I will have legs to run with."

Valma's joy and hopeful anticipation of heaven give new vibrancy to Paul's words in Philippians 1 when he referred to life-and-death issues. "If I am to go on living in the body, this will mean fruitful labor for me," he said. "I am torn between the two: I desire to depart and be with Christ, which is better by far" (vv. 22–23).

Each of us faces tough times that may cause us to long for the promise of heavenly relief. But as Valma showed us joy despite her current circumstances, we too can keep "running, skipping, praising the Lord"—both for the abundant life He gives us here and for the ultimate joy that awaits us.

DAVE BRANON

When God gives a new beginning, we find a joy that's never ending.

The Choice to Trust

MATTHEW 14:22–33

Trust in the LORD and do good; dwell in the land and enjoy safe pasture. . . .
Be still before the LORD and wait patiently for him; do not fret when people
succeed in their ways, when they carry out their wicked schemes.

PSALM 37:3, 7

When missionary Elisabeth Elliot was a young girl, her family spent a week at the New Jersey seashore. She had a wonderful time playing in the water because her father was there with her and she trusted him to keep her safe.

Her younger brother was afraid of the waves and refused to go in the water despite his father's coaxing. Then, on the last day of the vacation, he began to feel secure with his father at his side. But his shouts of glee suddenly changed to a wail. "Why didn't you make me go in?" he cried. That wouldn't have worked, though. Not until he chose to trust his father and was willing to keep trusting him could he enjoy the water.

The apostle Peter chose to trust Jesus and step out of the boat, and for a few moments he must have known the joy of walking on water with complete security. But when he took his eyes off the Lord, he lost that security and began to sink.

It follows that if we want to experience God's enablement, we must choose to trust Him and then actively continue that trust. The psalmist wrote, "Trust in the LORD and do good; . . . . Be still before the LORD and wait patiently for him" (37:3, 7).

Remember, trust is a choice and a continuing activity of believing and obeying God.

HERB VANDER LUGT

God tests our faith so that we may trust His faithfulness.

For Future Generations

2 TIMOTHY 1:1–7

*I am reminded of your sincere faith, which first lived in your grandmother
Lois and in your mother Eunice and, I am persuaded, now lives in you also.*
2 TIMOTHY 1:5

When a team of Christians visited Stavropol, Russia, in 1994 to hand out
Bibles, a local citizen said he recalled seeing Bibles in an old warehouse.
They had been confiscated in the 1930s when Stalin was sending believers
to the gulags. Amazingly, the Bibles were still there.

Among those who showed up to load them into trucks was a young
agnostic student just wanting to earn a day's wage. But soon he slipped
away from the job to steal a Bible. A team member went looking for him
and found him sitting in a corner weeping. Out of the hundreds of Bibles,
he had picked up one that bore the handwritten signature of his own
grandmother. Persecuted for her faith, she had no doubt prayed often for
her family and her city. God used that grandmother's Bible to convict that
young man.

God has no grandchildren. We must each become first-generation
believers through personal faith in Jesus. But the devotion to God of a
grandparent or parent is a powerful ally of His Spirit to bring our children
to Christ.

Paul encouraged Timothy by recalling the faith of his grandmother
and mother. Although Timothy's faith was his own, it was deeply linked
to theirs. What an admonition to us who are parents and grandparents to
be faithful!

DENNIS DEHAAN

**Better than having children bear your name is to
have your children bear Christ's name.**

A Storyteller

COLOSSIANS 1:13–23

Once you were alienated from God and were enemies in your minds because of your evil behavior. But now he has reconciled you.

COLOSSIANS 1:21–22

In the years following the American Civil War (1861–1865), Union Major General Lew Wallace served as a governor of the New Mexico territories; New Mexico not yet having been admitted as a state. His work there put him in contact with many of the characters that make up the Wild West's near-mythic history, including Billy the Kid and Sheriff Pat Garrett. It was here that Wallace wrote what has been called by some "the most influential Christian book" of the nineteenth century, *Ben-Hur: A Tale of the Christ.*

Wallace witnessed the worst impact of sin on humanity as he saw the violence of the Civil War and the Wild West. In life and in his bestselling book, Wallace understood that only the story of Jesus Christ has the power of redemption and reconciliation.

For the follower of Christ, the climax of our lives was the moment God "rescued us from the dominion of darkness and brought us into the kingdom of the Son he loves, in whom we have redemption, the forgiveness of sins" (Colossians 1:13–14).

Now we have the privilege of being storytellers of God's wonderful redemption.

RANDY KILGORE

The difference Christ makes in your life is a story worth telling.

The Small Giant

1 SAMUEL 17:32–37

*"The LORD who rescued me from the paw of the lion and
the paw of the bear will rescue me from the hand of this Philistine."
Saul said to David, "Go, and the LORD be with you."*

1 SAMUEL 17:37

The towering enemy strides into the Valley of Elah. He stands nine feet tall, and his coat of armor, made of many small bronze plates, glimmers in the sunlight. The shaft of his spear is wrapped with cords so it can spin through the air and be thrown with greater distance and accuracy. Goliath looks invincible.

But David knows better. While Goliath may look like a giant and act like a giant, in contrast to the living God he is small. David has a right view of God and therefore a right view of the circumstances. He sees Goliath as one who is defying the armies of the living God (1 Samuel 17:26). He confidently appears before Goliath in his shepherd's clothes, armed with only his staff, five stones, and a sling. His confidence is not in what he has but in who is with him (v. 45).

What "Goliath" are you facing right now? It may be an impossible situation at work, a financial difficulty, or a broken relationship. With God all things are small in comparison. Nothing is too big for Him. The words of the hymnwriter Charles Wesley remind us: "Faith, mighty faith, the promise sees, and looks to that alone; laughs at impossibilities, and cries it shall be done." God is able to deliver you if that's His desire, and He may do so in ways you don't expect.

POH FANG CHIA

**Don't tell God how big your giants are.
Tell your giants how big your God is.**

Show a Little Kindness

TITUS 2

In everything set them an example by doing what is good.
In your teaching show integrity, seriousness and soundness of speech.
TITUS 2:7–8

The considerate spirit and quiet good works of believers in Jesus Christ can make a tremendous impact on those who do not believe in Him. A little kindness speaks louder to some than fiery preaching.

A small congregation of Christ-followers in Japan put this principle into practice. They were planning to build a sanctuary. After the architect completed the plans, they went to all the neighbors, showed them the blueprints, and asked if anyone had any objections. No one did.

A few months later, however, before construction began, they heard that one man did have some concerns. They paid him a second visit and discovered he was worried that the structure would block the sunlight coming into his yard. Did they argue? No. Did they complain because he didn't speak out earlier? No. The church board went back to the architect and asked for a revision. At quite some additional expense, he redesigned the building with a lower roof. The surprised neighbor was pleased that he would not lose his sunlight.

In our hard-driving, rights-centered world, kind consideration toward others seems out of place. But it's always appropriate for us as Christians (Titus 2). And it can deliver a powerful witness.

DAVID EGNER

A Christian is a living sermon.

Power in Praise

2 CHRONICLES 20:15–22

After consulting the people, Jehoshaphat appointed men to sing to the LORD and to praise him for the splendor of his holiness as they went out at the head of the army, saying: "Give thanks to the LORD, for his love endures forever."

2 CHRONICLES 20:21

Willie Myrick was kidnapped from his driveway when he was nine years old. For hours, he traveled in a car with his kidnapper, not knowing what would happen to him. During that time, Willie decided to sing a song called "Every Praise." As he repeatedly sang the words, his abductor spewed profanity and told him to shut up. Finally, the man stopped the car and let Willie out—unharmed.

As Willie demonstrated, truly praising the Lord requires us to concentrate on God's character while forsaking what we fear, what is wrong in our lives, and the self-sufficiency in our hearts.

The Israelites reached this place of surrender when they faced attackers. As they prepared for battle, King Jehoshaphat organized a choir to march out in advance of their enemy's army. The choir sang, "Praise the LORD, for His mercy endures forever" (2 Chronicles 20:21 NKJV). When the music started, Israel's enemies became confused and destroyed each other. As the prophet Jahaziel had predicted, Israel didn't need to fight at all (v. 17).

Whether we're facing a battle or feeling trapped, we can glorify God in our hearts. Truly, "Great is the LORD and most worthy of praise" (Psalm 96:4).

JENNIFER BENSON SCHULDT

Worship is a heart overflowing with praise to God.

Our Influence

JAMES 1:1–8

When you ask, you must believe and not doubt, because the one who doubts is like a wave of the sea, blown and tossed by the wind.

JAMES 1:6

Adoniram Judson (1788–1850) was gifted with a brilliant mind. He learned to read at age three, could translate Greek at twelve, and enrolled in Brown University when he was seventeen. While there, he was befriended by Jacob Eames, a man who rejected the miracles of the Bible. When Judson graduated as valedictorian in 1807, he had been so influenced by Eames that he denied his Christian faith.

One night, when Judson was staying at a village inn, he was disturbed by a man moaning in the next room. The following morning, he asked the innkeeper about the ailing man. He was told that the man had died and that his name was Jacob Eames.

The startling coincidence of being near his friend at the point of his death stunned Judson. He felt compelled to search his own soul and to seek God's pardon for denying his faith. From that point on, he began to live for the Lord. God led him to pioneer missionary work in Burma. At the end of his life, Adoniram could look back on his ministry that had planted dozens of churches and influenced thousands to become believers.

What kind of influence are we having on others? Do our lives encourage faith in the Savior, or do we cause others to doubt?

DENNIS FISHER

Your life either sheds light or casts a shadow.

Wholehearted

NUMBERS 13:26–32; 14:20–24

Because my servant Caleb has a different spirit and follows me wholeheartedly,
I will bring him into the land he went to, and his descendants will inherit it.

NUMBERS 14:24

Caleb was a "wholehearted" person. He and Joshua were part of a twelve-man reconnaissance team that explored the Promised Land and gave a report to Moses and the people. Caleb said, "We should go up and take possession of the land, for we can certainly do it" (Numbers 13:30). But ten members of the team said they couldn't possibly succeed. In spite of God's promises, they saw only obstacles (vv. 31–33).

Ten men caused the people to lose heart and grumble against God, which led to forty years of desert wandering. But Caleb never quit. The Lord said, "Because my servant Caleb has a different spirit and follows me wholeheartedly, I will bring him into the land he went to, and his descendants will inherit it" (14:24). Forty-five years later God honored His promise when Caleb, at age eighty-five, received the city of Hebron "because he followed the LORD, the God of Israel, wholeheartedly" (Joshua 14:14).

Centuries later an expert in the law asked Jesus, "Which is the greatest commandment in the Law?" Jesus replied, "'Love the Lord your God with all your heart and with all your soul and with all your mind.' This is the first and greatest commandment" (Matthew 22:36–38).

Today Caleb is still inspiring us with his confidence in a God who deserves our wholehearted love, reliance, and commitment.

DAVID MCCASLAND

Commitment to Christ is a daily calling.

Just a Handful of Rice

LUKE 21:1–4

In the midst of a very severe trial, their overflowing joy and
their extreme poverty welled up in rich generosity.

2 CORINTHIANS 8:2

In the province of Mizoram in India lives a group of Christians who have discovered a unique way to give to the work of the Lord. As the woman of the house prepares meals for her family, meals that consist primarily of rice, she measures out just enough rice to feed her family.

Then, before she cooks that rice, she reaches into the dish, grabs a handful, and takes it out. This she sets aside until Sunday, when she takes it to church and combines it with the rice brought by other women. The church then sells it and uses the proceeds to support missionary projects. One of the items purchased was a computer that is being used to help the Mizo people complete a translation of the Bible in their language.

It would be easy for people without much money to look at the little they have and decide it's not worth giving. Likewise, it would have been easy for the widow in Luke 21 to feel inadequate with her two small coins when she saw the large amounts the rich people put in the temple treasury.

God isn't interested in the amount as much as He is in a heart of sacrifice. That's why Jesus said the widow put in more than all the others (v. 3). Can we honestly say that our giving is sacrificial?

DAVE BRANON

Sacrifice is the true measure of our giving.

Who Am I?

EXODUS 3:7–15

*But Moses said to God, "Who am I that I should go to Pharaoh
and bring the Israelites out of Egypt?"*

EXODUS 3:11

Years ago, world-famous evangelist Billy Graham (1918–2018) was scheduled to speak at Cambridge University in England, but he did not feel qualified to address the sophisticated thinkers. He had no advanced degrees, and he had never attended seminary. Billy confided in a close friend: "I do not know that I have ever felt more inadequate and totally unprepared for a mission." He prayed for God's help, and God used him to share the simple truth of the gospel and the cross of Christ.

Moses also felt inadequate when God recruited him for the task of telling Pharaoh to release the Israelites. Moses asked, "Who am I that I should go to Pharaoh?" (Exodus 3:11). Although Moses may have questioned his effectiveness because he was "slow of speech" (4:10), God said, "I will be with you" (3:12). Knowing he would have to share God's rescue plan and tell the Israelites who sent him, Moses asked God, "What shall I tell them?" God replied, "I AM has sent me to you" (vv.13–14). His name, "I AM," revealed His eternal, self-existent, and all-sufficient character.

Even when we question our ability to do what God has asked us to do, He can be trusted. Our shortcomings are less important than God's sufficiency. When we ask, "Who am I?" we can remember that God said, "I AM."

JENNIFER BENSON SCHULDT

When we focus on Christ, our identity becomes clearly focused.

"The Man from God"

JOHN 21:1–14

Jesus said to them, "Come and have breakfast." None of the disciples dared ask him, "Who are you?" They knew it was the Lord.

JOHN 21:12

When Jesus was on earth, He placed himself in a servant relationship with His fellowmen. By the shores of the Sea of Tiberias with His disciples, for instance, He served them breakfast. Just as He had done when He washed the disciples' feet, He was setting an example. And like Jesus, we are to serve one another, even our close friends and loved ones, for whom it is sometimes difficult to do humble tasks.

When he was a professor at Bryan College in Tennessee, Dr. William Brown (later, president of Bryan and then Cedarville University) told about a missionary who went to a tribe of Native Americans to present the gospel. At first he was received hesitantly and was referred to as "the white man." As the people got to know him better, they called him "the respectable white man." Later, when they saw his desire for their well-being, they spoke of him as "the white Indian." Then one of the people injured his foot. The missionary took the man into his home, washed his foot, and gave him medical attention. The people, amazed at his graciousness, began to call him "the man from God."

Like Jesus, that missionary went to serve (Mark 10:45). If we humble ourselves and follow our Lord's example, we too can become known as the man or the woman from God.

DAVID EGNER

A Christian can do great things for the Lord if he is willing to do little things for others.

World Hunger

PSALM 119:97–104

Like newborn babies, crave pure spiritual milk,
so that by it you may grow up in your salvation.
1 PETER 2:2

I had just completed a night of Bible conference ministry in Kuala Lumpur, Malaysia, and was chatting with some of the people who had attended. At the end of the line was a young man in his twenties. He shared with me that he had been a Christ-follower for only about four months, and he was eager to learn more of the teachings of the Bible. I referred him to the Our Daily Bread Ministries website with the Discovery Series topics as one possible resource for his personal study.

The next night the young man returned to the conference and shared that he had stayed up until 3:30 reading and processing the biblical truths he discovered in that online resource. With a big smile on his face, he declared that he just couldn't get enough of God's Word (1 Peter 2:2).

What spiritual hunger! That excited young man is a reminder to us of the wonder of the Bible and its heart-enriching truths. It's all too easy for us to ignore God's Book in a world filled with voices screaming for our attention. But only in the Bible can we find God's wisdom for our struggles, God's answers for our questions, and God's truths for our understanding. These truths are worth hungering for.

BILL CROWDER

Study the Bible to be wise; believe it to be safe; practice it to be holy.

What God Has Done

ACTS 26:6–23

"So then, King Agrippa, I was not disobedient to the vision from heaven."
ACTS 26:19

In a debate at Boston College, Christian scholar William Lane Craig convincingly set forth the historical arguments for believing in Jesus's resurrection, much as the apostle Paul did in Acts 26. Then Craig told the story of his conversion.

As a child he never went to church, but in his teens he began to be plagued by questions about death and the meaning of life. He started going to church, but the sermons didn't answer his questions. What he saw in his churchgoing classmates led him to conclude that most Christians were phonies. He became an angry loner. One day a girl who always seemed to be happy told him that her joy came from having Jesus in her life, and she assured him that Jesus wanted to live in him too.

Lane spent the next six months soul-searching and reading the New Testament. "I came to the end of my rope and cried out to God," he said. "I cried out all the bitterness and anger that was within me. And I felt this tremendous infusion of joy, and God became at that moment a living reality in my life—a reality that has never left me."

We tell others our logic for believing in Jesus, which is based on God's Word. But it's also important to tell them what He has done for us personally.

HERB VANDER LUGT

**When telling others what Jesus can do for them,
tell them what He has done for you.**

Ordinary People

JUDGES 6:11–16

*We have this treasure in jars of clay to show that this
all-surpassing power is from God and not from us.*

2 CORINTHIANS 4:7

Although Gideon was an ordinary person, his story as recorded in Judges
6 inspires me. He was a farmer, and a timid one at that. When God called
him to deliver Israel from the Midianites, Gideon's initial response was
"How can I save Israel? Indeed my clan is the weakest in Manasseh, and I
am the least in my father's house" (Judges 6:15 NKJV). God promised that
He would be with Gideon and that he would be able to accomplish what
he had been asked to do (v. 16). Gideon's obedience brought victory to
Israel, and he is listed as one of the great heroes of faith (Hebrews 11:32).

Many other individuals played a significant part in this plan to save
the Israelites from a strong enemy force. God provided Gideon with three
hundred men, valiant heroes all, to win the battle. We are not told their
names, but their bravery and obedience are recorded in the Scriptures
(Judges 7:5–23).

Today, God is still calling ordinary people to do His work and assuring
us that He will be with us as we do. Because we are ordinary people being
used by God, it's obvious that the power comes from God and not from us.

POH FANG CHIA

God uses ordinary people to carry out His extraordinary plan.

"Enough"

JAMES 1:9–11; 5:1–6

James, a servant of God and of the Lord Jesus Christ,
To the twelve tribes scattered among the nations: Greetings.

JAMES 1:1

After Bob Ritchie graduated from college, he spent the next two decades in the grasp of a love for money and advancement. He uprooted his wife and family five times for his career—always so he could make more money. Each time, they left warm church communities behind.

After a while, Bob and his family seldom had time for church. As God's people became strangers, so did the Lord. He became desperately lonely and isolated. Growing discontented with his life, he finally said, "Enough!"

Bob now testifies that God taught him the meaning of the word *downsize.* He stopped pursuing money, spent less time at work, cut back on his purchases, and learned to be content with what he had. The family again became faithful to the Lord and active in a church.

In his brief and practical epistle, James warned us not to be obsessed with amassing wealth (1:9–11; 5:1–6). Whether we're rich or poor, the desire for money can subtly take over our lives. Some believers have fallen into its clutches without being aware of it and are fading away in their pursuits (1:11).

Do you need to follow Bob's example? It may be time to say, "Enough!"

DAVE EGNER

He is truly rich who is satisfied with Jesus.

Full Surrender

ROMANS 11:33–12:2

*Therefore, I urge you, brothers and sisters, in view of God's mercy,
to offer your bodies as a living sacrifice, holy and pleasing to God—
this is your true and proper worship.*

ROMANS 12:1

When someone asked William Booth (1829–1912), founder of the Salvation Army, the secret of his success, Booth remained silent for several moments. Finally, with tear-filled eyes, he said, "There have been men with greater brains or opportunities than I, but I made up my mind that God would have all of William Booth there was."

Several years later, when General Booth's daughter heard about her father's comment regarding his full surrender to God, she said, "That wasn't really his secret—his secret was that he never took it back."

We may never be a William Booth; but all of us can, in response to God's grace and mercy in saving us, give Him our all—and never take it back.

The apostle Paul, in our Scripture reading for today, made an appeal based on what he had discussed earlier in his letter. In consideration of all that the Lord in His mercy has done for us, we are to give our bodies as living sacrifices to God.

Hymwriter Elisha A. Hoffman penned these penetrating questions: "Is your all on the altar of sacrifice laid? Your heart, does the Spirit control?" How would you answer them?

RICHARD DEHAAN

Christ showed His love by dying for us; we show ours by living for Him.

When God Supplied a Banquet

PSALM 37:3, 16–19

The lions may grow weak and hungry,
but those who seek the LORD lack no good thing.

PSALM 34:10

Missionary G. Christian Weiss and his wife served in a church-planting work in Minnesota during the 1950s. Money and supplies were running low, and the winter snows had all but locked them into their cabin. One night Mrs. Weiss set a bowl of boiled potatoes on the table. "This is it!" she said. They bowed their heads and gave thanks, asking God to supply their needs.

Suddenly they heard a sharp knock. Opening the door, they saw the wife of the manager of a nearby ranger station. She said, "We were expecting a crew of workers today, but they phoned to say they weren't able to get through. I had a big dinner prepared for them, and my husband and I will not be able to eat all that food before it spoils. Could you come over and have supper with us?" Gratitude flooded the hearts of the missionary couple as they made their way with difficulty through the drifts to the ranger outpost. For a second time they sat down to eat, but now their meal was a banquet—roast duck with all the trimmings, vegetables, and pie. Humble and grateful, Mr. Weiss bowed his head and returned thanks to God for His provision.

But what about the days to come? Would they have to worry about their meals then? No. The God who supplied the banquet would also supply their daily bread.

HENRY BOSCH

Man's poverty is no strain on God's provision.

Gaining Respect

DANIEL 1:1–16

But Daniel resolved not to defile himself with the royal food and wine,
and he asked the chief official for permission not to defile himself this way.
DANIEL 1:8

When a professional musician nicknamed "Happy" became a Christian, he quit playing in nightclubs and offered his services to a rescue mission. Some time later, he received a phone call from a club manager who wanted to hire him to do a show that would have brought in a lot of money. But Happy turned down the offer, telling the manager that he would be playing at the mission. Happy said, "He congratulated me. That surprised me. Here was a man who wanted me to play for him, and he was congratulating me for refusing his offer." The manager respected Happy's decision.

Daniel was a captive in a foreign land, but he did not forget his godly principles. He could not in good conscience eat meat that had been dedicated to a pagan god and had not been slaughtered in accordance with Hebrew laws. He asked for a simple fare of vegetables and water, and the steward risked his life to honor his request. I believe he did this because Daniel's noble conduct had earned his respect.

Consistency of character gains the respect of others. That is the best way to live.

HERB VANDER LUGT

If you're living for Christ you may lose some friends,
but you won't lose their respect.

Managing the Mess

RUTH 1:15–22

"I went away full, but the LORD has brought me back empty.
Why call me Naomi? The LORD has afflicted me; the Almighty
has brought misfortune upon me."

RUTH 1:21

When we meet Naomi in the Scriptures, her life is a mess. She and her husband had gone to Moab searching for food during a famine. While in that land, their two sons married Moabite women, and life was good—until her husband and sons died and she was stuck, widowed in a foreign land.

Though honest about her pain, Naomi obviously had a sense of who was in control: "The LORD has afflicted me; the Almighty has brought misfortune upon me" (Ruth 1:21).

The Hebrew word for "Almighty" (*Shaddai*) indicates God's sufficiency for any situation. The word "LORD" (*Yahweh*) refers to His faithfulness as the loving covenant-keeping God. I love how Naomi put these two names together. In the midst of her complaint, she never lost sight of the fact that her God was capable and faithful. Sure enough, He proved His capability to deliver her and His faithfulness to care for her.

If there seems to be no way out of your despair, remember that Naomi's God is your God as well. And He specializes in managing our messes to good and glorious outcomes. Thankfully, He is both capable and faithful. So, when your life is a mess, remember who your God is!

JOE STOWELL

Stand back and watch the Lord manage your mess
into a glorious outcome.

The Turning Point

LUKE 15:11–21

"The son said to him, 'Father, I have sinned against heaven and against you.
I am no longer worthy to be called your son.'"

LUKE 15:21

When I first met Joe, he was a hard-drinking man. Some of his neighbors saw him as a troublemaker. My initial efforts to help him were completely unsuccessful. He said he didn't want anything to do with Christ or Christians because he had seen too much hypocrisy in the church.

A short time after his wife's death, Joe surprised many people by coming to a church service. He received a cordial welcome and started to attend regularly. We put no pressure on him to become a Christian but trusted the Holy Spirit to do His work. About four weeks later, on a Monday morning, he rang our doorbell, came in, sat down, and said, "Pastor, the first time I met you I told you how rotten I thought everyone else was, but now I see how bad I am. Last night I got down on my knees and asked Jesus to save me."

Joe's life was transformed when he stopped making excuses and admitted his own sinfulness. That was also true of the wayward son in today's reading. When he hit bottom, he said, "I will set out and go back to my father and say to him: 'Father, I have sinned'" (Luke 15:18).

The turning point for all of us comes when we acknowledge our sin and accept God's offer of forgiveness.

HERB VANDER LUGT

The first step to receiving God's forgiveness is to admit that we need it.

"Just As I Am"

JOHN 6:35–40

All those the Father gives me will come to me, and whoever comes to me I will never drive away.

JOHN 6:37

Charlotte Elliott learned an important lesson about Jesus one sleepless night in 1834. She was unable to walk, so when her family held a bazaar in Brighton, England, to raise money to build a school, she could only watch from afar.

That night she was overwhelmed by her helplessness and could not sleep. But her sadness turned to joy when she realized that God accepted her just as she was.

Her experience inspired these well-loved words: "Just as I am, without one plea, but that Thy blood was shed for me, and that Thou bidd'st me come to Thee, O Lamb of God, I come! I come!" When she later published the poem in a hymnbook, she included with it John 6:37.

Jesus always accepts people as they are. In John 6, the people had come from miles around to hear Jesus. When the crowd became hungry, He miraculously fed them with a boy's unselfish gift of five loaves and two fish. Then the Lord offered himself as "the bread of life," promising that He would not turn away anyone who came to Him.

It's still true today. No one who comes to Jesus will be turned away. Come to Him with all your sin. He'll accept you just as you are.

DAVID EGNER

No one is too good or too bad to be saved.

The Greatest Power

1 JOHN 4:1-6

You, dear children, are from God and have overcome them, because the one who is in you is greater than the one who is in the world.

1 JOHN 4:4

John G. Paton (1824–1907), a missionary to the South Pacific islands of Vanuatu (then called New Hebrides), often lived in danger as he worked among hostile people who had never heard the gospel.

At one time three witch doctors, claiming to have the power to cause death, publicly declared their intentions to kill Paton with their sorcery before the next Sunday. To carry out their threat, they said they needed some food he had partially eaten. Paton asked for three pieces of fruit. He took one bite out of each, and then he gave them to the men who were plotting his death.

On Sunday, the missionary entered the village with a smile on his face and what he described as "more than my usual health and strength." The people looked at each other in amazement, thinking it couldn't possibly be Paton. When asked why they had failed, they replied that the missionary's God was stronger than theirs. From then on Paton's influence grew, and soon he had the joy of leading some of the villagers to the Lord.

The great power God has given us in the person of His Holy Spirit can help us go forward with confidence, conquering every foe in the name of Jesus.

HENRY BOSCH

**Sowing seeds of witness can grow into
a harvest of redemption.**

Russell

LUKE 6:30-36

*If you do good to those who are good to you, what credit is that to you?
Even sinners do that.*

LUKE 6:33

It started as small talk at an estate sale. When Patsy Wassenaar asked Russell about his family, tears filled his eyes. "Both my parents died, and I'm alone," he replied. Touched, Patsy knew in her heart that God wanted her to show mercy to this man. So she and her husband Gordon invited him to stay with them, which he did—for the rest of his life.

Russell had slipped through the cracks of society. He had lived with his parents until they died, avoiding people and accumulating old discarded items he hoped to repair and sell. His house was stuffed with things nobody wanted. And Russell figured he fit right in—nobody seemed to want him either.

But Patsy and Gordon gave him a "family," a comfortable place to live, and work to do each day. He continued to go to estate sales, but he was no longer ignored and alone.

Most of us will not be asked by God to take someone into our home like that, but we must not shy away from showing godly mercy and helping people like Russell. Becoming involved in someone's life may mean sacrifice. We aren't eager to have our lives interrupted, but we need to be willing to do good to those who need it the most.

When one of God's "unwanted" people crosses our path, let's be merciful as God is merciful.

DAVE BRANON

Life takes on new meaning when we invest it in others.

A Glimpse of God's Love

JOHN 9:24-34

"Let the one who boasts boast in the Lord."
2 CORINTHIANS 10:17

Nadine was in the last stages of cancer when I met her. The doctor said chemotherapy would no longer help. She was a dedicated Christian and had a wonderful peace from God. She spent her last weeks making scrapbooks for her adult daughters and planning her memorial service.

Nadine's joyful spirit was inviting to be around, and people looked forward to spending time with her. She kept her sense of humor and always shared how the Lord was meeting her needs. She gave everyone around her a glimpse of God's loving character.

When a man who had been born blind was healed by Jesus, he too had the opportunity to show others a glimpse of who God is (John 9:1–41). Neighbors asked, "How then were your eyes opened?" (v. 10). He told them about Jesus. When Pharisees questioned him, he told them how Jesus had given him sight, and concluded, "If this man were not from God, he could do nothing" (v. 33).

We may wonder how we can show others what God is like. God can be clearly seen in the way we handle life's difficulties, such as problems at work or home, or perhaps a serious illness. We can share with others how He is comforting us—and let them know that the Lord cares for them too.

Who in your life needs to see the love of God?

ANNE CETAS

You can be a glimpse of God's love to someone.

Lessons from Jonah

JONAH 1

*"In my distress I called to the Lord, and he answered me.
From deep in the realm of the dead I called for help,
and you listened to my cry."*

JONAH 2:2

Jonah's story is one of the most discussed accounts in the Bible. But for all the debate, one thing's sure: Jonah did a lot of soul-searching in that smelly underwater hotel. All of us can identify. Sometimes life just goes badly. When it does, like Jonah we need to ask ourselves some hard questions.

Is there sin in my life? In light of Jonah's blatant disobedience, God had to do something drastic to catch his attention and lead him to repentance.

What can I learn from this situation? The wicked people of Nineveh were enemies of God's people. Jonah thought they should be judged—not given a second chance. He obviously needed a lesson in God's compassion. "When God saw what they did and how they turned from their evil ways, he relented and did not bring on them the destruction he had threatened" (Jonah 3:10).

Can I display God's glory in this? Often our suffering is not about us but about people seeing the power of God working through our weakness. Jonah found himself in a helpless situation, yet God used him to lead a pagan nation to repentance.

Next time you find yourself in a "belly-of-a-whale" problem, don't forget to ask the hard questions. It could mean the difference between despair and deliverance.

JOE STOWELL

**We learn lessons in the school of suffering that
we can learn in no other way.**

Abandoned to God

PSALM 77

I cried out to God for help; I cried out to God to hear me.
PSALM 77:1

Walter Cizsek, a Christian in the former Soviet Union, was imprisoned and tortured for his faith in Christ. He was forced to make a soul-rending choice: cooperation or execution. Cooperate with liars and murderers? Never! But an agonizing death? How could he endure that?

On the verge of losing his faith in God, Walter began to pray desperately. Eventually he was able to abandon himself completely to the will of the Father. He writes that God's will was not "out there" but "in the situations in which I found myself. What He wanted was for me to accept these situations from His hands, to let go of the reins, and to place myself entirely at His disposal." Empowered by grace, Walter was able to do just that.

Have you ever felt abandoned by God? Have you ever felt like the psalmist who cried out in despair, "Has God forgotten to be merciful? Has he in anger withheld his compassion?" (Psalm 77:9). The psalmist's distress was alleviated when he remembered and meditated on the wonderful works of the Lord and realized that He is totally in control (vv. 10–20).

As we "let go of the reins" and place ourselves entirely at God's disposal, our feelings of abandonment by Him will fade away.

VERNON GROUNDS

No one who is abandoned to God will feel abandoned by God.

The Bible and Changed Lives

PSALM 119:1–16

I delight in your decrees; I will not neglect your word.
PSALM 119:16

William Wilberforce (1759–1833) was a clever debater, a shrewd politician, and a popular socialite. At twenty-one, he became a member of Parliament in England during a time of terrible moral and spiritual decline. The rich were making a mockery of marriage, the poor were downtrodden, and the slave trade was booming.

For a time, Wilberforce went along with these evils, thinking only of his personal ambitions. But when he was twenty-five, he traveled to France with one of his former teachers, Isaac Milner. During this trip, Wilberforce read and studied the Bible with Milner. Before long he surrendered his life to Christ and was transformed. The parties he once enjoyed now seemed indecent. The plight of the poor now troubled him. And he soon became the leader in the battle against slavery, which was abolished in England in 1833—primarily through his efforts.

Wilberforce was transformed after he read and then obeyed the Bible. Do you want to know God and do His will? Then start reading the Bible and taking its message seriously. If you are not yet a member of God's family, it will show you how to become one of His children. And if you are a Christian, reading and obeying God's Word will bring radiance and victory into your life.

HERB VANDER LUGT

The Spirit of God uses the Word of God to change the people of God.

Greatly Valued

2 SAMUEL 9

Then Ziba said to the king, "Your servant will do whatever my lord the king commands his servant to do." So Mephibosheth ate at David's table like one of the king's sons.

2 SAMUEL 9:11

A British factory worker and his wife were excited when, after many years of marriage, they discovered they were going to have their first child. According to author Jill Briscoe, who told this true story, the man eagerly relayed the good news to his fellow workers. He told them God had answered his prayers. But they made fun of him for asking God for a child.

When the baby was born, he was diagnosed as having Down syndrome. As the father made his way to work for the first time after the birth, he wondered how to face his coworkers. "God, please give me wisdom," he prayed. Just as he feared, some said mockingly, "So, God gave you this child!" The new father stood for a long time, silently asking God for help. At last he said, "I'm glad the Lord gave this child to me and not to you."

In a similar way to how this man accepted his son as God's gift to him, so David was pleased to show kindness to Saul's grandson who was "lame in both feet" (2 Samuel 9:3). Some may have rejected Mephibosheth because of his disability, but David's action showed that he valued him greatly.

In God's eyes, every person—made in God's image—is important. He sent His only Son to die for each person. May we remember with gratitude how much He values each human life.

DAVE BRANON

Everyone is valuable to God.

"Just God and Me"

PSALM 46

God is our refuge and strength, an ever-present help in trouble.
PSALM 46:1

Missionary Larry Smith stood outside the operating room doors of a hospital in Santiago, Chile. He had never felt more alone. His wife, Bev, was away and could not be reached. No one knew he was facing a life-or-death situation. No one—except God.

Earlier that day, Larry had been called home from the mission school where he was administrator. His son Doug had been hurt. Larry could see no injuries, though Doug was obviously in pain. When Doug's pain intensified, Larry thought, *I had better get him checked*, so he headed for the hospital. Doug's condition worsened quickly, so Larry sped to the emergency room.

By the time they arrived, his son was nearly unconscious. The medical staff took one look and sprang into action. The examining doctor said solemnly, "Your son has a ruptured spleen. We must operate immediately." Larry nodded, and they wheeled his son away.

"I realized then," Larry testifies, "that it was just God and me, so I cried out to Him. His presence gave me the confidence I needed." His son survived. But Larry Smith was reminded what it means to take refuge in God.

Psalm 46 assures us that whatever trial we face today, with God we are never alone.

DAVID EGNER

**We may face situations beyond our reserves
but never beyond God's resources.**

The Rest of the Story

ROMANS 6:1–14

Do not offer any part of yourself to sin as an instrument of wickedness, but rather offer yourselves to God as those who have been brought from death to life; and offer every part of yourself to him as an instrument of righteousness.

ROMANS 6:13

As a successful newsman, he seemed to have everything the world could offer.

One bright Sunday morning in 1971 while he and his wife were vacationing, they slipped into a little white clapboard church in Cave Creek, Arizona. The sight of the dozen or so people sitting on wooden folding chairs stirred boyhood memories. John 3:16 had been planted early in his mind, and one night he had knelt by his bed and received Jesus as his Savior. But that was years earlier.

The minister announced his subject—baptism. The newsman yawned but became attentive as the pastor talked of giving one's entire life to serve Christ. The newsman mused, "Long years ago I had asked to be saved, but had I offered to serve? I began to realize how much of me I had been holding back." That morning the issue became clear and Paul Harvey, one of America's best-loved broadcasters, surrendered his life to Christ.

A year later, Paul Harvey said, "Though I had learned John 3:16 early in life, it took me till last year to learn John 14:15 as well: 'If you love Me, keep My commandments' (KJV). The Christian life is one of obedience, not partnership."

If we want to know the true and complete joy of living for Christ, we must surrender every area of our life to Him. Now you know the rest of the story.

DENNIS DEHAAN

Christ offered himself for our sins; we offer ourselves for His service.

The Power of Kindness

ROMANS 12:17–21

Be kind and compassionate to one another, forgiving each other,
just as in Christ God forgave you.
EPHESIANS 4:32

A young factory worker noticed one day that a valuable tool was missing from his toolbox. Later he saw it in the toolbox of a fellow employee. The young man who lost the tool was the only Christian in the shop, and he wanted to have a good testimony for Christ. So he said to the other man, "I see you have one of my tools, but you may keep it if you need it." Then he went on with his work and put the incident out of his mind.

During the next two weeks, the person who had taken the tool tried to soothe his conscience. First, he offered the young man something of equal value, then he offered to help him on some home projects, and finally he slipped some money into his coat pocket. Eventually, the coworkers became good friends, and the one-time tool thief admitted he couldn't resist the man's kindness.

Kindness is probably the most effective tool Christians have in their kit of virtues. But even when it doesn't bring about reconciliation, as it did with those two workers, it is always the right response. No matter how we are treated, we are to follow Christ's example (Ephesians 4:32).

We need the grace to extend love to others, even as God for Christ's sake has loved us! Titus 3:4–5 says, "When the kindness and love of God our Savior appeared, he saved us." Our Lord is our ultimate example of kindness.

HENRY BOSCH

Need to repair a relationship? Try kindness.

When I'm Afraid

PSALM 56

When I am afraid, I put my trust in [God].
PSALM 56:3

David fled from the home of the priests in Nob with Saul in hot pursuit. He made his way to Gath, the home of his enemies, where he was instantly recognized and brought before King Achish.

David's fame was celebrated everywhere in story and song. He had slain thousands of Philistines (1 Samuel 21:11), a reputation established at the expense of bereaved Philistine women and children. Here was an opportunity to take revenge.

David lost his nerve. In terror, he "pretended to be insane . . . , making marks on the doors of the gate and letting saliva run down his beard" (v. 13). Achish dismissed him with contempt: "Must this man come into my house?" (v. 15). Broken and utterly humiliated, David fled to Adullam in Judah. Close by was a hill honeycombed with caves. Into one of those holes he crept—alone.

As he experienced the solitude of that cave, at the nadir of his life and surrounded by enemies, David began to reflect on God's tender, faithful love. "When I am afraid, I put my trust in you," he wrote (Psalm 56:3). "You number my wanderings; put my tears into Your bottle" (v. 8 NKJV).

Perhaps you're "in a cave" today. You too can say, "In God I trust and am not afraid" (v. 11).

DAVID ROPER

Loneliness is being unaware of the One who is with us everywhere.

Of Chocolates and Bibles

1 PETER 1:22–25

For you have been born again, not of perishable seed, but of imperishable, through the living and enduring word of God.
1 PETER 1:23

Chocolates have been produced by the Cadbury company near Birmingham, England, for nearly two hundred years. Millions of people have enjoyed them, but few know the unusual story of Helen Cadbury, daughter of the company's president.

At age twelve, Helen Cadbury received Jesus Christ as her personal Savior. She immediately became interested in witnessing and in growing spiritually, so she began carrying her huge Victorian Bible to school. Because it was so cumbersome, her father gave her a small New Testament she could put in her pocket. Helen's Christian friends admired it and acquired their own so they could carry them and read the Word every day. Soon they were calling themselves the Pocket Testament League, and they began giving New Testaments to people who promised to read them. A policeman was the first to receive Christ after being given a free copy by one of Helen's friends.

The Pocket Testament League has become a worldwide ministry with millions of members. And the basic idea of sharing God's Word with others is good for all of us. Carry a Bible or New Testament with you, read it, and be a witness to its power.

DAVID EGNER

One measure of your love for God is your desire to share His Word with others.

Just a Coincidence?

NEHEMIAH 2:1-8

The king said to me, "What is it you want?" Then I prayed to the God of heaven, . . . "May I have a letter to Asaph, keeper of the royal park, so he will give me timber to make beams for the gates of the citadel by the temple and for the city wall . . . ?" And because the gracious hand of my God was on me, the king granted my requests.

NEHEMIAH 2:4, 8

A missionary in Africa was on his way to a village when he came to a narrow, turbulent river at floodstage. All the bridges had been washed away. Needing desperately to get across, he dropped to his knees and asked God to provide a way. Just then he heard a loud crash. A huge tree, its roots undermined by the rushing water, had fallen directly across the stream.

Believing he had seen a miracle, he thanked God for answering his prayer. But what if he told this story to a group of nonbelievers? They would probably say that the falling tree was a naturally produced event and that the timing was just a coincidence.

I am convinced that this falling tree was an answer to prayer. God often answers our petitions in such a way that only those who have spiritual insight can see His hand.

Consider Nehemiah. Standing before the king, he silently prayed. A little later, he left the monarch's presence with everything he needed to rebuild the walls of Jerusalem and help the Jews who returned there. No open miracle. Just the king being surprisingly helpful and generous. Who influenced him? God did. Why? Because Nehemiah prayed.

God answers our prayers. So keep praying!

HERB VANDER LUGT

Prayer moves the hand that moves the world.

Fruitfulness

JOHN 15:1–14

Remain in me, as I also remain in you. No branch can bear fruit by itself; it must remain in the vine. Neither can you bear fruit unless you remain in me.

JOHN 15:4

While visiting Russia, Joe Stowell, longtime president of Cornerstone University, met Christians who had spent ten years in prison for their faith. They told him they were forced to break rocks. As they swung their hammers, they often sang about Jesus. This so displeased the prison commander that he ordered them outside at 2 a.m. to sing before jeering guards. The believers sang with all their hearts.

One night the commander came alone to the barracks. "Tell me about this Christ," he said. The believers led that Russian commander to the Lord. He had seen the reality of their close relationship with Christ.

Before Jesus went to the cross, He used the analogy of a vine and its branches to encourage His disciples to stay in close relationship with Him. In the days to come, their world would be turned upside down. I believe the Lord was saying, "Rely on everything I've told you. Stay true to Me. Live in My love. If you do, your lives will produce fruit."

We may not always see dramatic conversions or immediate results when we abide in Christ, but wherever branches remain in the vine, there is life and fruit.

Lord, help us to abide in fellowship with You so that we may be fruitful.

DENNIS DEHAAN

Fruitfulness for Christ depends on fellowship with Christ.

Keep at It!

ISAIAH 55:6–13

So is my word that goes out from my mouth: It will not return to me empty,
but will accomplish what I desire and achieve the purpose for which I sent it.
ISAIAH 55:11

They knew Tom Dotson pretty well in the prisons of Michigan. They should have. He spent one-third of his first thirty-eight years as an inmate.

After he was released, Tom gave his testimony at an annual banquet for jail chaplains in Muskegon, Michigan. He said he had grown up in a Christian home but had rebelled and rejected the gospel. His wife, who sang for the banquet, had stayed with him in spite of his repeated failures. And a prison chaplain faithfully worked with him.

Finally, Tom genuinely surrendered to Jesus Christ. He stayed out of jail from that day forward.

In his testimony, Dotson spoke directly to Christian workers. "Continue on in your ministry with people like me," he urged, "no matter how frustrating. We may have lots of setbacks. But don't give up. There's power for change in even the most frustrating person through the sacrifice of Christ, the One who really sets us free." Then, looking right at the chaplain who had patiently witnessed to him, Tom said tenderly, "Thank you for not giving up on me."

Are you about to give up on someone? Don't! God will "freely pardon" all who come to Him (Isaiah 55:7). His powerful Word can bring change (v. 11), freeing men and women from the prison of sin (John 8:32). Keep at it!

DAVID EGNER

Instead of giving up on a person, give that person to God.

Safe in His Arms

PSALM 95

He tends his flock like a shepherd: He gathers the lambs in his arms and carries them close to his heart; he gently leads those that have young.
ISAIAH 40:11

Roy and Aleta Danforth first went to the African nation of Congo as missionaries in 1979. They were heartbroken when they had to leave the country in 1997. A tribal war that began in Rwanda was sweeping toward them across the country. Soldiers were finally seen in their area, so the Danforths and their fellow missionaries had to say goodbye to their good friends.

They had also been forced to evacuate a few years earlier, and now they were leaving once more. Aleta says she felt that she was on a roller coaster, and the ups and downs were overwhelming her.

While giving a report to her church after arriving in the US, she tearfully described the wild up-and-down emotions she had been experiencing. Then she remembered that on most roller coasters, no matter how high or how fast you go, you are kept snugly in place by a safety bar and a harness. *I'm even more secure*, Aleta thought, *because God has wrapped His arms around me. He is holding me as a shepherd holds a lamb. I am secure in His love.*

Have your emotions been on a wild roller-coaster ride? Let Aleta's experience show you that you are secure in God's loving, everlasting arms (Psalm 95:7; Isaiah 40:11).

DAVID EGNER

No matter how low you feel, underneath are the everlasting arms.

Loving the Unlovable

LUKE 19:1–10

"For the Son of Man came to seek and to save the lost."
LUKE 19:10

Zacchaeus was easy to dislike. As a tax collector for an oppressive occupying government, he made himself rich by overcharging his countrymen. Yet, to the consternation of the crowd, Jesus honored him by going to his house and eating with him.

A judge with a reputation for toughness tells how he learned to relate to unlovable people. In a Sunday morning homily his clergyman urged the congregation to try to look at people through the eyes of Jesus.

A few days later the judge was about to give a stiff sentence to an arrogant young man who kept getting in trouble. But then he remembered what the minister had suggested. The judge said, "I looked this young man in the eye and told him I thought he was a bright and talented human being. And then I said to him, 'Let's talk together about how we can get you living in more creative and constructive ways.' We had a surprisingly good conversation."

Jesus saw Zacchaeus as a sinner with an empty hole that only He could fill, and through His kindness Zacchaeus was transformed. The judge could not report any such change, but who knows the long-term outcome? He set a good example for all of us, because he saw the man through the eyes of Jesus.

HERB VANDER LUGT

True compassion will put love into action.

God's Protective Power

2 THESSALONIANS 3:1–5

*The Lord is faithful, and he will strengthen you
and protect you from the evil one.*
2 THESSALONIANS 3:3

Lorrie Anderson, missionary to the Candoshi Shapra people of Peru, was looking for a quiet place for her daily time of Bible reading and prayer, so she went down by the edge of the river.

After reading the Bible, she took up her prayer list. Eyes closed, she did not see the deadly anaconda weaving through the water until it struck, burying its fangs into her flesh. It withdrew to strike, hitting her arm again and again as it held her, screaming, in its coils. It reared up for the death blows. Then suddenly the giant snake, never known to release its prey, relaxed its grip and slithered off through the water.

While Lorrie was being treated, a witch doctor from a nearby village burst into the hut and stared at her. She couldn't believe Lorrie had survived. She said her son-in-law, also a witch doctor, had chanted to the spirit of the anaconda that morning and sent it to kill the young missionary. "I'm certain," Lorrie said, "that except for the protection of God, it would have worked."

That same God is on our side in the battle with that old serpent, the devil (Revelation 20:2). The Lord defends us both physically and spiritually in ways we often do not recognize or understand. How thankful we can be for God's protective power!

DAVID EGNER

**We need not fear the perils around us because
the power of God surrounds us.**

Formula for Success

ROMANS 6:1–14

Count yourselves dead to sin but alive to God in Christ Jesus.
ROMANS 6:11

What does Paul mean in Romans 6:11 when he says we must count ourselves "dead to sin"? Maybe this story by Bible teacher Keith Brooks will help explain it.

Twentieth-century Bible teacher and author Keith L. Brooks (1888–1954) told how this truth was borne out in something that happened to John Foster, a foreman in a pottery factory. The owner of the business wrote his formulas for making pottery in a little book that he kept in his private office and guarded jealously. One day Foster was confronted by an almost irresistible temptation.

Unaware that the owner had been called from his office, Foster walked in to look for him. What he found was the formula book lying open on the desk. The thought struck him that if he quickly copied some of the formulas, he could use them to begin his own pottery business. The thought of riches loomed before him. An internal struggle ensued, but it ended quickly. Reckoning himself *dead to sin*, he closed the book, lifted it heavenward, and said, "Hallelujah! Victory through Christ!" Although he continued for many years at his same position and salary, great joy filled his heart because he had applied the truth of Romans 6:11.

Read Romans 6. Then start regarding yourself as dead to sin but "alive to God." Sin will lose its attraction. You'll have a formula for success.

PAUL VAN GORDER

**Think less of the power of things OVER you and
more of the power of Christ IN you.**

Good and Bad Laughter

ECCLESIASTES 3:1–8

There is a time for everything, and a season for every activity under the heavens: . . .
a time to weep and a time to laugh, a time to mourn and a time to dance.
ECCLESIASTES 3:1, 4

Doctors and psychologists tell us that laughter is good for us. This is undoubtedly true, because the Bible says that "a cheerful heart is good medicine" (Proverbs 17:22).

But the Scriptures distinguish between good and bad laughter. The author of Ecclesiastes declared that the laughter of people who have no place for God in their lives has no more value than the noise of crackling thorns in a fire (Ecclesiastes 7:6). God disapproves of any humor that belittles people or makes light of immorality. Sin is never a laughing matter.

Joe E. Brown was a top-notch movie and Broadway comedian of the World War II era. When entertaining American troops in the South Pacific, he was asked by a soldier to tell some "dirty jokes." He responded, "Son, a comedian like me lives for applause and laughter. . . . But if telling a dirty story is the price I must pay for your laughter, then I'm not interested. I've never done an act that I couldn't perform before my mother, and I never will." The soldiers rocked the jungle with their cheers.

Lord, give us a cheerful heart. And help us be discerning so we will laugh
for the right reasons and about the right things.
HERB VANDER LUGT

Wholesome laughter has great face value.

The Mule Knew the Way

JOB 23:1–10

But he knows the way that I take;
when he has tested me, I will come forth as gold.
JOB 23:10

Many years ago, I was invited to preach in a remote mission station in the hills of Kentucky. To get there, I first took a passenger train. After that, I rode in the cab of a logging-train engine over a winding track that crossed several rickety wooden trestles spanning roaring streams. The engineer, sensing my uneasiness, assured me that he made the run every day.

Then things got interesting. When we reached the end of the track, it was dark. I was met by my missionary host, who introduced me to my next means of transportation—an old skinny mule. As he helped me into the saddle, he said, "Don't use the reins, and don't try to guide the mule. He knows this road much better than you do."

It was pitch dark, and I could not see one step ahead. So I just trusted the intelligence of the mule, and we finally arrived at the mission station.

When it was time for the return trip, the missionary took me back to the road over which the mule and I had traveled. My heart skipped a beat when I saw the narrow, dangerous, rocky trail I had traveled along the rim of the mountain at night. One slip and I would have landed in a chasm a hundred feet below!

I learned a lesson that day. If we could see the dangers ahead we would despair—so sometimes the Lord leaves us in the dark. We must travel on in faith, trusting the one who knows the way! If your path is difficult today—let Him lead.

M. R. DeHaan

The Lord may lead you around, but He'll lead you aright!

An Unusual Couple?

ACTS 18:1–3, 18–28

He began to speak boldly in the synagogue. When Priscilla and Aquila heard him, they invited him to their home and explained to him the way of God more adequately.

ACTS 18:26

The more we see marriage problems all around us, the more we wonder where to look for a marriage that is working.

How about the story of a couple who not only made their marriage work but who also used their unity to assist the early church? Their names were Aquila and Priscilla.

Notice the characteristics that made them so helpful to Paul, and which, I believe, reflected the strength of their marriage.

They were selfless and brave. They "risked their lives" for Paul (Romans 16:4).

They were hospitable. A church met in their home (1 Corinthians 16:19).

They were flexible. Twice they had to move—once by force from Rome (Acts 18:2) and once by choice to go on a missionary trip with Paul (v. 18).

They worked together. They were tentmakers (v. 3).

They both were committed to Christ and teaching others about Him. They invited Apollos to their home, where they "explained to him the way of God more accurately" (v. 26).

Priscilla were a unit—a team—an inseparable twosome. That may make them an unusual couple, but it's a difference we who are married should all hope to imitate.

DAVE BRANON

Marriage works best when a couple has a single purpose.

Down but Not Destroyed

2 CORINTHIANS 4:7–15

We are hard pressed on every side, but not crushed;
perplexed, but not in despair.

2 CORINTHIANS 4:8, 9

These bodies of ours truly are "jars of clay" (2 Corinthians 4:7). They are fragile and weak and susceptible to injury and disease. But physical limitations need not limit the spirit. Many believers have learned that to be "hard pressed" does not mean "crushed."

Leon J. Wood (1918–1977) was an example of that during the closing years of his life. While this brilliant Old Testament scholar was in his prime as an author and as the dean of a seminary, he contracted Amyotrophic Lateral Sclerosis—Lou Gehrig's disease. Bit by bit, it struck down Wood's body. When he could no longer run, he had to give up tennis. Walking became difficult as he grew weaker and weaker. Finally, he was confined to his bed. But as his body weakened, his faith and resolve strengthened. He continued to study, to teach, and to write. Some of his most significant books were written in the latter stages of his illness. The last seminary class he taught met at his bedside. His spirit remained strong to the end. He was not "crushed."

Perhaps you too are hard pressed by some disease or crippled by some serious setback. Don't let it destroy you. Choose to hold fast to God's goodness. Trust Him. Obey Him. In so doing, you will demonstrate the power of God and bring encouragement to others.

DAVID EGNER

When adversity strikes us, God is ready to strengthen us.

Get Your Hands Dirty

LUKE 5:27–32

The Pharisees and the teachers of the law who belonged to their sect complained to his disciples, "Why do you eat and drink with tax collectors and sinners?"

LUKE 5:30

Aloof Christians make poor witnesses. Non-Christians need to interact with flesh-and-blood followers of Jesus who think, talk, and act like He did.

When F. B. Meyer (1847–1929) became pastor of Christ Church in England, only middle-class and wealthy people attended services. He decided to change this by making friends with the poor people who lived nearby. One morning a garbage collector shouted from his wagon, "Good morning, Brother Meyer." The preacher replied, "Good morning, dear brother." When the man jumped down, Meyer extended his hand. The garbage collector drew back, saying, "Excuse me, sir, my hand is not fit for the likes of you." "There's lots of soap and water at Christ Church," Meyer responded. "Please give me your hand." So they shook hands, and the two walked together down the street. Soon they met four other men, and the garbage collector held up his hand. "Look here, mates," he said, "the new parson has shaken that filthy hand." One replied, "Well, if he'll do that, he'll do to listen to." And they all came to hear the gospel.

Jesus was not afraid to dirty His hands (or His reputation) in order to call despised tax collectors and sinners to repentance and faith. Are we willing to do the same to draw people to Jesus, our wonderful Savior?

DENNIS DEHAAN

**While we are praying for sinners to come to Christ,
He is pleading for us to go to sinners.**

Make My Brown Eyes Blue

MATTHEW 16:24–28

For whoever wants to save their life will lose it,
but whoever loses their life for me will find it.

MATTHEW 16:25

As a young girl, Amy Carmichael (1867–1951) wished she had blue eyes instead of brown. She even prayed that God would change her eye color and was disappointed when it didn't happen. At age twenty, Amy sensed that the Lord was calling her to serve Him as a missionary. After serving in various places, she went to India. It was then that she realized God's wisdom in the way He had made her. She realized that she may have had a more difficult time gaining acceptance from the brown-eyed people if her eyes had been blue. She served God in India for fifty-five years.

We don't know for sure that Amy was more readily accepted because of her eye color. But we do know and believe that it is the Lord "who made us, and we are his" (Psalm 100:3). As we submit to His wisdom in everything, we can serve Him effectively.

Amy knew what submission was. When asked about missionary life, she replied, "Missionary life is simply a chance to die." Jesus said, "Whoever wants to save their life will lose it, but whoever loses their life for me will find it" (Matthew 16:25).

That describes the devoted Christian's life as well—total surrender to God's plans and will for us. May we submit to Him today.

ANNE CETAS

Our lives are never more secure than when they are abandoned to God.

Sinners Like Us

LUKE 15:1–7

This man welcomes sinners and eats with them.
LUKE 15:2

I have a friend—her name is Edith—who told me about the day she decided to follow Jesus.

Edith cared nothing for religion. But one Sunday morning she walked into a church near her apartment looking for anything that might satisfy her discontented soul. The text that day was Luke 15:1–2, which the pastor read from the King James Version: "Then drew near unto him all the publicans and sinners for to hear him. And the Pharisees and scribes murmured, saying, This man receiveth sinners, and eateth with them."

That's what it said, but this is what Edith heard: "This man receives sinners and *Edith* with them." She sat straight up in her pew! Eventually she realized her mistake, but the thought that Jesus welcomed sinners—*and that included Edith*—stayed with her. That afternoon she decided to "draw near" to Jesus and listen to Him. She began to read the Gospels, and soon she decided to put her faith in Him and follow Him.

The religious folks of Jesus's day were scandalized by the fact that He ate and drank with sinful, awful people. Their rules prohibited them from associating with such folk. Jesus paid no attention to their made-up rules. He welcomed the down-and-out and gathered them to Him, no matter how far gone they were.

It's still true, you know: Jesus receives sinners and _____ (your name).

DAVID ROPER

God pursues us in our restlessness, receives us in our sinfulness, holds us in our brokenness. —Scotty Smith

A Complete Salvation

TITUS 3:1–8

He saved us, not because of righteous things we had done,
but because of his mercy. He saved us through the washing of rebirth and
renewal by the Holy Spirit, . . . so that, having been justified by his grace,
we might become heirs having the hope of eternal life.

TITUS 3:5, 7

John Newton, author of the well-known hymn "Amazing Grace," was a miserable man at the age of twenty-three. He had been involved in an immoral lifestyle and was engaged in the heartlessly cruel African slave trade as a seaman. But he was fed up with his sinful way of life.

A crisis came on March 10, 1748, on board a ship that was caught in a violent storm. Thinking all was lost, Newton cried out in terror, "Lord, have mercy on us!" Suddenly the word *mercy* struck him with great force. If anybody needed it, he did. At that moment he believed on Jesus Christ as his Savior. God forgave his sins and broke the power of his wicked lifestyle.

The apostle Paul referred to both the mercy and the grace of God in salvation. He declared that it is by God's grace we are justified and delivered from the guilt of our sins (Titus 3:7). But he also said it is God's mercy that delivers us from a lifestyle that he described as "foolish, disobedient, deceived, serving various lusts and pleasures, living in malice and envy, hateful and hating one another" (v. 3 NKJV).

Let's thank God daily for His grace and His mercy. Together they provide for us a complete salvation.

HERB VANDER LUGT

Grace and mercy are unearned blessings given to unworthy sinners.

You're Not Home Yet

PHILIPPIANS 3:17–4:1

But our citizenship is in heaven.
PHILIPPIANS 3:20

Today's heroes are often overrated. Many sports personalities, entertainers, and movie stars receive acclaim that is out of proportion to the value of their achievements. On the other hand, many Christians have done work of eternal significance through prayer and faithful service for the Lord, yet have spent their entire lives in obscurity.

Just after the end of his presidency, Theodore Roosevelt went on a long hunting safari to Africa. On Roosevelt's return to the US, Henry Morrison, who was retiring after forty years of missionary work in a remote jungle village was traveling on the same vessel. When the ship docked at New York Harbor, cheering throngs greeted the popular former chief executive, but no one was there to welcome Morrison and his wife.

Momentarily the man of God was filled with self-pity. He thought, *When a president comes home after a hunting trip, thousands come out to greet him. But Lord, when one of your missionaries comes home after a lifetime of service, no one is there to meet him.* Immediately it was as if the Lord whispered, "But Henry, you are not home yet."

Do you sometimes feel a little like that faithful missionary? Look again at the blessed reality expressed in Philippians 3:20. Your citizenship is not of this world. Someday you'll receive the real welcome.

DENNIS DEHAAN

The greatest use of life is to spend it for something that will outlast it.

The Truth about Honesty

1 PETER 2:11–19

Finally, brothers and sisters, whatever is true, whatever is noble, whatever is right, whatever is pure, whatever is lovely, whatever is admirable— if anything is excellent or praiseworthy—think about such things.

PHILIPPIANS 4:8

A news story told of a supervisor in an office instructing his secretary to alter some questionable financial records. When she refused, he asked incredulously, "Don't you ever lie?" For many people, honesty in public as well as in private life is an obsolete virtue—a moral remnant of bygone days.

Honesty has many aspects. It means speaking out if remaining silent would convey the wrong impression. It involves representing a situation accurately. It also includes making a reasonable effort to return something we find to its rightful owner.

I was deeply moved when I read about Sa'ad, a sensitive, hardworking man who worked long hours collecting trash in Cairo, Egypt, so he could eke out a livelihood for his wife and children. Often he cleared little more than fifty cents a day. One day he found a gold watch valued at nearly $2,000, but he returned it to its owner. Why? Sa'ad, a Christian, knew it was wrong to keep what didn't belong to him.

This kind of honesty must be evident in our lives as Christians. Remember, Jesus, our Savior, is the way, the truth, and the life (John 14:6). Truthfulness, therefore, must be the way of life with all who follow Him.

DENNIS DEHAAN

Some people are honest only because they have never had a good chance to steal anything.

"For This, I Have Jesus"

ISAIAH 49:13–20

Shout for joy, you heavens; rejoice, you earth;
burst into song, you mountains! For the LORD comforts his people
and will have compassion on his afflicted ones.

ISAIAH 49:13

There is rarely a problem-free season in our lives, but sometimes the onslaught is terrifying.

Rose saw her entire family, except for her two little daughters, slaughtered in the Rwandan Genocide of 1994. She became a widow among many widows with little money. But she refused to be defeated. She adopted two orphans and simply trusted God to provide for the food and school fees for her family of five. She translated Christian literature into the local language and organized an annual conference for other widows. Rose wept as she told me her story. But for every problem in her life she has one simple remedy. "For this," she said, "I have Jesus."

God knows exactly what you are facing. God's knowledge of us is so intimate it is as if our names were written on the palms of His hands (Isaiah 49:16). God is aware of every detail of our lives. And He has given us His Spirit to guide, to comfort, and to strengthen us.

Think of the challenges you face at this moment, and then write these words beside each one as a reminder of His faithfulness and care: "For this, I have Jesus."

MARION STROUD

Those who see God's hand in everything are content
to leave everything in God's hand!

Shipwrecked for God's Glory

PHILIPPIANS 1:1–12

Now I want you to know, brothers and sisters, that what has happened to me has actually served to advance the gospel.

PHILIPPIANS 1:12

When Alexander Duff (1806–1878) embarked on his first missionary journey from Scotland to India in 1830, he discovered that God sometimes allows difficulties to beset his people.

As he sailed for India on the *Lady Holland*, he had his clothes, his prized possessions, his library of 800 volumes all on board. Within a few miles of India's coast, however, he and his fellow travelers were shipwrecked. The passengers were rescued, but all their belongings were lost. When Duff reached shore, he looked back, hoping to see his luggage floating toward shore. Suddenly he spied something very small. Nearer and nearer it came, while anxious eyes watched it. Finally, Duff waded into the water and secured it. It was his packaged Bible.

He took this to be a token of the Lord's blessing. So heartened, he got to work. The very next day, reading from that Bible, he began his first meeting with a group of five boys under a banyan tree. Within a week the class had grown to 300 listeners! Eventually a chapel stood on that spot, and a thousand students of the gospel raised their voices in prayer and praise to Jesus Christ.

Alexander Duff's shipwreck had "actually served to advance the gospel."

HENRY BOSCH

**There are no accidents in God's dealings;
all things have divine purpose!**

Misunderstood

EXODUS 17:1–4

So then, those who suffer according to God's will should commit themselves to their faithful Creator and continue to do good.

1 PETER 4:19

Even though Moses gave up the treasures and honors of Egypt to lead his people out of bondage, they didn't appreciate what he had done. He was obedient to the will of God and did everything he could for them, yet they murmured against him. What should we do today if we were to receive the same kind of treatment?

Years ago a magazine article told a story about noted preacher Charles H. Spurgeon (1834–1892). It said that he and his wife were called "miserly" because they sold all the eggs their chickens laid and wouldn't give any away. Because they always made a profit on their butter, milk, and eggs, rumors circulated that they were greedy.

The Spurgeons, however, took the criticism graciously, and only after the death of Mrs. Spurgeon was the truth revealed. The records showed that their entire profits had been used to support two needy, elderly widows whose husbands had spent their lives in serving the Lord. Yet because the Spurgeons did not want to call attention to their giving (Matthew 6:3), they had refused to defend themselves.

Are you being misunderstood today in spite of your pure motives and faithful service? Don't be discouraged. God knows the motives of your heart. Commit your situation to Him and keep on doing good (1 Peter 4:19).

HENRY BOSCH

God judges us not by what others say, but by what we do.

2 A.M. Friends

COLOSSIANS 4:2–15

Epaphras, who is one of you and a servant of Christ Jesus, sends greetings.
He is always wrestling in prayer for you, that you may stand firm in all the
will of God, mature and fully assured.

COLOSSIANS 4:12

A friend told me about a group of people who share a strong bond of faith in Christ. One of them, a ninety-three-year-old woman, said, "I feel like I can call any of you at 2 a.m., and I don't even have to apologize if I feel the need for any type of assistance." Whether the need is prayer, practical help, or someone to be there during a time of need, these friends are unconditionally committed to each other.

The same sense of commitment shines through Paul's letter to the followers of Jesus in Colosse. Writing from prison in Rome, Paul says he is sending Tychicus and Onesimus to encourage them (Colossians 4:7–9). He said that Aristarchus, Mark, and Justus send their greetings (vv. 10–11). And Epaphras is "always wrestling in prayer for you, that you may stand firm in all the will of God, mature and fully assured" (v. 12). These are bold assurances of practical help and deep-seated love.

Are you part of a "2 a.m. group"? If so, give thanks for the faithfulness of friends. If not, ask the Lord to connect you with another person with whom you can share a commitment to pray and care. I suspect it will soon grow to include others. Share the love of Christ with one another.

Anything. Anytime. Anywhere. All in Jesus's name!

DAVID MCCASLAND

Greater love has no one than this: to lay down one's life
for one's friends. —John 15:13

The Dedicated Penny

MARK 12:38–44

For if the willingness is there, the gift is acceptable according to what one has, not according to what one does not have.

2 CORINTHIANS 8:12

Pastor and songwriter Wendell P. Loveless (1892–1997) related the following incident: "A little girl who loved the Lord longed to share the message of salvation with those who had never heard it. So she contributed a penny to a missionary to help with the work of evangelizing the people of Burma. That small coin was all she had, but she gave it from her heart. The missionary was deeply touched by the child's earnestness and decided he would do the most he could with the money. He bought a gospel tract for a penny and personally gave it to a young chieftain."

Apparently, the Christian did not know that the tribal leader couldn't read. But God instilled within the ruler a burning desire to know the meaning of the leaflet, so he traveled 250 miles to find someone who could translate it for him. After he heard the gospel message, it wasn't long before the young chief trusted Jesus. Returning to his people, he told them what the Lord had done for his soul. Later, he invited missionaries to come and preach to his entire village, and many tribesmen who heard the good news accepted the Savior. All this and probably much more resulted from one dedicated penny given in Christ's name by a little girl who wanted the lost to hear about Jesus!

Don't wait until you can do "great things" to start working for the Master. God can do wonders with dedicated little things.

HENRY BOSCH

Christ often uses the smallest tools to perform the largest tasks.

A New Man

COLOSSIANS 1:3–14

Continue in your faith, established and firm, and do not move from the hope held out in the gospel. This is the gospel that you heard and that has been proclaimed to every creature under heaven, and of which I, Paul, have become a servant.

COLOSSIANS 1:23

As a group of teenagers visited a home for the elderly in Montego Bay, Jamaica, one teen noticed a lonely looking man at the end of the room. He appeared to have little left in this world but a bed from which he could not move because of his disability.

The teen began right away to share the story of God's love and read some Bible passages to him. "As I shared with him," she would say later, "I started to feel his eagerness to hear more." Responding to his interest, she explained Jesus's sacrificial death for us. "It was hard for this man, with no hope and no family," she recalled, "to understand that Someone he's never met would love him enough to die for his sins."

She told him more about Jesus—and then about the promise of heaven (including a new body) for all who believe. He asked her, "Will you dance with me up there?" She saw him begin to imagine himself free of his worn-out body and crippling limitations.

When he said he wanted to trust Jesus as his Savior, she helped him pray a prayer of forgiveness and faith. When she asked him if she could get a picture with him, he replied, "If you help me sit up. I'm a new man."

Praise God for the life-changing, hope-giving, available-to-all gospel of Jesus Christ! It offers new life for all who trust Him (Colossians 1:5, 23).

DAVE BRANON

Jesus offers new life.

Taking the First Step

2 CORINTHIANS 5:11-21

God was reconciling the world to himself in Christ, not counting people's sins against them. And he has committed to us the message of reconciliation.

2 CORINTHIANS 5:19

Tham Dashu sensed something was missing in his life. So he started going to church—the same church his daughter attended. But they never went together. In earlier days, he had offended her, which drove a wedge between them. So, Tham would slip in when the singing started and leave promptly after the service ended.

Church members shared the gospel story with him, but Tham always politely rejected their invitation to put his faith in Jesus. Still, he kept coming to church.

One day Tham fell gravely ill. His daughter plucked up the courage and wrote him a letter. She shared how Christ had changed her life, and she sought reconciliation with her dad. That night, Tham put his faith in Jesus and the family was reconciled. A few days later, Tham died and entered into the presence of Jesus—at peace with God and his loved ones.

The apostle Paul wrote that we are to "try to persuade others" about the truth of God's love and forgiveness (2 Corinthians 5:11). He said that it is "Christ's love [that] compels us" to carry out His work of reconciliation (v. 14).

Our willingness to forgive may help others realize that God desires to reconcile us to himself (v. 19). Would you lean on God's strength to show others His love today?

POH FANG CHIA

**Our willingness to seek reconciliation with others
shows God's heart to them.**

Not Saying Goodbye

PHILIPPIANS 4:1–9

Whatever you have learned or received or heard from me, or seen in me—
put it into practice. And the God of peace will be with you.

PHILIPPIANS 4:9

Francis Allen led me to Jesus, and now it was nearly time for Francis to meet Jesus face to face. I was at his home as it grew time for him to say goodbye. I wanted to say something memorable and meaningful.

For nearly an hour I stood by his bed. He laughed hard at the stories I told on myself. Then he got tired, we got serious, and he spent his energy rounding off some rough edges he still saw in my life. I listened, even as I tried to sort out how to say goodbye.

He stopped me before I got the chance. "You remember, Randy, what I've always told you. We have nothing to fear from the story of life because we know how it ends. I'm not afraid. You go do what I've taught you." Those challenging words reminded me of what the apostle Paul said to the believers in Philippi: "The things which you learned and received and heard and saw in me, these do" (Philippians 4:9 NKJV).

Francis had the same twinkle in his eye this last day I saw him as he had the first day I met him. He had no fear in his heart.

So many of the words I write, stories I tell, and people I serve are touched by Francis. As we journey through life, may we remember those who have encouraged us spiritually.

RANDY KILGORE

Live so that when people get to know you,
they will want to know Christ.

How Are You Running?

HEBREWS 12:1-4

Let us run with perseverance the race marked out for us.
HEBREWS 12:1

Millions of people became familiar with Eric Liddell through the prize-winning 1981 movie *Chariots of Fire*. It depicted this Scottish athlete's devotion to Jesus Christ and his refusal under severe pressure to violate his spiritual convictions—even at the expense of Olympic glory.

Ian Charleson, who played the role of Eric Liddell in the film, had to learn to run with his head tilted back in the style of that Olympic champion. On the sixth day of filming, Charleson concluded that Eric's unconventional running style was inspired by trust. He "trusted to get there," said Charleson. "He ran with faith. He didn't even look where he was going."

That trust carried over into Eric's spiritual life. It was trust that took him to China as a missionary. Head up, trusting his Savior, he died young in a Japanese concentration camp, still faithfully serving God.

"Let us run," Hebrews 12:1 exhorts us. Run as Paul did as he copied his example Jesus (1 Corinthians 11:1). Run head up, trusting our Coach to get us to the goal He has set before us. Run not to gain the approval and applause of people nor to win any of this world's trophies. Run so as to win "a crown that will last forever" (9:25). How are you running?

VERNON GROUNDS

Expect great things from God; attempt great things for God.
—William Carey

Granville Sharp

JAMES 1:19–27

Do not merely listen to the word, and so deceive yourselves. Do what it says.
JAMES 1:22

When I was a Bible college student, a name occasionally mentioned in Greek class was that of Granville Sharp (1735–1813). He was a renowned Greek scholar whose studies resulted in principles of biblical interpretation that continue to guide our understanding of the original language of the New Testament.

To study the Scriptures and learn the powerful truths they contain is noble, but no matter how deeply we study, it is not enough. James challenged us to understand this when he wrote: "Do not merely listen to the word, and so deceive yourselves. Do what it says. Anyone who listens to the word but does not do what it says is like someone who looks at his face in a mirror and, after looking at himself, goes away and immediately forgets what he looks like" (James 1:22–24).

Granville Sharp understood this and put his faith into practice. In addition to being a biblical scholar, he also fought to eradicate slavery in England. Sharp said, "A toleration of slavery is, in effect, a toleration of inhumanity." His biblical understanding of the worth of a human soul and the justice of a holy God compelled him to act on his beliefs.

We can benefit from Sharp's passion for the Word—and for living out the truth that Word contains.

BILL CROWDER

We don't really know the Bible unless we obey the Bible.

The Fruit of Christlike Love

1 JOHN 4:7–11

Dear friends, since God so loved us, we also ought to love one another.
1 JOHN 4:11

Eleanor Chestnut, a medical missionary in China, beautifully exemplified Christlike love. A beggar had come to the hospital badly burned, but no one was willing to donate skin for a graft. So the next morning the nurses were surprised to learn that the operation had been performed. Then they noticed that Dr. Chestnut was limping and realized that she had surgically removed some of her own skin to save the victim's life. They were amazed at such a sacrifice, for they couldn't understand why she would do this for a total stranger.

Later, during an uprising in her community, this gallant missionary again manifested a selflessness that profoundly impressed the Chinese people. In the midst of the chaos, she saw a little boy bruised and bleeding. Immediately she ripped some material from her dress, knelt down, and bound up the youngster's wound. A few hours afterward, she was attacked and killed. Fifty years passed, and people in China still talked about the foreign doctor whose loving concern for others made them think of Jesus.

How can we be that unselfish? By abiding in Christ! This means being conscious of our union with Him and spending time in communion with Him. Only as we practice the presence of Christ can we bear the precious fruit of Christlike love.

HERB VANDER LUGT

Love for God is evidenced by our love for others.

We Thank the Lord

PROVERBS 3:1–12

Trust in the LORD with all your heart
and lean not on your own understanding.

PROVERBS 3:5

Anna Anderson's husband died early in their marriage, leaving her with three young daughters and a difficult future. Although trained in Virginia as a teacher, she lacked full credentials to work in the Philadelphia schools, so she took in laundry, did ironing, and later scrubbed floors at a large department store. As African Americans, the Anderson family often experienced racial prejudice and discrimination.

Whenever doors of opportunity closed, Anna believed that if they would trust the Lord with all their heart and acknowledge Him in all their ways, He would direct their paths (Proverbs 3:5–6). She taught her daughters to depend on God, follow Him, and always be thankful.

When her firstborn, Marian Anderson, rose to international acclaim as a classical singer, Anna continued to pray for her and always gave God credit for her success. Reporters who asked Anna how she felt after attending Marian's concerts at Carnegie Hall and her debut with the Metropolitan Opera heard her say, "We thank the Lord." Her reply was not a cliché but sincere gratefulness to God.

Rather than lament what she lacked, Anna Anderson expressed gratitude for what she had and used it for God's glory. Today, we can follow her example with faith, confidence, and a heartfelt, "We thank the Lord."

DAVID McCASLAND

Gratitude is a mark of godliness.

Julie's Prayer

JOHN 14:12-14

*I will do whatever you ask in my name, so that the Father
may be glorified in the Son.*

JOHN 14:13

Several years ago, a film crew from the television program *Day of Discovery*
traveled to China on a special assignment—to retrace the life of missionary
Eric Liddell, the 1924 Olympic gold medalist whose story was told in the
Academy Award-winning movie *Chariots of Fire*. The crew took with them
Eric's three daughters: Patricia, Heather, and Maureen—allowing them to
revisit some of the places where the two older sisters had lived in China.
Also along on the trip was their elderly Aunt Louise.

On one occasion, after the entourage had arrived in Beijing, they had
to walk quite a distance with their luggage. As they did, Aunt Louise grew
short of breath. Julie Richardson, a *Day of Discovery* crew member, sat
down beside her, put her hand on her knee, and prayed simply, "Dear Jesus,
help Aunt Louise to breathe." Immediately, she began to catch her breath.

Later, Heather retold the story and shared that Julie's prayer had
rekindled her faith. Julie's simple act of faith reminded Heather of the
continual connection we have with Jesus—a reality she had set aside in
her life.

Sometimes we need reminders that God is near. When trials come and
God seems far away, remember Julie's prayer and the truth that we are just
one prayer from connecting with the God of the universe (John 14:13).

DAVE BRANON

God delights in the earnest prayers of His people.

My All

MATTHEW 27:45–54

Therefore, I urge you, brothers and sisters, in view of God's mercy,
to offer your bodies as a living sacrifice, holy and pleasing to God—
this is your true and proper worship.

ROMANS 12:1

As a young man, Isaac Watts (1674–1748) found the music in his church sadly lacking, and his father challenged him to create something better. Isaac did. His hymn "When I Survey the Wondrous Cross" was called by English poet Matthew Arnold the greatest in the English language.

Watts's third verse ushers us into the presence of Christ at the crucifixion.

See from His head, His hands, His feet,
Sorrow and love flow mingled down.
Did e'er such love and sorrow meet
Or thorns compose so rich a crown?

The crucifixion Watts describes so elegantly stands as history's most awful moment. The Son of God strains for breath, held by crude spikes driven through His flesh. After tortured hours, a supernatural darkness descends. Finally, mercifully, the Lord of the universe dismisses His anguished spirit. An earthquake rattles the landscape. In the city, the thick temple curtain rips in half (Matthew 27:51). These events compel the centurion who crucified Jesus to say, "Surely he was the Son of God!" (v. 54).

Watts's song concludes eloquently, "Love so amazing, love so divine demands my soul, my life, my all."

TIM GUSTAFSON

It is our privilege to give everything we have to the
One who gave us everything on the cross.

His Word the Last Word

PSALM 63:1–11

*On my bed I remember you; I think of you through the watches of the night.
Because you are my help, I sing in the shadow of your wings.*

PSALM 63:6–7

Dawson Trotman (1906–1956), a dynamic Christian leader of the mid-twentieth century and founder of The Navigators, emphasized the importance of the Bible in the life of every Christian. Trotman ended each day with a practice he called "His Word the last word." Before going to sleep he meditated on a memorized Bible verse or passage, then he prayed about its place and influence in his life. He wanted the last words he thought about each day to be God's words.

The psalmist David wrote, "On my bed I remember you; I think of you through the watches of the night. Because you are my help, I sing in the shadow of your wings" (Psalm 63:6–7). Whether we are in great difficulty or enjoying a time of peace, our last thought at night can ease our minds with the rest and comfort God gives. It may also set the tone for our first thought the next morning.

A friend and his wife conclude each day by reading aloud a Bible passage and daily devotional with their four children. They welcome questions and thoughts from each child and talk about what it means to follow Jesus at home and school. They call it their version of "His Word the last word" for each day.

There can be no better way to end our day!

DAVID McCASLAND

**The Spirit of God renews our minds when we
meditate on the Word of God.**

Garden of Prayer

ACTS 12:5-17

So Peter was kept in prison, but the church was earnestly praying to God for him.
ACTS 12:5

When I was a pastor, I often visited residents in nursing homes. I'll never forget one dear elderly lady I met. She was blind and had been bedridden for seven years, yet she remained sweet and radiant. One day she told me about a dream she had. She was in a beautiful garden, where the grass was a luxuriant carpet beneath her and the fragrance of flowers filled the air.

She dropped to her knees, entranced by the scene. As her thoughts were drawn heavenward, she felt the need to pray for her own pastor, for me, and for others. When she awakened, however, she discovered that she was still in her hospital bed. With a smile she said to me, "You know, Pastor, at first I was a bit disappointed. But in a sense the dream was true. This old bed has been a garden of prayer these seven years!" Prayer had made her room a holy place of meditation and blessing.

Prayer also made a difference when Peter was in prison (Acts 12). It isn't always easy to pray, for real intercession takes self-discipline. Many of us lapse into saying fine-sounding words without truly praying. God often drives us to our knees through the press of circumstances, where we are to "look to the LORD and his strength; seek his face always" (1 Chronicles 16:11).

HERB VANDER LUGT

God and prayer go together; to neglect one is to neglect the other.

Faith That Works

HABAKKUK 3:8–19

*Though the fig tree does not bud and there are no grapes on the vines,
though the olive crop fails and the fields produce no food, though there are no
sheep in the pen and no cattle in the stalls, yet I will rejoice in the LORD,
I will be joyful in God my Savior.*

HABAKKUK 3:17–18

I read about a family who lost three children to diphtheria in the same week. Only a three-year-old girl escaped the disease. On the following Easter morning, the father, mother, and child attended church. Because the father was the Sunday school superintendent, he led the session when all the classes met together. As he read the Easter message from the Bible, many were weeping, but the father and mother remained calm and serene.

When Sunday school was over, a fifteen-year-old boy was walking home with his father. "The superintendent and his wife must really believe the Easter story," said the boy. His dad answered, "All Christians do." "Not the way they do!" replied the teen.

How we react under trial demonstrates the depth of our convictions. This is not to say that a true Christian will not weep at the loss of a loved one. However, knowing that all believers who die go into Christ's presence, we need not "grieve like the rest of mankind, who have no hope" (1 Thessalonians 4:13). We can say, "Thank you, Lord," because we know He can be trusted to do what is best. The prophet said it well: "Though the fig tree does not bud and there no grapes on the vines; . . . yet I will rejoice in the LORD" (Habakkuk 3:17–18).

RICHARD DEHAAN

Faith in Christ knows that the best is yet to come.

Confident Prayer

MATTHEW 7:7–11

Pray in the Spirit on all occasions with all kinds of prayers and requests. With this in mind, be alert and always keep on praying for all the Lord's people.

EPHESIANS 6:18

As one of Africa's first explorers, David Livingstone (1813–1873) loved that continent's people and longed to see them reached for Jesus Christ. His journals reveal his spiritual concern and deep faith.

In late March 1872, he wrote, "He will keep His word—the gracious One, full of grace and truth—no doubt of it. He said, 'Him that cometh unto Me, I will in no wise cast out' and 'Whatsoever ye shall ask in my name I will give it.' He will keep His word; then I can come and humbly present my petition, and it will be all right. Doubt is here inadmissible, surely."

Livingstone had rock-like confidence in the Father's promises. In our praying we too can exercise the trust that God will not deny our requests when they are in keeping with His will. By the way, we must read the Bible faithfully so we can know His will.

We can defeat doubt when we remind ourselves that no matter what happens in life, God cares deeply about us and longs to give us the wisdom to handle what comes our way (1 Peter 5:7; James 1:5). Our faith will grow stronger as we realize that our heavenly Father is gracious, delighting to give good gifts to His children (Matthew 7:11). Humbly but confidently, we can come to Him with our requests—whether we are serving God in a faraway land or right at home.

VERNON GROUNDS

When we love God as our Father, we won't treat Him as our servant.

God's Love and Ours

ROMANS 5:1-11

But God demonstrates his own love for us in this:
While we were still sinners, Christ died for us.

ROMANS 5:8

Franklin Graham regrets it now, but in his youth he was wild and rebellious. One day he went roaring up to his dad's house on his Harley Davidson motorcycle to ask for some money. Dressed in his leathers, dusty and bearded, he burst into his father's living room—and walked right into a meeting of Billy's executive board.

Without hesitation, Billy Graham identified Franklin as his son. Then he proudly introduced him to every member of the board. Billy did not apologize for his son or show any shame or guilt. Franklin wrote later in his autobiography, *Rebel with a Cause*, that the love and respect his father gave him that day never left him, even during his rebellious years.

Our children don't have to earn our love. To withhold love for our own selfish purposes is to follow the enemy, not God. God's love for us is undeserved. We did nothing to earn it; no good in us merited it. "God demonstrates His own love for us in this: While we were still sinners, Christ died for us" (Romans 5:8). In all our relationships, especially with our children, we must genuinely show that same kind of love.

We are called to treat our children, and all people, with love and respect. It helps to remember what we were when Christ died for us.

DAVID EGNER

God's love changes prodigal sons into precious saints.

The Power of Prayer

1 TIMOTHY 2:1–8

I urge, then, first of all, that petitions, prayers,
intercession and thanksgiving be made for all people.

1 TIMOTHY 2:1

A clergyman in England told his young sons about a missionary who had gone from their church to Sri Lanka, an island nation off the southeast coast of India. He described the hardships she would face and told them that she would encounter poisonous snakes.

Freddie, who was only five years old, kept thinking about those dangerous reptiles. That night during his bedtime prayer, his father heard him say in a quivering voice, "O dear God, please take care of Miss Price. Keep her safe from those snakes."

One day as the missionary was returning from a meeting, she saw lurking across her path a small but deadly snake. Within striking range and with its head raised, the serpent was poised for the attack. Suddenly, it lowered its head and fled into the long grass. She praised the Lord for her deliverance!

Some time later, the mail brought this word from her pastor: "Little Fred never forgets to pray for you. Two Sundays ago he asked the Lord most earnestly to keep you from being harmed by the snakes!" Miss Price concluded that this was the exact day she had encountered the critter. She rejoiced that God had delivered her in answer to Freddie's earnest supplication.

When the Lord brings someone's need to mind, we should take a moment right away and pray. That's one way to experience the power of prayer.

DENNIS DEHAAN

God who prepares the answers to our prayers also prompts the asking.

Lincoln's Test

LUKE 24:13–27

"Did not the Messiah have to suffer these things
and then enter his glory?"

LUKE 24:26

Abraham Lincoln was a backwoodsman who rose from humble beginnings to the heights of political power. During the dark days of the US Civil War, he served as a compassionate and resolute president. Depression and mental pain were his frequent companions. Yet the terrible emotional suffering he endured drove him to receive Jesus Christ by faith.

Lincoln told a crowd in his hometown in Illinois: "When I left Springfield, I asked the people to pray for me; I was not a Christian. When I buried my son, the severest trial of my life, I was not a Christian. But when I saw the graves of thousands of our soldiers, I then and there consecrated myself to Christ. I do love Jesus." Life's most painful tragedies can bring us to a deeper understanding of the Savior.

When two men walked the road to Emmaus, they were dumbfounded by the senseless murder of Jesus of Nazareth. Then a stranger joined them and provided scriptural insight about the suffering Messiah (Luke 24:26–27). The stranger was Jesus himself, and His ministry to them brought comfort.

Heartache has a way of pointing us to the Lord Jesus, who has shared in our sufferings and can bring meaning to seemingly senseless pain.

DENNIS FISHER

Suffering can teach us what we can't learn in any other way.

True Sacrifice

PHILIPPIANS 2:17–30

He almost died for the work of Christ. He risked his life to make up for the help you yourselves could not give me.

PHILIPPIANS 2:30

Teenagers amaze me. So many of them love life with grand passion and face it with unrelenting optimism. Sometimes they demonstrate the Christian life in ways adults can only hope to emulate.

Such is the case with Carissa, a teen who loved soccer, basketball, friends, family, and Jesus. One day, her mother was diagnosed with cancer. Carissa was just twelve years old, but she began helping to care for her mom.

During the next few years, Carissa often fed her mom, dressed her, and helped her do what she couldn't do for herself. "It was so hard to learn," she said. "Can you imagine, a mother and daughter literally changing roles? I truly learned to be a humble servant."

Sometimes, while her friends were out having fun, Carissa was helping her dad take care of her mom. She continued to do so until the summer when she was sixteen years old, when Carissa and her family said goodbye to Mom for the last time. As Carissa puts it, "God took her home and made her perfect."

Carissa reminds me of Epaphroditus, who sacrificially cared for Paul's needs (Philippians 2:25–30). What examples of caring, love, and compassion! Not all of us, of course, could set aside our lives to give as they did. But their sacrifice can teach us all about the value of servanthood.

DAVE BRANON

When you do little things for others, you do big things for Jesus.

Blessed by a Large Tip

MATTHEW 5:43–48

"But I tell you, love your enemies and pray for those who persecute you."
MATTHEW 5:44

A Christian worker went into a restaurant to buy an inexpensive meal. A waitress approached him and in a rather brusque voice demanded, "Can I help you?" "Yes, ma'am." "You want our special for the day?" "Yes, ma'am." "Coffee with your order?" "Yes, ma'am," he replied absentmindedly, for his thoughts were occupied.

Suddenly the uncongenial waitress flared up, exclaiming sarcastically, "Is that all you can say?" Before he could catch himself, he once again replied, "Yes, ma'am!" She stamped away in disgust and anger.

When the food was ready, she almost threw it on the table and showed contempt with every action.

As he was leaving, he placed a rather large tip of cash on the table as he left. As he was paying the cashier, the discourteous waitress called, "Sir, you left this money on the table."

"Isn't that the usual place to leave a tip?" he replied, smiling at her warmly. The girl blushed and began to apologize for her hateful actions. He commented, "I figured you must have some heavy burdens on your heart or you wouldn't have been so easily upset. I thought a good tip might encourage you." Sensing his concern, she poured out her heart to him, and he was able to witness to her about his faith!

Who knows what surprises are in store when we practice Matthew 5:44.

HENRY BOSCH

Those who deserve love least, need it most.

Always for Us

RUTH 1

What, then, shall we say in response to these things?
If God is for us, who can be against us?
ROMANS 8:31

Naomi, her husband, and their two sons left Israel and moved to Moab because of a famine (Ruth 1:1–2). One son married Ruth; the other married Orpah. Eventually Naomi's husband and sons died (vv. 3, 5), so she decided to return to Israel. But she felt that her daughters-in-law would be better off staying in Moab (vv. 6–13). She tried to dissuade them from going with her by saying, "No, my daughters. It is more bitter for me than for you, because the Lord's hand has turned against me!" (v. 13).

Was Naomi right in her thinking about God? Perhaps the family had displayed a lack of faith by moving to pagan Moab, but God certainly was not against her. He proved this by wonderfully providing for her and Ruth after they returned to Israel.

(Read the rest of the book—it's short.)

You may be unemployed, terminally ill, have a disabled child, or care for a loved one with Alzheimer's. God hasn't promised to keep us from such problems. But He has proven that He is always "for us" as Christians by what He did through Jesus (Romans 5:8–9). Nothing, not even death, can separate us from His love (8:35–39).

The Lord is never "against us," not even when He chastens us (Hebrews 12:5–6). He is always for us!

HERB VANDER LUGT

The One who died to save you will never be against you.

Passing through Deep Waters

JOB 1:6–22

When you pass through the waters, I will be with you; and when you pass through the rivers, they will not sweep over you. When you walk through the fire, you will not be burned; the flames will not set you ablaze.

ISAIAH 43:2

When the trials of life surround us, especially when we have suffered a huge loss, we can agree with David, who said, "Save me, O God; for the waters have come up to my neck" (Psalm 69:1).

Scottish missionary John G. Paton surely felt this way during his first few months of service on the island of Tanna in what are now called the Vanuatu islands in the South Pacific Ocean. Not long after arriving in Tanna, Paton and his wife Mary rejoiced in the birth of a baby son they named Peter. But the joy was short-lived. Soon death took both Mary and Peter. Grieving, John had to dig their graves and bury his loved ones with his own hands. In writing of this experience, he testified, "If it had not been for Jesus and the fellowship and grace He afforded me, I am certain I would have gone mad or died of grief beside their lonely graves." Leaning on God's strength, Paton found that the promises of the Word were able to sustain him through the heartache and sorrow of his tragic loss.

Have you been going through deep waters? The Lord is near, and He beckons you to walk close to Him. His sovereign purpose in these trials is not to let you drown but to help you pass through the waves of woe and on to higher ground!

HENRY BOSCH

There is nothing like the high tide of trial to test our spiritual stature.

Cross the Divide

MARK 2:13–17

While Jesus was having dinner at Levi's house,
many tax collectors and sinners were eating with him and his disciples,
for there were many who followed him.

MARK 2:15

Two young men with mischief on their minds approached a missionary's outreach bus parked in a downtown area of a German city.

The missionaries were there to offer refreshments as a way to open up conversations about Christ. The two visitors, wearing skull-and-crossbones bandannas, were there to offer trouble.

But the missionaries didn't respond to the ruffians as they expected. The Christians welcomed them warmly and talked with them. Surprised, the guys hung around long enough to hear the gospel. One trusted Jesus that day. The other, the next day.

Those two young men and the missionaries who reached them were light-years apart culturally. The guys were German; the missionaries, American. The guys were involved in a culture of darkness and death; the missionaries were shining the light. The cultural divide was crossed with cookies and nonjudgmental love.

Look at the people around you. How can you show those on the other side of the cultural fence unconditional, unquestioning love? How can you eliminate the barriers and help them see that Jesus's love knows no boundaries?

Cross the divide. Take Christ to the culture—even if it doesn't look anything like yours.

DAVE BRANON

Our witness for Christ is a light for a world in darkness.

Strawberry Jam

2 PETER 1:1–8

*Be kind and compassionate to one another, forgiving each other,
just as in Christ God forgave you.*
EPHESIANS 4:32

When we see a need, we should respond by showing kindness and doing what we can to help. Even when there is no apparent need, we should look for ways to bring cheer by doing thoughtful things for others.

Our friend Donna showed us a wonderful kindness when my wife Shirley broke her ankle. It was a severe break, and Shirley was limited to a wheelchair and crutches for the entire summer. The accident occurred while we were visiting friends in Canada, and by the time the surgery was performed and we got back to Grand Rapids, strawberry season was past. Both Shirley and I commented that we would miss the freezer jam we usually made every year.

Then one day Donna came to our door with a dozen jars of strawberry freezer jam. She knew we hadn't been able to make any, and she just wanted us to have some. We enjoyed Donna's jam all winter, but we appreciated her thoughtfulness even more.

Christians should be kind to one another because God is kind to us. His lovingkindness is unfailing (Isaiah 54:10) and "is better than life" (Psalm 63:3). In His kindness God gives us the rain (Acts 14:17). His kindness also brings us salvation (Ephesians 2:7).

What deed of kindness can you do today to encourage a fellow believer in Christ?

DAVID EGNER

A little kindness can make a big difference.

Confronted by the Cross

LUKE 23:33–43

*When they came to the place called the Skull, they crucified him there,
along with the criminals—one on his right, the other on his left.*

LUKE 23:33

World-famous Russian author Aleksandr Solzhenitsyn (1918–2008) was
sent to a Siberian prison because he criticized communism. Languishing
there under intolerable conditions year after year, he decided to end his life.
But suicide, he firmly believed, would be against God's will. He thought it
would be better for a guard to shoot him.

So at a public assembly of the prisoners, he sat in a front row, planning
to get up and walk toward an exit, compelling a guard to kill him. But to
his surprise, another prisoner sat down, blocking his exit. That unknown
man leaned over, and to Solzhenitsyn's astonishment drew a cross on the
dirt floor.

The cross! Wondering if that fellow prisoner might be a messenger
from God, Solzhenitsyn resolved to endure his imprisonment. There in
prison he became a Christian and was eventually set free to bear witness
to the world.

Are you in the grip of difficult circumstances? Have you wondered
if life is worth living? Focus your heart on the cross—it is the message
of God's love, forgiveness, and saving grace for you. Invite the Christ of
Calvary with His transforming power into your life. Discover for yourself
that the Christ of the cross can change you.

VERNON GROUNDS

Calvary's cross is the only bridge to eternal life.

Tuned In

ACTS 10:1–23

While Peter was still thinking about the vision, the Spirit said to him, "Simon, three men are looking for you."

ACTS 10:19

God speaks to us primarily through His Word, the Bible. Sometimes, however, He directs in ways we do not expect.

Gary Dougherty, who worked for several years at Our Daily Bread Ministries, was walking home from church one evening when he saw a young man coming from the opposite direction. A strong urge came over Gary to talk with him about becoming a Christian. He hesitated at first, but then he said to this total stranger, "Pardon me, but I believe God wants me to tell you how to become a Christian."

"I just asked my girlfriend's mother that question," said the man, "but she didn't know."

"You mean you want to become a Christian?" Gary asked.

"Yes, I do!" he replied. Still incredulous, Gary asked him again and then shared the plan of salvation with him. That night a young man met Jesus as his Savior.

Some might call this a coincidence, but there's a biblical parallel in Acts 10 with Cornelius and Peter, two men who were in touch with God's Spirit.

Not all believers have equally dramatic experiences. But if God's Word, prayer, and obedience are a daily part of our lives, we will be tuned in to the Spirit's leading and be ready to convey God's love to others.

DENNIS DEHAAN

When you open your heart to the Lord, He opens your eyes to the lost.

"I Dreaded Going Back"

JEREMIAH 32:17–25

"Ah, Sovereign LORD, you have made the heavens and the earth by your great power and outstretched arm. Nothing is too hard for you."
JEREMIAH 32:17

It was in a Sunday morning service that missionary Lois Walsh was bidding farewell to the church. Within a few hours the plane would be in the air, carrying her, her husband, and their three young children on the first leg of their journey back to Brazil. The weeks preceding had been hectic, filled with hard work and difficult obstacles. Now Lois stood before us, looking fresh and unruffled. I wondered what she was going to say.

First she thanked the church people for their friendship and help during their time at home in the States. Then she admitted honestly, "I dreaded going back." It was not the missionary work, she explained, but all the effort of moving her children. Furthermore, a month after arriving on the field, they would have to move again. She had wondered how she could do it. Then she called our attention to Jeremiah 32:17. "One day," she said, "I felt weak and inadequate. In my Bible reading, however, I came to Jeremiah 32. I thought about the power of our Creator God. And I came to verse 17: 'There is nothing too hard for you.' I realized anew that I wouldn't have to do it alone—all the strength of God was at my disposal. He is my Helper."

Are you facing difficult problems? Are you overwhelmed? Is the emotional strain getting to you? Remember, nothing is too hard for God!

DAVE EGNER

When adversity is ready to strike, God is ready to strengthen.

Trust Him with Your Heart

PSALM 34:15–22

The LORD is far from the wicked, but he hears the prayer of the righteous.

PROVERBS 15:29

Even as longtime sportswriter Waddy Spoelstra (1910–1999) and his wife Jean reached their eighties, they demonstrated each day the importance of a life of faith in Jesus Christ.

Jean had suffered from congestive heart failure for several years. After she had a medical checkup one year, her doctor announced, "Your heart is good and your lungs are clear. It seems that both are in the process of healing." When Waddy responded with "Praise the Lord," the physician replied, "That's it. You two have positive attitudes. You believe in answered prayer. As I've said before, prayer is a big part of medical care."

It's exciting to hear a doctor acknowledging the connection between prayer and patient care. It's not a new idea, though. Studies have shown that prayer can accelerate the healing process, whether it's the patient or others who do the praying.

But we don't really need studies to prove that prayer works. God's Word tells us it does.

Have you spent time talking to the Lord about your trials? He knows how to meet your needs—whether through His direct intervention (Psalm 34:17) or through the comfort of His presence (v. 18). Trust Him today with your heart.

DAVE BRANON

Daily prayers are the best remedy for daily cares.

Rock Bottom

PSALM 119:65–72

It was good for me to be afflicted so that I might learn your decrees.
PSALM 119:71

I was in my early thirties, a dedicated wife and mother, a Christian worker at my husband's side. Yet inwardly I found myself on a trip nobody wants to take, the trip downward. I was heading for that certain sort of breakdown that most of us resist, the breakdown of my stubborn self-sufficiency.

Finally, I experienced the odd relief of hitting rock bottom, where I made an unexpected discovery: The rock on which I had been thrown was none other than Christ himself. Cast on Him alone, I was in a position to rebuild the rest of my life, this time as a God-dependent person rather than the self-dependent person I had been. My rock-bottom experience became a turning point and one of the most vital spiritual developments of my life.

Most people feel anything but spiritual when they hit bottom. Their misery is sometimes reinforced by fellow Christians who take a shortsighted view of what the sufferer is going through and why. But our heavenly Father is well-pleased with what He intends to bring out of such a painful process. A person who knows the secret of the God-dependent life can say, "It is good for me to be afflicted, so that I may learn your decrees" (Psalm 119:71).

JOANIE YODER

**When a Christian hits rock bottom,
he finds that Christ is a firm foundation.**

Well Done, David Schumm

ISAIAH 35:3–10

Say to those with fearful hearts, "Be strong, do not fear; your God will come,
he will come with vengeance; with divine retribution he will come to save you."

ISAIAH 35:4

At David Schumm's memorial service, we celebrated the optimism, perseverance, and faith of a man with severe cerebral palsy. For all of David's seventy-four years, the simple tasks of daily life required great effort. Through it all, he kept smiling and helping others by giving more than 23,000 hours as a hospital volunteer, along with encouraging at-risk teens.

David selected Isaiah 35:3–10 to be read at his service: "Strengthen the weak hands, and make firm the feeble knees. Say to those who are fearful-hearted, 'Be strong, do not fear! Behold, your God will come with vengeance, with the recompense of God; He will come and save you. . . . Then the lame shall leap like a deer, and the tongue of the dumb sing. For waters shall burst forth in the wilderness, and streams in the desert" (vv. 3–4, 6 NKJV). This promise, given to the people of Israel while in captivity, reminds us of our hope for the time when Christ will return for those who trust and follow Him.

During David's last weeks, he often pointed visitors to a large picture of Jesus near his bed, saying, "He's coming to get me soon." This is the hope Jesus Christ gives to all His children, which calls forth our thanks and praise to Him!

DAVID MCCASLAND

Live as if Christ died yesterday and is coming back today.

Giving It to God

MARK 10:17–22

At this the man's face fell. He went away sad, because he had great wealth.
MARK 10:22

A hero to a generation of people who grew up after World War II, Corrie ten Boom (1892–1983) left a legacy of godliness and wisdom. A victim of the Nazi occupation of the Netherlands, she survived to tell her story of faith and dependence on God during horrendous suffering.

"I have held many things in my hands," Corrie once said, "and I have lost them all; but whatever I have placed in God's hands, that, I still possess."

Corrie was well acquainted with loss. She lost family, possessions, and years of her life to hateful people. Yet she learned to concentrate on what could be gained spiritually and emotionally by putting everything in the hands of her heavenly Father.

What does that mean to us? What should we place in God's hands for safekeeping? According to the story of the rich young man in Mark 10, everything. He held abundance in his hands, but when Jesus asked him to give it up, he refused. He kept his possessions, and he failed to follow Jesus—and as a result he "went away sad" (v. 22).

Like Corrie ten Boom, we can find hope by putting everything in God's hands and then trusting Him for the outcome.

DAVE BRANON

No life is more secure than a life surrendered to God.

Charlie's Walk on the Moon

GENESIS 5:21–32

Enoch walked faithfully with God; then he was no more,
because God took him away.

GENESIS 5:24

The documentary *In the Shadow of the Moon* includes the story of Charlie Duke, one of the Apollo 16 astronauts launched to the moon in 1972. While the command ship orbited the moon, Duke and another astronaut landed the lunar module *Orion* on the moon's surface. After three days of running experiments and collecting lunar rocks, the Apollo 16 crew safely returned to earth.

Later, Charlie had a spiritual transformation. He said it began when his friend invited him to a Bible study. After the meeting, Charlie prayed to Christ, "I give you my life, and if you're real come into my life." He then experienced an indescribable peace. It was so profound that he began to share his story with others. Charlie told them, "My walk on the moon lasted three days and it was a great adventure, but my walk with God lasts forever."

The Bible tells us of another man who walked with God. "Enoch walked faithfully with God; then he was no more because God took him away" (Genesis 5:24). His spiritual walk with God was so close that God took him directly into eternity (see Hebrews 11:5).

We can learn a lesson from Charlie and Enoch. For believers, no matter where our journey leads, our walk with God will last for eternity!

DENNIS FISHER

Keep eternity's goal in sight by walking daily in God's light.

The Singers

PSALM 40:1–5

He put a new song in my mouth, a hymn of praise to our God.
Many will see and fear the LORD and put their trust in him.

PSALM 40:3

Singing is a vital part of a Christian's life. Whether believers like the old hymns of the faith or prefer newer choruses, they sing because of changed hearts, and the joy of their life in Christ must find expression in song.

In his book *Psalms of the Heart*, George Sweeting illustrated this truth from the experience of two Moody Bible Institute graduates, John and Elaine Beekman. God called them to missionary work among the Chol Indians of southern Mexico. Sweeting reports that they rode mules and traveled by dugout canoes to reach this tribe. They labored twenty-five years with other missionaries to translate the New Testament into the language of the Chol Indians, and they were able to start a thriving church there—with thousands of professing believers in Jesus. What's interesting is that when the missionaries arrived, the Chol Indians didn't know how to sing. With the coming of the gospel, however, the believers became known as "the singers." Sweeting commented, "Now they have something to sing about."

We who have trusted Christ as Savior have the song of redemption ringing in our hearts. May we too, as we express the joys of our relationship to Christ, be known as "the singers."

DAVID EGNER

The truest expression of Christianity is not a sigh but a song.

Amazing Abigail

1 SAMUEL 25:14–35

Blessed are the peacemakers, for they will be called children of God.
MATTHEW 5:9

Abigail was a remarkable woman! She was a true peacemaker whose courage spared the future king of Israel from committing a terrible sin. Here's her story:

David had been forced to live in the wilderness to escape King Saul's jealous wrath. A group of about six hundred men and their families had gathered around him. For several months they camped near Carmel where the flocks of Nabal (Abigail's husband) were grazing. David's men had helped Nabal's shepherds protect the sheep from robbers. Now the shearing time had come, and David sent messengers to request some compensation from Nabal, who was a wealthy man. But he refused and treated David's men with disdain.

In anger David rashly decided to kill Nabal and all the men in his household. When Abigail heard what was happening, she quickly gathered a large supply of food, intercepted David and his fighting men, and humbly apologized for her husband's surly behavior. David immediately realized that she had prevented him from carrying out a vengeful decision, and he praised God (1 Samuel 25:32).

Are we as quick to resolve a conflict? Jesus said, "Blessed are the peacemakers, for they will be called children of God" (Matthew 5:9).

HERB VANDER LUGT

You can be a peacemaker if you have God's peace in your heart.

Fair Play

TITUS 2:7-8, 11-14

In everything set them an example by doing what is good.
TITUS 2:7

When Singaporean runner Ashley Liew found himself at the head of the pack during a marathon at the Southeast Asian Games, he knew something was wrong. He quickly realized that the lead runners had taken a wrong turn and were now behind. Ashley could have taken advantage of their mistake, but a strong sense of sportsmanship told him it would not be a genuine victory. He wanted to win because he was faster—not because those ahead of him had made a mistake.

Acting on his convictions, he slowed down to let them catch up.

In the end, Ashley lost the race and missed out on a medal. But he won the hearts of his countrymen—and an international award for his act of fair play. It spoke well of his faith as a Christian, and it must have prompted some to ask, "What made him do that?"

Ashley's act challenges me to share my faith through my actions. Little acts of thoughtfulness, kindness, or forgiveness can glorify God. As Paul put it simply, "Show integrity, seriousness and soundness of speech that cannot be condemned" (Titus 2:7–8).

Our positive actions toward others can show the world that we are able to live differently because of the Holy Spirit's work in us. He will give us the grace to reject ungodliness and wrong passions, and to live upright lives that point people to God (vv. 11–12).

LESLIE KOH

Live so that others will want to know Jesus.

A Consistent Life

2 KINGS 4:8–17

She said to her husband, "I know that this man who often comes our way is a holy man of God."

2 KINGS 4:9

Wouldn't it be great if those who know us could say what the woman of Shunem said in 2 Kings 4:9: "I know this man who often comes our way is a holy man of God." Unfortunately, we sometimes give people who are observing us reason instead to say something like this: "If Mr. So-and-So who goes to your church is a follower of Jesus, then I want nothing to do with your religion!" We never want to be a stumbling block to the world because of what we say or do.

A missionary in India was once teaching the Bible to a group of women. Halfway through the lesson, one of the ladies got up and walked out. A short time later, she came back and listened more intently than ever. At the close of the hour the missionary inquired, "Why did you leave the meeting? Weren't you interested?" "Oh yes," the lady replied. "I was so impressed with what you had to say about Christ that I went out to ask your driver whether you really lived the way you talked. When he said you did, I hurried back so I wouldn't miss out on anything."

The world will listen to our testimony for the Lord only if we are exemplifying Him in our daily conduct. Can people say of us that we are "holy [people] of God"?

HENRY BOSCH

If you want the world to heed, put your creed into your deed!

Facing Our Past

ACTS 9:20–30

When he came to Jerusalem, he tried to join the disciples, but they were all afraid of him, not believing that he really was a disciple.

ACTS 9:26

Chuck Colson, founder of Prison Fellowship, spent forty years helping people hear and understand the gospel of Jesus Christ. When he died in April 2012, one newspaper article carried the headline, "Charles Colson, Nixon's 'dirty tricks' man, dies at eighty." It seemed surprising that a man so transformed by faith should be identified with things he did as a politically ruthless presidential aide decades earlier before he knew the Savior.

The apostle Paul's conversion and his early Christian witness were greeted with skepticism and fear. When he began preaching that Jesus is the Son of God, people said, "Is this not he who destroyed those who called on this name in Jerusalem, and has come here for that purpose?" (Acts 9:21 NKJV). Later, when Paul went to Jerusalem and tried to join the disciples, they were afraid of him (v. 26). In years to come, Paul never ignored his past, but he spoke of it as evidence of the mercy of God (1 Timothy 1:13–14).

Like Paul, we don't need to parade our failures or to pretend they didn't happen. Instead, we can thank the Lord that through His grace and power, our past is forgiven, our present is changed, and our future is bright with hope for everything He has prepared for us.

DAVID MCCASLAND

Only God can transform our lives.

Peanuts and Cathedrals

LUKE 19:11–27

"'Well done, my good servant!' his master replied. 'Because you have been trustworthy in a very small matter, take charge of ten cities.'"

LUKE 19:17

Famed botanist George Washington Carver (c. 1864–1943) once asked God to tell him about the universe. According to Carver, the Lord replied, "George, the universe is just too big for you to understand. Suppose you let Me take care of that." Humbled, he replied, "Lord, how about a peanut?" The Lord said, "Now, George, that's something your own size. Go to work on it, and I'll help you." When Carver was done studying the peanut, he had discovered over 300 products that could be made with that little bit of God's universe.

Faithfulness in little things is never lost to the work of Christ. When a cathedral in Milan, Italy, was completed, vast throngs of people assembled to witness its dedication. In the crowd was a little girl who pointed to the beautiful edifice and cried with childish glee, "I helped build that!" "What!" exclaimed a guard in brilliant uniform. "What did you do?" "I carried the dinner pail for my father while he worked on it," she replied.

If we are living for Jesus, we have every right to "think big" about our part in God's plan. Diligently using our small efforts in Christ's service is great work—whether we dissect a peanut or help build a cathedral.

DENNIS DEHAAN

God isn't looking for extraordinary men for ordinary work, but ordinary men for extraordinary work.

The Jesus Story

LUKE 1:1–4; 24:44–53

These are written that you may believe that Jesus is the Messiah, the Son of God, and that by believing you may have life in his name.

JOHN 20:31

I like to think of the New Testament as "the Jesus story." The Gospels tell it, and the Epistles explain it. It's a believable, life-changing story for all who are truly seeking God. Its beauty has been acknowledged even by people who are not Christians. An Asian Buddhist, after reading the Gospel of Matthew, summed up his reaction this way: "I cried. Jesus was a wonderful person."

Reading the story of Jesus brought me strength while serving in the US Army during World War II. I put in many successive twenty-hour days working in an overseas hospital. Helping men who had serious wounds drained me emotionally, and at times I felt spiritually empty. Doubts would fill my mind. I knew I needed help, and I found it in the New Testament. I had read it before, but somehow it was different this time. I came face-to-face with Jesus, whose words and works so beautifully reflected God's love. How wonderful that Jesus lived a sinless life and died on the cross for me! The Jesus story renewed my spirit.

Since leaving the armed forces and serving for many years in the pastoral ministry and in the work of *Our Daily Bread*, I have told the Jesus story again and again to individuals and congregations.

Do you love that story? Does it revive you? Are you telling it?

HERB VANDER LUGT

**We must not withhold from the world the best news
that ever came into it!**

Firstfruits Giving

PROVERBS 3:5–10

Honor the LORD with your wealth, with the firstfruits of all your crops.
PROVERBS 3:9

A Christian living in an underdeveloped part of the world earned money by making and selling a special kind of bean cake. She had always been conscientious in her giving to her local church, but her income ceased after she suffered a severe foot injury in an accident. It was many long months before she could resume her work.

Eagerly she awaited the day she could sell her tasty cakes again. She promised her pastor that she would give one-third of her earnings to the Lord instead of just ten percent. She said her goal for the first week of business was to make a profit of three shillings.

The pastor was surprised, therefore, when the woman returned after only two days with one shilling as an offering for the Lord. "You surely haven't earned three shillings already!" he exclaimed. The woman was perplexed by his response. "Do you think I would give my Lord the last of the three?" she asked. "This is the first one, and it belongs to Him—the other two I make will be for me."

God may not lead you to give that large a portion of your income. But whatever the amount, I challenge you to practice "firstfruits" giving (Proverbs 3:9).

HENRY BOSCH

We show who we love by what we do with what we have.

One Thumb—but Thankful

PSALM 145:1-10

Give thanks in all circumstances; for this is God's will for you in Christ Jesus.
1 THESSALONIANS 5:18

Songwriter Wendell P. Loveless told of a woman who had been confined to her bed for more than sixteen years. She was in constant pain and unable to move her limbs. Yet she was one of the most thankful people Loveless had ever met. She rejoiced that God had left her a great blessing—the use of the thumb on her right hand. The other hand was stiff and completely useless. With a two-pronged fork fastened to a stick she could put on her glasses, feed herself, sip her tea through a tube, and turn the pages of a large Bible. Although it took great effort, everything she did was with the use of just one thumb.

She once said to a visitor, "I have so much to be thankful for." When asked why, she replied, "Now that my sins are forgiven, I can lie back and daily drink in the great love of Jesus my Savior." Asked if at times she became despondent, she replied, "I'm perfectly content to lie here as long as the Lord keeps me in this world, and I'm also ready to leave whenever He calls me."

Perhaps you are afflicted and greatly limited. Genuine contentment isn't learned all at once. But it always includes being thankful for whatever blessings we have—even if it is just one thumb.

HENRY BOSCH

Praising God turns burdens into blessings.

Commissioned for Missions

ACTS 1:19

*"You will receive power when the Holy Spirit comes on you;
and you will be my witnesses in Jerusalem, and in all Judea and Samaria,
and to the ends of the earth."*

ACTS 1:8

A pastor in Belton, Texas, had a deep desire for his people to become actively involved in fulfilling Christ's commission to take the gospel to the ends of the earth. As he was preaching a message on missions one Sunday, he was moved to pause and pray. He asked God to lay His hand on some young men and women in the church and send them out to share the message of the gospel in other countries. Then he extended his hands toward the audience and earnestly pleaded, "Who will go? Oh, who will go?" Immediately a lovely young lady, a student at a local college, stood and said, "Dad, I will go." The pastor, at first shocked, thought to himself, *Lord, I didn't mean Annie!* But that was only a temporary reaction. In fact, he rejoiced that she had answered God's call. In the years that followed, she faithfully served as a missionary in South America.

God's grand design for the spread of the gospel is not restricted to believers we call "missionaries." It is every Christian's job. We are all to obey Christ's command to be witnesses—wherever we are called to serve.

Whether God asks you to serve Him in another country or in your hometown, the key is to be willing. Who will be His witnesses? All of us. God commissions each of His children, and He will choose the place.

PAUL VAN GORDER

**There's one thing you cannot do about missions:
Get rid of your responsibility.**

Fearing the Worst

GALATIANS 6:2–10

Carry each other's burdens, and in this way you will fulfill the law of Christ.
GALATIANS 6:2

When I learned I needed chemotherapy to battle cancer, my biggest fear was losing my hair. I knew this was a vain thought and should have been a minor concern, but I rationalized that it was okay to grieve what the Bible calls a woman's glory (1 Corinthians 11:15).

I knew, however, that the loss I was grieving was not my glory but my identity. My hair, which reached to my knees, was so much a part of who I was that I was afraid of losing myself when I lost it. In the past I'd had nightmares about having my hair cut. What would happen when it was really gone? I feared the worst.

But the worst never happened. I had my hair cut short—a little anxiety but no nightmares. And then it fell out—some sadness, but no despondency.

Several weeks later my dear friend Marge said to me, "Julie, I can't tell you how often I have grieved the loss of your hair. It's so much a part of you."

Suddenly I realized that Marge was fulfilling the command of Galatians 6:2, "Carry each other's burdens." She was coming alongside me with prayers and empathy to ease my burden.

Satan wants to defeat us with heavy burdens, but fellow believers by their love and support can minimize the suffering he causes.

JULIE ACKERMAN LINK

Bearing one another's burden helps make the burden bearable.

Breakfast from God

EXODUS 16:1–6

*My God will meet all your needs according to the riches
of his glory in Christ Jesus.*
PHILIPPIANS 4:19

Things looked bleak for the children in George Müller's orphanage at Ashley Down in nineteenth-century England. It was time for breakfast, and there was no food. A small girl whose father was a close friend of Müller was visiting in the home. Müller took her hand and said, "Come and see what our Father will do." In the dining room, long tables were set with empty plates and empty mugs. Not only was there no food in the kitchen but neither was there any money in the home's account. Müller prayed, "Dear Father, we thank Thee for what Thou art going to give us to eat."

Immediately, they heard a knock at the door. When they opened it, there stood the local baker. "Mr. Müller," he said, "I couldn't sleep last night. Somehow I felt you had no bread for breakfast, so I got up at 2 o'clock and baked fresh bread. Here it is." As Müller was thanking God for the bread, the milkman arrived. His cart had broken down in front of the orphanage, and he wanted to give the children the milk so he could empty the cart and repair it.

Why could George Müller pray with such confidence? Because he had seen God take care of the children many times before. When we look back and see how God has cared for us, our faith is strengthened. He who can provide breakfast for orphans will not disappoint our trust.

PAUL VAN GORDER

Faith expects from God what is beyond all expectation.

It's What We Do

PSALM 112

*Whoever fears the LORD has a secure fortress,
and for their children it will be a refuge.*

PROVERBS 14:26

My father was critically injured when he took a bullet in the leg as a second lieutenant leading his men on Hill 609 in North Africa during World War II. Dad was never again 100 percent physically. I was born several years after this, and when I was young I didn't even know he had been wounded. I found out later when someone told me. Although he felt constant pain in his leg, my dad never complained about it, and he never used it as an excuse for not providing for our family.

My parents loved the Savior and raised us to love, trust, and serve Him. Through good times and bad, they simply trusted God, worked hard, and loved us unconditionally. Proverbs 14:26 says that "Whoever fears the LORD has a secure fortress, and for their children it will be a refuge." My parents did that for our family. No matter what difficulties they faced, they provided a safe place for us spiritually, emotionally, and physically.

We parents can provide a safe haven for our families with the help of our perfect heavenly Father, whose love for His children is deep and eternal. It's what we are called to do.

DAVE BRANON

The Father's love knows no limit.

God Loves Atheists

ROMANS 5:1–10

But God demonstrates his own love for us in this:
While we were still sinners, Christ died for us.

ROMANS 5:8

A man who claimed to be an atheist stood on the street and cried out, "If there is a God in heaven, I challenge Him to strike me dead in five minutes!" After the allotted time had gone by and nothing had happened, this scoffer cried out with a sneer, "You see, there is no God, or by this time He would have struck me dead!"

Just then a woman stepped up to him and asked, "Do you have any children?" The man replied, "One son." She asked, "If your son gave you a knife and said to kill him, would you do it?" He quickly answered, "Of course not." "Why not?" The man replied, "I love him too much!" The lady explained, "Well, it's also because God loves YOU so much that He refuses to accept your foolish challenge. He wants you saved, not lost."

Romans 5:6–8 tells us, "At just the right time, when we were still powerless, Christ died for the ungodly. Very rarely will anyone die for a righteous person, though for a good person someone might possibly dare to die. But God demonstrates his own love for us in this: While we were still sinners, Christ died for us." God loved us so much that He sent His Son into a world knowing full well that wicked men would reject Him.

God loves us! He cares for us! He will provide!

RICHARD DEHAAN

God loves us not for what we are, but for what He can make of us!

Miracle Rain

1 KINGS 18:1, 41–45

Remember the former things, those of long ago;
I am God, and there is no other; I am God, and there is none like me.
ISAIAH 46:9

Life is hard for villagers who live on a hilly terrain in the Yunnan Province of China. Their main sources of food are corn and rice. But one year a severe drought hit the region and the crops withered. Everyone was worried, and many superstitious practices were carried out as the people attempted to end the drought. When nothing worked, people started blaming the five Christians in the village for offending the spirits of the ancestors.

These five believers gathered to pray. Before long, the sky darkened and thunder was heard. A heavy downpour started and lasted the whole afternoon and night. The crops were saved! While most of the villagers did not believe God sent the rain, others did. Those people desired to find out more about the Lord.

In 1 Kings 17 and 18 we read of a severe drought in Israel. But in this case, we are told, it was a result of God's judgment on His people (17:1). They had begun to worship Baal, the god of the Canaanites, believing that this deity could send the rain for their crops. Then God, through His prophet Elijah, showed that He is the one true God who determines when rain falls.

Our all-powerful God desires to hear our prayers and answer our pleas. And though we do not always understand His timing or His purposes, God always responds with His best for our lives.

POH FANG CHIA

Through prayer, we draw upon the power of the infinite God.

"I Wish You Knew My Jesus"

MATTHEW 28:16–20

The first thing Andrew did was to find his brother Simon and tell him,
"We have found the Messiah" (that is, the Christ).

JOHN 1:41

The words of a song written by Mildred L. Dillon should express the desire of every believer for those who do not know Christ as their Savior. The song says,

I wish you knew my Jesus
And loved Him as I do,
For if you knew my Jesus,
Then you would love Him too.

It is this longing that has led many men and women to leave the comforts of home and the warmth of family relationships to go around the world to proclaim Jesus to people who need the Savior. In the book *450 Stories from Life*, H. M. Robbins tells of a missionary who read Bible passages about the life and death of Jesus to a group of villagers in South America. At the conclusion of the service, he was approached by a man who asked, "Did you know the Man in the Book?" The missionary replied that he did. Later, when he told Robbins about the incident, he said, "Thank God, I did know the Man in the Book. I knew Him as my Lord and Savior. And I was able to introduce Him to these people who had never experienced His love and forgiveness."

People all around us need Jesus. Let's ask God to fill us with the longing, "I wish you knew Him too." Then we can become instruments in God's hand to introduce Christ to those who do not know Him.

RICHARD DEHAAN

If your Christianity is worth having, it's worth sharing.

Ruth's Story

ROMANS 10:1–13

"Everyone who calls on the name of the Lord will be saved."
ROMANS 10:13

Ruth could not tell her story without tears. She was in her mid-eighties and unable to get around much anymore, and Ruth may not have appeared to be a central figure in our church's life. She depended on others for rides, and because she lived alone most of her life, she didn't have a huge circle of influence.

But when she told us her story of salvation—as she often did—Ruth stood out as a remarkable example of God's grace. Back when she was in her thirties, a friend invited her to go to a meeting one night. Ruth didn't know she was going to hear a preacher. "I wouldn't have gone if I knew," she reflected. She already had "religion," and it wasn't doing her any good. But go she did. And she heard the good news about Jesus that night.

More than fifty years later, she still cried tears of joy when she talked of how Jesus transformed her life. That evening, she became a child of God. As long as she lived (she died in April 2018) and as often as she retold that story, it never grew old.

It doesn't matter if our story is similar to Ruth's or not. What does matter is that we take the simple step of putting our faith in Jesus and His death and resurrection. The apostle Paul said, "If you declare with your mouth, 'Jesus is Lord,' and believe in your heart that God raised him from the dead, you will be saved" (Romans 10:9).

That's what Ruth did. You can do that too. Jesus redeems, transforms, and gives us new life.

DAVE BRANON

Belonging to Christ is not rehabilitation; it's re-creation.

Thanks in Everything

1 CHRONICLES 16:8–14

Give thanks to the LORD, for he is good; his love endures forever.
1 CHRONICLES 16:34

Scottish minister Alexander Whyte (1836–1921) was known for his uplifting prayers in the pulpit. He always found something for which to be grateful.

One Sunday morning the weather was so gloomy that one church member thought to himself, "Certainly the preacher won't think of anything for which to thank the Lord on a wretched day like this." Much to his surprise, however, Whyte began by praying, "We thank Thee, O God, that it is not always like this." True to form, Whyte found cause for thanksgiving.

Because of a detached retina, my sight in one eye is severely impaired. Shortly after heart bypass surgery, I suffered the complete blockage of an artery and the collapse of its replacement. More recently, I was diagnosed as having Parkinson's disease, which has made it impossible for me to continue teaching on radio and television. *(Editor's Note: Richard wrote this in 1988 at age 65; he died in July 2002.)*

Now, I can imagine some people saying, "Certainly no one can think of anything for which to thank the Lord in circumstances like that!" But they would be wrong. I have countless blessings—so many that I can echo the words of David, "Give thanks to the LORD, for He is good!" Can you?

RICHARD DEHAAN

If we pause to think, we'll have cause to thank.

More Than a Conqueror

2 CORINTHIANS 12:1–10

In all these things we are more than conquerors through him who loved us.
ROMANS 8:37

Fanny Crosby (1820–1915), beloved composer of some of the great songs of the faith, was truly "more than a conqueror." When she was only six weeks old, faulty treatment of an eye infection resulted in lifelong blindness. By age eight, having fought and defeated discouragement, she wrote this poem:

> *Oh, what a happy soul am I! Although I cannot see,*
> *I am resolved that in this world contented I will be.*
> *How many blessings I enjoy*
> *That other people don't.*
> *To weep and sigh because I'm blind,*
> *I cannot—and I won't!*

Instead of weeping and sighing, Fanny Crosby dedicated her blindness to God. Out of her rich Christian experience she composed thousands of gospel hymns. In her testimonial song "Blessed Assurance," she seemed to forget that she was blind. Phrases like "Visions of rapture now burst on my sight" or "Watching and waiting, looking above" expressed what she called "a foretaste of glory divine."

Do you wish to know and apply her secret? Consider this: While many of us seek Christ for what we can get, Fanny sought Christ for what she could become through Him—more than a conqueror (Romans 8:37).

Even in times of distress, God's grace is sufficient (2 Corinthians 12:9), and He is lovingly working to make us more like His Son. We can become more than conquerors.

JOANIE YODER

Seek Christ not for what you can get but for what you can become.

Altered Attitude

GENESIS 39:20–23; 40:1–4

The LORD was with [Joseph]; he showed him kindness and granted him favor in the eyes of the prison warden.

GENESIS 39:21

As Christians, we sometimes lose sight of God's help in what we think is a bad situation.

A young missionary wife living in very primitive surroundings became severely depressed, and it appeared that she and her husband would have to return home. But understanding that his skills were in great demand, she wanted to make sure he could continue to be used in God's work. So she began to pray.

She felt that the Holy Spirit was encouraging her to do all she could to adjust to her environment. First, she started taking a renewed interest in the language and customs of the people. Then she studied the trees, plants, and animals of that area. She also found ways to help her new friends, and she began witnessing to them. Before long, she had a newfound appreciation for the work she and her husband were doing. What changed? Not her surroundings. She had! Trusting God and acting in faith had given her a new outlook. And this made everything different.

Think of Joseph in Egypt. He too had to adjust his thinking when he found himself in a place he didn't want to be in. He trusted God, who promised to be with him, and he looked for opportunities to do good while in prison. With God's help, he transformed what could have been a miserable time into one of real blessing. Sometimes what we need is an altered attitude—not a new environment.

HERB VANDER LUGT

The Lord may calm your storm, but more often He'll calm YOU.

Why Me?

LUKE 17:11–19

One of them, when he saw he was healed, came back,
praising God in a loud voice.
LUKE 17:15

A few years ago, an unkempt, poorly adjusted youth named Tim (not his real name) was converted to Christ in an evangelistic crusade. Several days later, still unkempt but bathed in the love of Christ, he was sent to my home so that I could help him find a good church. And so it was that he began attending with me.

Although Tim needed and received much loving help in personal grooming and basic social graces, one characteristic remained unchanged—his untamed love for his Savior.

One Sunday after church Tim rushed to my side, looking somewhat perplexed. He exclaimed, "Why me? I keep asking myself, why me?" *Oh, no*, I thought, *he's become another complaining Christian.* Then with arms outstretched, he went on to say, "Out of all the people in the world who are greater and smarter than I am, why did God choose me?" With that he joyfully clapped his hands.

Over the years I've heard many Christians, including myself, ask "Why me?" during tough times. But Tim is the first one I've heard ask that question when talking about God's blessings. Many were converted the same night as Tim, but I wonder how many among them have humbly asked, "Why me?" May we ask it often.

JOANIE YODER

Afflictions become blessings when blended with acceptance.

Legacies of Love

2 TIMOTHY 1:1–5

*Let your light shine before others, that they may see your good deeds
and glorify your Father in heaven.*
MATTHEW 5:16

I was paging through my great-grandmother's Bible when a treasure fell into my lap. On a small scrap of paper, in a young child's handwriting, were the words, "Blessed are the poor in spirit: for theirs is the kingdom of heaven. Blessed are they that mourn: for they shall be comforted" (Matthew 5:3–4 KJV). Scribbled beside those verses in wobbly cursive was my mother's signature.

My great-grandmother had a habit of teaching her grandchildren to write out Scripture verses so they would learn them and take them to heart. But the story behind this verse brought tears to my eyes. My grandfather died when my mother was very young, and her little brother (my uncle) died just weeks later. It was in that tragic season that my great-grandmother pointed my mother to Jesus and the comfort only He can give.

Paul wrote Timothy, "I am reminded of your sincere faith, which first lived in your grandmother Lois and in your mother Eunice and, I am persuaded, now lives in you also" (2 Timothy 1:5). Faith isn't inherited, but it is *shared*. Timothy's mother and grandmother *shared their faith with him*, and he believed.

When we encourage those close to us to have hope in Jesus, we offer them a legacy of love. Through a simple note, my mother left evidence of my great-grandmother's love for her Savior and her family. Oh, to share Him with those who come after us!

JAMES BANKS

When we share our faith, we share the greatest treasure of all.

A Life of Integrity

PSALM 26

I lead a blameless life; deliver me and be merciful to me.
PSALM 26:11

He was a politician noted for his integrity. Although this description might be viewed by some as a contradiction in terms, it certainly was used often and correctly to describe US Congressman Paul Henry (1942–1993). After the three-term member of the House of Representatives lost a battle with brain cancer, political commentator David Broder said, "He was a model of what a public servant should be."

There was good reason for Paul Henry's integrity. He was a Christian who devoted his life and service to the Lord. In many ways his life mirrored the characteristics mentioned in Psalm 26.

The psalmist David said that he (1) walked in God's truth, (2) avoided sinful entanglements, and (3) enjoyed worshiping God. In a similar way, Paul Henry (1) sought to live by biblical principles, (2) was on guard against the influence of those who were ungodly, and (3) regularly worshiped at his local church.

The integrity David wrote about and Paul Henry demonstrated should be a goal for us as believers in Jesus. As we grow more and more like the One we worship, our lives will be marked by truth and right thinking. Each day we should ask God to help us to live a life of integrity.

DAVE BRANON

Integrity is the mark of true character.

"Jesus and I"

2 TIMOTHY 4:16–18

But the Lord stood at my side and gave me strength, so that through me the message might be fully proclaimed and all the Gentiles might hear it. And I was delivered from the lion's mouth.

2 TIMOTHY 4:17

Many years ago, a Christian magazine published an article about missionary Dan Crawford, who had the difficult task of following in the steps of David Livingstone, a larger-than-life missionary pioneer. Crawford didn't have the imposing personality of his famous predecessor, so at first he had trouble winning the loyalty of the tribal people. Even the people in his church back home weren't sure he could carry on the work. With God's help, however, he did a magnificent job.

When he died, a well-worn copy of the New Testament was found in his pocket. A poem, evidently his own, handwritten on the inside cover, revealed the secret of his success: "I cannot do it alone!/ The waves dash fast and high;/ The fog comes chilling around,/ And the light goes out in the sky,/ But I know that we two shall win in the end—/ Jesus and I./ Coward, and wayward, and weak,/ I change with the changing sky, / Today so strong and brave,/ Tomorrow too weak to fly;/ But—HE never gives in! So we two shall win—/ Jesus and I!"

Facing a new task? Burdened by trials? You'll find that depending completely on the Lord will make all the difference. Because He is there to strengthen and comfort, you can say, "I know that we two shall win in the end—Jesus and I!"

HENRY BOSCH

The fact of His presence is the focus of our strength.

Whom Shall I Send?

ISAIAH 6:1-8

Then I heard the voice of the Lord saying, "Whom shall I send?
And who will go for us?" And I said, "Here am I. Send me!"
ISAIAH 6:8

As a young pastor, I served a fledgling new congregation that included my parents. My father was very active in the church's "people ministries"— evangelism, hospital and nursing-home visitation, bus ministry, relief for the poor, and more. Although he had never been formally trained in ministry, Dad had a natural ability to connect with people who were in the midst of hard times. That was his passion—the downtrodden people who are often overlooked. In fact, on the day he died, my last conversation with him was about someone he had promised to call on. He was concerned that his promise be kept.

I believe that my father's service was one that followed the heart of Christ. Jesus looked out over the masses of the forgotten people of the world and felt compassion for them (Matthew 9:36–38). He commanded His followers to pray that the heavenly Father would send workers (like my dad) to reach those weighed down with the cares of life.

My father became the answer to those prayers in many hurting people's lives, and we can be as well. When the prayer goes out for someone to represent Christ's love, may our heart respond: "Lord, here am I. Send me!"

BILL CROWDER

True service is love in working clothes.

Ruler of the Waves

JOB 38:1–18

"[God] said, 'This far you may come and no farther; here is where your proud waves halt.'"

JOB 38:11

King Canute of Denmark was one of the most powerful men on earth in the eleventh century. In a now-famous tale, it is said that he ordered his chair to be placed on the shore as the tide was rising. "You are subject to me," he said to the sea. "I command you, therefore, not to rise on to my land, nor to wet the clothing or limbs of your master." But the tide continued to rise, drenching the king's feet.

This story is often told to draw attention to Canute's pride. Actually, it's a story about humility. "Let all the world know that the power of kings is empty," Canute says next, "save Him by whose will heaven, earth and sea obey." Canute's story makes a point: *God* is the only all-powerful One.

Job discovered the same thing. Compared to the One who laid Earth's foundations (Job 38:4–7), who commands morning to appear and night to end (vv. 12–13), who stocks the storehouses of the snow and directs the stars (vv. 22, 31–33), we are small. There is only one Ruler of the waves, and it is not us (v. 11; Matthew 8:23–27).

Canute's story is good to reenact when we begin feeling too clever or proud about ourselves. Walk to the beach and tell the tide to halt or try commanding the sun to step aside. We'll soon remember who is really supreme, and we'll thank Him for ruling our lives.

SHERIDAN VOYSEY

God is great, we are small, and that is good.

How to Be Rich and Successful

1 TIMOTHY 6:11–19

But godliness with contentment is great gain.
1 TIMOTHY 6:6

Some rich and successful people don't have much money and aren't famous. Leslie Flynn told how the leaders of an alumni association discovered this through a questionnaire sent to a missionary in Colombia, South America.

Here are some of the questions they asked and the answers they received: (1) Do you own your own home? Yes. (He had paid the tribes people $125 for his palm-thatched dwelling in the Amazon basin.) (2) Do you rent quarters elsewhere? Yes. (He and his family occasionally stayed in a house where missionaries were crowded together for conferences.) (3) Do you own a boat? Yes. (He had a dugout canoe tied up at the riverbank.) (4) Do you plan to travel abroad during the next two years? Yes. (His family was going home on furlough.) (5) What is your income? Under $10,000 per year. (6) How many automobiles do you own? None.

Flynn suggests that the computer probably spit out an analysis with the notation, "Data incompatible." But this man is both rich and successful! He possesses great spiritual wealth as a child of God and as a citizen of heaven. He is successful because he is doing the work to which God called him— a work of eternal value.

You can be like that missionary no matter what you do or how much you earn. Dedicate yourself and all you have to God. Then make it your sole purpose to do His will. You too can be rich and successful.

HERB VANDER LUGT

To be rich in God is better than to be rich in goods.

More Joy in Heaven

LUKE 15:4–7

I tell you that in the same way there will be more rejoicing in heaven over one sinner who repents than over ninety-nine righteous persons who do not need to repent.

LUKE 15:7

I dreaded the idea of attending a memorial service for an old friend. Fred had rejected the need for Jesus in his life, and because of that I was sure he was lost forever. Yet Fred's many friendships had included followers of Jesus. At the service, as one of those friends spoke of a conversation he had in Fred's last months, my eyes filled with tears.

Fred had asked him, "Do you think I'll go to heaven?" The friend had honestly replied, "No, Fred. I don't think so." As they talked, Fred's wall of resistance began to fall, and he said, "Philip, I believe that what the Bible says is true." After a lifetime of rejecting the free gift of salvation, Fred finally accepted Jesus as his Savior.

With happy tears, I thought about the verse: "There will be more rejoicing in heaven over one sinner who repents than over ninety-nine righteous persons who do not need to repent" (Luke 15:7). Jesus and the angels were rejoicing with me.

As Fred had requested, we stood and sang, "Jesus loves me, this I know, for the Bible tells me so!" To my friend, those familiar words had become a personal reality.

Let's bring more joy to heaven by spreading the good news: Jesus loves us—this we know!

CINDY HESS KASPER

All heaven rejoices over one sinner who repents.

One Good Joe

HEBREWS 10:19–23

Let us hold unswervingly to the hope we profess,
for he who promised is faithful.

Joe was a behind-the-scenes kind of person—quiet, unassuming, often unnoticed. To see him, you wouldn't think he had been carrying a heavy burden for more than eleven years. But Joe carried it well.

Every so often I would think about Joe. I hardly knew him, but just knowing what he had to live with encouraged my faith in God. Joe was being faithful to his wife, who for eleven years lay in the hospital following brain surgery. With the exception of just two or three days, Joe visited her in the hospital every day until she died.

Such unfailing fidelity is the stuff God-fearing men and women are made of. It's the fruit of the Spirit rooted in the hearts of people who hold firm to God's love through life's trials. One Sunday at church before Joe's wife died, I told him what an inspiration he was to me. He said humbly, "It's all by God's grace."

As we appropriate God's grace in Jesus Christ and persevere in faith, He gives us what we need to keep the promises we make according to His will. And when one day He says to us, "Well done," we will respond, "It's all because You were faithful in keeping Your promises to us."

DENNIS DEHAAN

Because God is faithful to us, we can be faithful to our promises.

When Love Speaks Loudest

PHILIPPIANS 2:1–11

Not looking to your own interests but each of you to the interests of the others.
PHILIPPIANS 2:4

Missionary Doug Nichols was a patient in a tuberculosis ward in India in 1967. Patients and staff saw him as a rich American taking up space in their hospital. Their hostility was evident as they refused the gospel tracts he offered them.

One morning at two o'clock, a very sick Indian man struggled to get out of bed to go to the bathroom, but he was too weak to make it. Soon the stench from his bed filled the room. Other patients yelled at him. Nurses showed their anger for having to clean up the mess. One slapped him.

The next night the old man tried again to get up, but again fell backward. He began to cry. Doug, weak himself, went over, picked him up, and carried him to the bathroom and then back to his bed.

What a change came over that hospital ward! One patient gave Doug a steaming cup of Indian tea, motioning that he wanted a tract. Nurses, interns, and doctors asked for booklets or gospels of John. And several eventually received Christ.

What changed their attitude? Doug had exemplified the Savior, who "made himself of no reputation" but took "the form of a bondservant" and "humbled himself" (Philippians 2:7–8).

We are called to do the same. Sometimes loving is unpleasant, but that's when it speaks the loudest.

DENNIS DEHAAN

Love without action is not love.

Faithful Service

2 TIMOTHY 2:1–10

Join with me in suffering, like a good soldier of Christ Jesus.
2 TIMOTHY 2:3

Having served in World War I, C. S. Lewis was no stranger to the stresses of military service. In a public address during World War II, he eloquently described the hardships a soldier has to face: "All that we fear from all the kinds of adversity . . . is collected together in the life of the soldier on active service. Like sickness, it threatens pain and death. Like poverty, it threatens ill lodging, cold, heat, thirst, and hunger. Like slavery, it threatens toil, humiliation, injustice, and arbitrary rule. Like exile, it separates you from all you love."

The apostle Paul used the analogy of a soldier suffering hardship to describe the trials a believer may experience in service to Christ. Paul—now at the end of his life—had faithfully endured suffering for the sake of the gospel. He encouraged Timothy to do the same: "You therefore must endure hardship as a good soldier of Jesus Christ" (2 Timothy 2:3 NKJV).

Serving Christ requires perseverance. We may encounter obstacles of poor health, troubled relationships, or difficult circumstances. But as a good soldier we press on—with God's strength—because we serve the King of Kings and Lord of Lords who sacrificed himself for us!

DENNIS FISHER

God's love does not keep us from trials, but sees us through them.

The Death of Doubt

JOHN 11:1–16

So the other disciples told him, "We have seen the Lord!"
But he said to them, "Unless I see the nail marks in his hands and put my
finger where the nails were, and put my hand into his side,
I will not believe."

JOHN 20:25

We know him as Doubting Thomas (see John 20:24–29), but the label isn't entirely fair. After all, how many of us would have believed that our executed leader had been resurrected? We might just as well call him "Courageous Thomas." After all, Thomas displayed impressive courage as Jesus moved purposefully toward His death.

At the death of Lazarus, Jesus had said, "Let us go back to Judea" (John 11:7), prompting a protest from the disciples. "Rabbi," they said, "a short while ago the Jews there tried to stone you, and yet you are going back?" (v. 8). It was Thomas who said, "Let us also go, that we may die with him" (v. 16).

Thomas's intentions proved nobler than his actions. Upon Jesus's arrest, Thomas fled with the rest (Matthew 26:56), leaving Peter and John to accompany Christ to the courtyard of the high priest. Only John followed Jesus all the way to the cross.

Despite having witnessed the resurrection of Lazarus (John 11:38–44), Thomas still could not bring himself to believe that the crucified Lord had conquered death. Not until he saw the risen Lord, could he exclaim, "My Lord and my God!" (John 20:28).

We can draw hope from Jesus's response to Thomas: "Because you have seen me, you have believed; blessed are those who have not seen and yet have believed" (v. 29).

TIM GUSTAFSON

Real doubt searches for the light; unbelief is content with the darkness.

Tears of a Teen

ROMANS 9:1–5

I have great sorrow and unceasing anguish in my heart.
ROMANS 9:2

As I sat with four teenagers and a twenty-something homeless man at a soup kitchen in Alaska, I was touched by the teens' compassion for him. They listened as he talked about what he believed and then they gently presented the gospel to him—lovingly offering him hope in Jesus. Sadly, the man refused to seriously consider the gospel.

As we were leaving, one of the girls, Grace, expressed through her tears how much she didn't want the man to die without knowing Jesus. From the heart, she grieved for this young man who, at least at this point, was rejecting the love of her Savior.

The tears of this teen remind me of the apostle Paul, who served the Lord humbly and had great sorrow in his heart for his countrymen, desiring that they trust in Christ (Romans 9:1–5). Paul's compassion and concern must have brought him to tears on many occasions.

If we care enough for others who have not yet accepted God's gift of forgiveness through Christ, we will find ways to share with them. With the confidence of our own faith and with tears of compassion, let's take the good news to those who need to know the Savior.

DAVE BRANON

Sharing the gospel is one person telling another the good news.

A Fair Trade

PSALM 119:161–168

I rejoice in your promise like one who finds great spoil.
PSALM 119:162

Scott and Mary Crickmore poured fifteen years of their lives into helping to translate the New Testament in the Maasina dialect. It was for the Fulani tribe in the West African nation of Mali.

After the initial draft, Mary visited nearby villages and read it to people. She sat in huts with a group of men or women listening to them discuss what they understood. That helped her to make sure the words they were using in the translation were accurate and clear.

Some people would think that the Crickmores' sacrifice was too great—giving up their comfortable lifestyle, changing their diet to mush and rice, and living in less-than-ideal circumstances for those fifteen years. But the Crickmores say it was "a fair trade," because now the Fulani people have the Word of God in a language they can read.

The psalmist delighted in God's Word. He stood in awe of it, rejoiced over it, loved it, and obeyed it (Psalm 119:161–168). He found great peace and hope in the Word.

The Fulani people are now able to discover the "great treasure" (v. 162 NKJV) of God's Word. Would you agree with the Crickmores that any effort and sacrifice to get the Bible to others is "a fair trade"?

ANNE CETAS

**One measure of our love for God is what we're willing to do
to share His Word with others.**

China's Billy Graham

PHILIPPIANS 3:1–11

Whatever were gains to me I now consider loss for the sake of Christ.
PHILIPPIANS 3:7

In 1927, John Sung boarded a ship from the US—bound for Shanghai, China. He had been in the States for more than seven years, earning three degrees in that time, including a PhD.

As the ship neared its destination, Sung threw all his diplomas, medals, and fraternity keys overboard, keeping only his doctorate diploma from Ohio State University to show his father. He had received Jesus Christ and was determined that for the rest of his life he would live only for what counted for eternity.

Many older Christians still living in East and Southeast Asia came to know Christ through the ministry of John Sung, who has been called China's Billy Graham for his evangelistic work. His actions demonstrate what Paul wrote in Philippians 3:7, "Whatever were gains to me I now consider loss for the sake of Christ."

Not everyone can do what John Sung did. But like Paul we all should regard the things of this life "as rubbish" (v.8) and live our lives so they will count for eternity.

There are people within your sphere of influence whose lives you can impact for God. He has placed them within your reach to point them to Jesus.

Think of someone you can speak to about Jesus Christ and what He has done for you.

C.P. HIA

Only one life 'twill soon be past; only what's done for Christ will last.

Worth Dying For

PHILIPPIANS 1:19–26

For to me, to live is Christ and to die is gain.

PHILIPPIANS 1:21

Sophie Scholl was a young German woman during the 1940s. She saw the deterioration of her country under the iron rule of the Nazi regime, and she was determined to make a difference. She and her brother, with a small group of friends, began to peacefully protest not only the actions but also the values the Nazis had forced upon the nation.

Sophie and others were arrested and subsequently executed for speaking out against the evil in their land. Although she wasn't eager to die, she saw that the conditions in her country had to be addressed—even if it meant her death.

Sophie's story raises a critical question for us as well. What would we be willing to die for? Jim Elliot, Nate Saint, Pete Fleming, Roger Youderian, and Ed McCully gave their lives in the jungles of Ecuador in 1956 because they were committed to spreading the gospel. Elliot revealed the heart that drove such sacrifice when he wrote, "He is no fool who gives what he cannot keep to gain that which he cannot lose." The apostle Paul put it this way: "For to me, to live is Christ and to die is gain" (Philippians 1:21).

Some things really are worth dying for—and in them we gain the reward of the One who declares, "Well done, good and faithful servant!" (Matthew 25:21, 23).

BILL CROWDER

Those who faithfully bear the cross in this life will wear the crown in the life to come.

A Helping Hand

LUKE 5:17–26

*Anyone who withholds kindness from a friend
forsakes the fear of the Almighty.*

JOB 6:14

A college student named Kelly shattered her arm in the first volleyball game of the season. This meant she couldn't work at her part-time job. Then her car stopped running. To top it all off, the young man she had been dating stopped calling. Kelly felt so low that she began spending hours alone in her room crying.

Laura, a Christian friend on the volleyball team, became concerned about Kelly and decided to help her. So she planned a party. She and some friends collected money, and a couple of guys got Kelly's car running again. They found a temporary job she could do, using just one hand. And they gave her tickets to see her basketball hero when his team came to town. Before long, Kelly was herself again. When she asked why they did all this for her, Laura was able to tell her about the love of Jesus.

Kelly's story reminds me of the paralyzed man who was healed by Jesus. The afflicted man's friends cared enough about him to bring him to the Savior (Luke 5:17–26).

Do you have a friend in need? Think of some ways you can help. Show the love of Christ and then share the gospel. You never know what might happen when you lend a helping hand.

DAVID EGNER

Real love puts actions to good intentions.

God's Giving Standard

2 CORINTHIANS 8:1–15

For you know the grace of our Lord Jesus Christ, that though he was rich, yet for your sake he became poor, so that you through his poverty might become rich.

2 CORINTHIANS 8:9

What is sacrificial giving? The early congregations of Macedonia set the pace for other first-century churches. They gave not only what they were able but also beyond their ability (2 Corinthians 8:3).

Stanford Kelly, a missionary to Haiti, provides a modern example of that kind of generosity. After taking up an offering in the little congregation where he served, Kelly found a gift of $13. That was the equivalent of one month's wages. The gift surprised him every bit as much as a $5,000 check would startle a pastor in a wealthier nation.

The extraordinary gift prompted Kelly to search out the giver, who was a farmer. When he questioned the man about his gift, the peasant was reluctant to answer. Kelly probed until he discovered that the man had sold his horse, even though the animal helped provide the man's livelihood. Kelly asked, "Why didn't you come to church to give the gift yourself?" The farmer replied, "Because I had no shirt to wear."

None of us can match the Lord's standard of giving. He gave up everything He had to bring us redemption. Keep that in mind as you prayerfully plan to give to God's work. How does your giving compare to God's giving standard?

HADDON ROBINSON

Your standard of giving is more important than your standard of living.

What a Ride!

1 THESSALONIANS 1

The Lord's message rang out from you not only in Macedonia and Achaia—
your faith in God has become known everywhere. Therefore we do not need
to say anything about it.

1 THESSALONIANS 1:8

Francis Asbury (1745–1816) rode 6,000 miles a year on horseback for nearly half a century. Despite ill health, he drove himself tirelessly. He sustained himself with venison jerky because it wouldn't spoil during his extended travels. Asbury is remembered for introducing the Methodist "circuit-riding preacher" (a minister who had a regular route of churches where he would present gospel sermons) as an effective way to capture the American frontier for Christ. Planting new churches in remote areas was central to his approach.

At the close of Asbury's ministry, he had recruited more than 700 traveling preachers. In 1771, when Asbury had first arrived in the colonies from his native England, there had been only about 600 Methodists in America. Forty-five years later, there were 200,000!

In many ways, Asbury's strategy for planting churches reflects the approach of the apostle Paul. To the church he had planted in Thessalonica, Paul wrote, "From you the word of the Lord has sounded forth, not only in Macedonia and Achaia, but also in every place" (1 Thessalonians 1:8 NKJV; see Acts 17:1–10).

The days of the "circuit-riding preacher" have come and gone. But each of us has a "frontier" where friends, relatives, and neighbors are our mission field. Can you think of someone today who needs to hear the good news?

DENNIS FISHER

Those who love Christ have a love for the lost.

Behind the Building

1 PETER 4:8–11

Therefore, my dear brothers and sisters, stand firm. Let nothing move you. Always give yourselves fully to the work of the Lord, because you know that your labor in the Lord is not in vain.

1 CORINTHIANS 15:58

Where we were working was hot, dirty, and it smelled bad. We had traveled thousands of miles to do some work projects, and on this day we were painting the back of a classroom building at a school for the deaf. The only people who would ever see this part of the building would be the guy who cut the grass and any unfortunate person who would have to work on the septic pit.

Yet, as the teenagers diligently painted away, one of the girls, Melissa, put it in perspective by saying, "Nobody will ever come back here to see this, but God will see it. So let's make it look nice." And so we did.

Sometimes we sit at our desk and think no one sees our work. Or we stand at a line assembling item after endless item. Perhaps we take care of crying babies in the church nursery. Or we live the best Christian life we can—without anyone noticing.

Often our work is "behind the building." But if that is what God has called us to do, we need to work with all our heart. As part of our calling to love others deeply (1 Peter 4:8), offer hospitality (v. 9), and use our gifts to serve others (v. 10), our task is to work with God's strength to bring praise and glory to God, not ourselves. The important thing is that God likes what He sees.

DAVE BRANON

No service for Christ goes unnoticed by Him.

Grass on Your Path?

DANIEL 6:1–10

Now when Daniel learned that the decree had been published,
he went home to his upstairs room where the windows opened toward Jerusalem.
Three times a day he got down on his knees and prayed, giving thanks to his God,
just as he had done before.

DANIEL 6:10

In one region of Africa, the first converts to Christianity were diligent about praying. In fact, the believers all had their own special places outside the village where they went to pray in solitude. The villagers reached these "prayer rooms" by using their own private footpaths through the brush. When grass began to grow over one of these trails, it was evident that the person to whom it belonged was not praying very much.

Because these new Christians were concerned for each other's spiritual welfare, a unique custom sprang up. Whenever anyone noticed an overgrown "prayer path," he or she would go to the person and lovingly warn, "Friend, there's grass on your path!"

In today's Scripture we read this about Daniel: "Three times a day he got down on his knees and prayed, giving thanks to his God" (6:10). We too must maintain a regular schedule of meeting the Lord in prayer. We should see if there has been any tendency to neglect our times with God.

Have you met with the Lord yet today? Do you regularly come to "God's throne of grace" to "receive mercy and find grace to help us in our time of need"? (Hebrews 4:16). Is there any "grass on your path"?

RICHARD DeHAAN

No day is well spent without spending time with God.

Heaven's Greatest Delights

REVELATION 22:1–5

However, as it is written: "What no eye has seen, what no ear has heard, and what no human mind has conceived"—the things God has prepared for those who love him.

1 CORINTHIANS 2:9

What will be one of heaven's supreme joys?

Joni Eareckson Tada, disabled as a teenager in a diving accident, has been a quadriplegic for more than fifty years. One would imagine that her greatest longing would be the ability to walk, even run—free from the confinement of her wheelchair.

But Joni tells us that her greatest desire is to offer a "praise that is pure." She explains: "I won't be crippled by distractions, or disabled by insincerity. I won't be handicapped by a ho-hum half-heartedness. My heart will join with yours and bubble over with effervescent adoration. We will finally be able to fellowship fully with the Father and the Son. For me, this will be the best part of heaven."

How that speaks to my divided heart and grips my unfocused spirit! What a blessing to offer "a praise that is pure," with no wandering thoughts, no self-centered requests, no inability to soar above my earth-bound language!

In heaven, "no longer will there be any curse. The throne of God and of the Lamb will be in the city, and his servants will serve him" (Revelation 22:3). May the prospect of heaven enable us to experience a foretaste of that God-glorifying worship even here and now.

VERNON GROUNDS

To see Jesus will be heaven's greatest joy.

A Mere Happening?

RUTH 2:1-12

In all your ways submit to him, and he will make your paths straight.
PROVERBS 3:6

Huang, a nonbeliever, was a visiting scientist at the University of Minnesota. While there, he met some Christians and enjoyed their fellowship. So when they learned he would be returning to Beijing, they gave him the name of a Christian to contact who was also moving there.

On the flight back to Beijing, the plane encountered engine trouble and stopped in Seattle overnight. The airline placed Huang in the same room with the very person he was to contact! Once they arrived in Beijing, the two began meeting weekly for a Bible study, and a year later Huang gave his life to Christ. This was not just a mere happening; it was by God's arrangement.

In Ruth 2, we read that Ruth came to "a field belonging to Boaz" (v. 3). Boaz asked his servants who she was (v. 5), which prompted his special consideration toward her. When Ruth asked him the reason for such kindness, Boaz replied, "I've been told all about what you have done for your mother-in-law . . . . May the LORD repay you for what you have done. May you be richly rewarded by the LORD" (vv. 11–12).

Did the events in the lives of Ruth and Huang just happen? No, for none of God's people can escape God's plans to guide and to provide.

ALBERT LEE

A "mere happening" may be God's design.

He Did It

2 TIMOTHY 2:1–10

And the things you have heard me say in the presence of many witnesses entrust to reliable people who will also be qualified to teach others.
2 TIMOTHY 2:2

At the memorial service for LeRoy Eims, longtime staff member with The Navigators, I pondered why hundreds of colleagues and friends had come from across the US to pay tribute. Why did so many people love him so deeply?

As a young Christian, LeRoy had been challenged to disciple others one on one. He took seriously Paul's charge to Timothy: "The things you have heard me say in the presence of many witnesses entrust to reliable people who will also be qualified to teach others" (2 Timothy 2:2). LeRoy embraced that clear, simple command of Scripture and practiced it faithfully for more than fifty years.

Scores of people who packed the church that afternoon had lived in LeRoy and Virginia Eims' home. They had been embraced, encouraged, and instructed by him. As his spiritual children, they had multiplied his ministry by investing themselves in others, just as he had in them.

One sentence in a written tribute captured the essence of the man: "His life was characterized by singleness of purpose, great creativity and a wonderful sense of humor."

LeRoy's example spurs us on to a lifetime of faithfully following the Lord. He did it! And by God's grace, so can we.

DAVID MCCASLAND

You can teach more with your life than with your lips.

The Power That Works

EPHESIANS 3:14–21

*Now to him who is able to do immeasurably more than all we ask or imagine,
according to his power that is at work within us, to him be glory in the church
and in Christ Jesus throughout all generations, for ever and ever! Amen.*

EPHESIANS 3:20–21

A trip through the jungles of Thailand brought four Christian women
face-to-face with death. As they made their way through the dense foliage
to follow up on some new converts, they were ambushed at gunpoint by
three communist rebels. When the men found that the women had no
money, they angrily told them they were going to kill them.

The women pleaded with their captors not to shoot, but the men were
adamant. Then one of the workers asked the men if they could tell them
about God's love before they were shot. Surprisingly, the gunmen agreed!
So Kleun Anuyet explained that Jesus had died on the cross because He
loved them.

The men did an astonishing thing—they dropped their guns, and tears
began to flow. The ringleader said, "If Jesus has that much love, then I want
it too." Soon all three accepted Christ as Savior. Today they are serving
God as fulltime Christian workers.

When Paul prayed for the Ephesians, he referred to "the power that
is at work within us" (3:20). It was that indwelling strength that allowed
those brave women to witness of God's love while staring down the barrel
of a gun.

Let's think about the last time we relied on God's exceedingly abundant
power to work in us.

DAVE BRANON

Our needs can never exhaust God's supply.

Questions for God

JUDGES 6:11–16, 24

The LORD turned to him and said, "Go in the strength you have and save Israel out of Midian's hand. Am I not sending you?" . . . The LORD answered, "I will be with you, and you will strike down all the Midianites."

JUDGES 6:14, 16

What would you do if the Lord showed up in the middle of your workday with a message? This happened to Gideon. "The angel of the LORD appeared to him and said, 'Mighty hero, the LORD is with you!'" Gideon could have responded with a wordless nod and gulp, but instead he said, "If the LORD is with us, why has all this happened to us?" (Judges 6:12–13 NLT). Why had God seemingly abandoned His people?

God didn't answer that question. After Gideon had endured seven years of enemy attacks, starvation, and hiding in caves, God didn't explain why He never intervened. God could have revealed Israel's past sin as the reason, but instead He gave Gideon future hope: "Go with the strength you have, . . . I will be with you." (vv. 14, 16 NLT).

Do you ever wonder why God has allowed suffering in your life? Instead of answering that question, God may satisfy you with His nearness and remind you that you can rely on His strength when you feel weak. When Gideon finally believed that God was with him and would help him, he built an altar and called it "The LORD is peace" (v. 24).

There is peace in knowing that wherever we go, we go with God, who promised never to leave or forsake His followers.

JENNIFER BENSON SCHULDT

What could be better than getting answers to our "why" questions? Trusting a good and powerful God.

"Plumb Bobs" for the Heart

PSALM 119:9–16

I have hidden your word in my heart that I might not sin against you.
PSALM 119:11

Charlie Riggs has been called "the man behind Billy Graham." For nearly forty years, Riggs was the director of counseling and follow-up for Graham's evangelistic meetings. In his counselor training classes, Charlie taught thousands of people the basic principles of how to live for Christ and share their faith with others.

At Charlie's ninetieth birthday celebration, many tributes mentioned his lifelong practice of memorizing Scripture. His goal was not merely to know the Bible, but to know Christ and live by His Word.

Charlie followed the concepts found in Psalm 119:9–11: "How can a young man cleanse his way? By taking heed according to Your word. . . . Your Word I have hidden in my heart, that I might not sin against You" (NKJV). Charlie likened the Scriptures to "plumb bobs" for his heart. Like the weight that holds a builder's plumb line straight and true, these divine principles never change, no matter what the circumstances. He measured his thoughts, feelings, and behavior by God's Word, not the other way around.

Charlie Riggs's life was quiet and steady behind the scenes. His example challenges us today to hide God's Word in our hearts and let it guide our lives. Charlie demonstrated what it means to live according to plumb.

DAVID MCCASLAND

The Bible: Know it in your head, stow it in your heart, show it in your life, and sow it in the world.

The Price

1 CORINTHIANS 10:23–33

*Therefore, I urge you, brothers and sisters, in view of God's mercy,
to offer your bodies as a living sacrifice, holy and pleasing to God—
this is your true and proper worship.*

ROMANS 12:1

A pastor once sent me the following clear explanation of being a "living sacrifice."

"I know something of the price of missionary effort. Of the first twelve workers sent out by the Africa Inland Mission, I was the only one left after two and one-half years. I had been attacked by lions and rhinoceroses, I had been surrounded by tribesmen with their poisoned arrows and bows, not knowing what minute they would let go. For fourteen months I never saw any bread, and for two months at one time I had to live on beans and sour milk. For weeks I was without the commonest of necessities and had to eat anything from ants to rhino. But while getting the Bible for the first time into a great tribe that had never heard it before—I can never think of those forty years in terms of sacrifice."

For this man, the serenity of being in the center of God's will discounted the trials and difficulties—making those struggles almost unworthy of consideration. The Lord compensated him so marvelously in other ways that he testifies that it is but his "reasonable service" (Romans 12:1 NKJV).

If you find it hard to rejoice in the service God has entrusted to you—consider what this man did: He presented his body as a living sacrifice.

HENRY BOSCH

**Only as we give our bodies to Christ and "die" to all about us,
do we live to God above us!**

Who Is My Neighbor?

LUKE 10:30–37

The expert in the law replied, "The one who had mercy on him."
Jesus told him, "Go and do likewise."
LUKE 10:37

Mary enjoyed her midweek church group meeting when she and several friends gathered to pray, worship, and discuss questions from the previous week's sermon. This week they were going to talk about the difference between "going" to church and "being" the church in a hurting world. She was looking forward to seeing her friends and having a lively discussion.

As she picked up her car keys, the doorbell rang. "I'm so sorry to bother you," said her neighbor, Sue, "but are you free this morning?" Mary was about to say that she was going out when Sue continued, "I have to take my car to the repair shop. Normally I would walk or cycle home, but I've hurt my back and can't do either at the moment." Mary hesitated for a heartbeat and then smiled. "Of course," she said.

Mary knew her neighbor only by sight. But as she drove her home, she learned about Sue's husband's battle with dementia and the utter exhaustion that being a caregiver can bring with it. She listened, sympathized, and promised to pray. She offered to help in any way she could.

Mary didn't get to church that morning to talk about sharing her faith. Instead, as Luke 10:37 suggests, she took a little bit of Jesus's love to her neighbor who was in a difficult situation.

MARION STROUD

Faith is seen in our actions.

A Surprise Answer

1 JOHN 3:16–23

[We] receive from him anything we ask,
because we keep his commands and do what pleases him.

1 JOHN 3:22

When the mother of Christian apologist and author Josh McDowell died, he was not sure of her salvation. He became depressed. Was she a Christian or not? "Lord," he prayed, "somehow give me the answer so I can get back to normal. I've just got to know." It seemed like an impossible request.

Two days later, Josh drove out to the ocean and walked to the end of a pier to be alone. There sat an elderly woman in a lawn chair, fishing. "Where's your home originally?" she asked. "Michigan—Union City," Josh replied. "Nobody's heard of it. I tell people it's a suburb of—" "Battle Creek," interrupted the woman. "I had a cousin from there. Did you know the McDowell family?"

Stunned, Josh responded, "Yes, I'm Josh McDowell." "I can't believe it," said the woman. "I'm a cousin to your mother." "Do you remember anything at all about my mother's spiritual life?" asked Josh. "Why sure— your mom and I were just girls—teenagers—when a tent revival came to town. We both went forward to accept Christ." "Praise God!" shouted Josh, startling the surrounding fishermen.

God delights to give us what we ask when it is in His will. Never underestimate His desire to respond to our prayers. A surprise may be just around the corner.

DENNIS DEHAAN

If you get definite with God, He'll get definite with you.

Mell's Smiley Face

ROMANS 5:15

We also glory in our sufferings, because we know that
suffering produces perseverance.

ROMANS 5:3

Some people think you shouldn't draw in your Bible, but I'm glad my daughter Melissa drew in hers. In the margin next to Romans 5, she used a green ink pen to draw a simple smiley face, and she circled verse three.

How could she have known that her family and friends would need this passage when she left us so suddenly in a car accident at age seventeen? How could she know that these verses would tell her story, while guiding our lives and the lives of others over the past few years?

Romans 5 begins by explaining our justification through faith, which gives us peace with God through Jesus (v. 1). Melissa had that peace. And right now she is enjoying the fruits of her faith, as verse two describes: We "rejoice in hope of the glory of God" (NKJV). Imagine the smiley face she could draw now!

And then there's the rest of us—all of us left behind when loved ones precede us in death. Somehow, we "glory in our sufferings." Why? Our suffering brings perseverance, which brings character, which brings us hope (vv. 3–4).

We feel helpless in times of tragedy, but we are never hopeless. God pours His love into our hearts—and with it the great hope of His glory. It's all part of God's mysterious yet marvelous plan.

DAVE BRANON

God often digs wells of joy with the spade of sorrow.

Set the Sail

MARK 11:20–24

*Therefore I tell you, whatever you ask for in prayer,
believe that you have received it, and it will be yours.*

MARK 11:24

When we ask God for something that we know is in His will, we must also be ready to receive the answer.

When Hudson Taylor went to China, he made the voyage on a sailing ship. As it neared the channel between the southern Malay Peninsula and the island of Sumatra, the missionary heard an urgent knock on his stateroom door. He opened it, and there stood the captain of the ship.

"Mr. Taylor," he said, "we have no wind. We are drifting toward an island where the people are heathen, and I fear they are cannibals."

"What can I do?" asked Taylor.

"I understand that you believe in God. I want you to pray for wind."

"All right, Captain, I will, but you must set the sail."

"Why, that's ridiculous! There's not even the slightest breeze. Besides, the sailors will think I'm crazy." Nevertheless, the captain finally agreed. Forty-five minutes later he returned and found the missionary still on his knees. "You can stop praying now," said the captain. "We've got more wind than we know what to do with!"

Hudson Taylor believed that God answers prayer. What about you? Do you really expect Him to respond? Pray. And then "set the sail."

PAUL VAN GORDER

When you pray for rain, carry an umbrella.

The Little Things Too

2 KINGS 6:1–7

My God will meet all your needs according to the riches
of his glory in Christ Jesus.

PHILIPPIANS 4:19

Pastor Harold Springstead was driving along on his way to preach at a little country church when he felt a sudden vibration. A tire had gone flat. As the seventy-eight-year-old pastor maneuvered his car to a stop, a trucker pulled up behind him. A young man jumped out, assessed the situation, and cheerfully changed the tire. Pastor Springstead got to the service in plenty of time, and it was not until later that he realized his car didn't even have a jack!

It was a minor problem. He was a retired faithful servant of God. It was a tiny congregation. We might think God would be too busy with larger and more important needs than to be concerned about a flat tire. But His promise to provide for the needs of His people covers little things as well as big ones.

The same God who helped Elisha retrieve the borrowed ax head (2 Kings 6:5–7), who supplied food for a faithful widow (1 Kings 17:8–16), and who provided wine at a small-town wedding (John 2:1–10) meets our needs as well.

Think back over the past few days. Has the Lord taken care of some minor needs in your life? Has He solved some nagging problem? Thank Him! As today unfolds, remember that He provides the little things too.

DAVID EGNER

Nothing is too great for God to accomplish;
nothing is too small for His attention.

Faithful Prayer

1 TIMOTHY 2:1–7

For kings and all those in authority, that we may live peaceful and quiet lives in all godliness and holiness.

1 TIMOTHY 2:2

In June 2009, ninety-five-year-old Emma Gray died. For more than two decades, she had been the cleaning lady in a big house. Each night as she did her work, she prayed for blessings, wisdom, and safety for the man she worked for.

Although Emma worked in the same place for twenty-four years, the occupants of the residence changed every four years or so. Over the years, Emma offered her nightly prayers for six US Presidents: Eisenhower, Kennedy, Johnson, Nixon, Ford, and Carter.

Emma had her personal favorites, but she prayed for them all. She followed the instruction we read in 1 Timothy 2 to pray for "all those in authority" (v. 2). The verses go on to speak of how living "peaceful and quiet lives" and being a godly and reverent person "is good, pleases God our Savior . . . who wants all people to be saved and to come to a knowledge of the truth" (vv. 2–4).

Because God "hears the prayer of the righteous" (Proverbs 15:29), who knows how He used Emma's faithful prayers? In Proverbs 21:1, we read: "The king's heart is in the hand of the LORD, like the rivers of water; He turns it wherever He wishes" (NKJV).

Like Emma, we are to pray for our leaders. Is there someone God is calling you to pray for today?

CINDY HESS KASPER

To influence leaders for God, intercede with God for leaders.

Age Is Not a Factor

1 CORINTHIANS 12:12–26

If one part suffers, every part suffers with it;
if one part is honored, every part rejoices with it.
1 CORINTHIANS 12:26

After owning and working at his dental lab for forty years, Dave Bowman planned to retire and take it easy. Diabetes and heart surgery confirmed his decision. But when he heard about a group of young refugees from Sudan who needed help, he made a life-changing decision. He agreed to sponsor five of them.

As Dave learned more about these young Sudanese men, he discovered that they had never been to a doctor or a dentist. Then one day in church someone mentioned the verse, "If one part suffers, every part suffers with it" (1 Corinthians 12:26). He couldn't get the verse out of his mind. Sudanese Christians were suffering because they needed medical care, and Dave sensed that God was telling him to do something about it. But what?

Despite his age and bad health, Dave began exploring the possibility of building a medical center in Sudan. Little by little, God brought together the people and the resources, and in 2008 Memorial Christian Hospital opened its doors to patients. Since then, hundreds of sick and injured people have been treated there.

Memorial Christian Hospital stands as a reminder that God cares when people suffer. And often He works through people like us to share His care—even when we think our work is done.

JULIE ACKERMAN LINK

God cares when people suffer.

Nine Days in the Jungle

ROMANS 1:8-15

Now, brothers and sisters, I want to remind you of the gospel I preached to you, which you received and on which you have taken your stand.

1 CORINTHIANS 15:1

Slicing through a thick jungle in Irian Jaya was not on missionary Phil Fields' list of relaxing ways to spend part of his furlough. Yet that's what he did for nine days one year while his family stayed in Kansas. Phil had spent the previous four years in Irian Jaya, translating the gospel of Mark into the Orya language. Then he went to the United States to have it published. Returning to Irian Jaya, he recruited two nationals to help him deliver copies of Mark to the 1,600 Orya-speaking people scattered throughout the jungle.

But why? What would cause this former college music professor to give up the comforts of modern life to translate and distribute God's Word in such obscurity? One of the nationals traveling with him suggested an answer. He said, "Do you think this man would leave his good country and travel to our land, then do all the work he has done to translate this book into Orya if what he was sharing was a falsehood?" Phil gave up "the good life" and risked his family's life because he wanted the Oryas to read for themselves the good news of God's love.

No sacrifice is too great to make the gospel known to those who've never heard. Phil Fields is doing his part. Are we willing to do ours?

DAVE BRANON

We must go to sinners if we expect sinners to come to the Savior.

Not Trying, but Trusting

ROMANS 4:1-8

To him who does not work but believes on Him who justifies the ungodly,
his faith is accounted for righteousness.

ROMANS 4:5 NKJV

The founder of Radio Bible Class (now Our Daily Bread Ministries), Dr. M. R. DeHaan (1891–1965), was in his study one day when a man came to see him. The visitor told him he had served five years in prison, was released, and then was arrested again and sentenced to fifteen years in the penitentiary for robbery. He had wanted to "go straight" but couldn't.

He said that one Sunday morning while listening to the radio in his cell he heard Dr. DeHaan say, "We are not saved by trying, nor by doing anything, but simply by receiving the Lord Jesus by faith."

The man said he called the chaplain and told him he wanted to be saved. The chaplain was not a believer himself, however, so he replied, "Make up your mind to do better." But the prisoner had tried again and again and had failed.

That night he couldn't sleep. Finally, he cried out in desperation, "Lord Jesus, the best I know how, I receive You as my Savior and Lord." Peace flooded his soul, and he knew he had been forgiven.

That man learned for himself that salvation is gained not by trying to do better but by trusting Christ, who died for our sins. Have you trusted Him? If so, you can rejoice today because of what Jesus has done for you.

PAUL VAN GORDER

Salvation is not what we achieve but what we receive.

Tissue Boxes

PSALM 31:9–18

But I trust in you, LORD; I say, "You are my God." My times are in your hands; deliver me from the hands of my enemies, from those who pursue me.
PSALM 31:14–15

As I sat in the surgical waiting room, I had time to think. I had been here recently, when we received the jarring news that my only brother, much too young, was "brain dead."

And so on this day, waiting for news about my wife who was undergoing a serious surgical procedure, I penned a lengthy note to her. Then, surrounded by nervous chatter and oblivious children, I listened for the quiet voice of God.

Suddenly, news! The surgeon wanted to see me. I went to a secluded room to wait. There, on the table, sat two tissue boxes, conspicuously available. They weren't for the sniffles. They were for cold, hard phrases like I heard when my brother died—"brain dead" and "nothing we can do."

In such times of grief or uncertainty, the honesty of the psalms makes them a natural place to turn. Psalm 31 was the heart cry of David, who endured so much that he wrote, "My life is consumed by anguish" (v. 10).

But David had the bedrock of faith in the one true God. "I trust in you, LORD; I say, 'You are my God.' My times are in your hands" (vv. 14–15).

This time, the surgeon gave us good news: My wife could expect a full and complete recovery. Of course, we're relieved and grateful! But even if she hadn't been "okay," our times still remain in God's capable hands.

TIM GUSTAFSON

**When we put our problems in God's hands,
He puts His peace in our hearts.**

Arms of Love

1 JOHN 3:16-20

Dear children, let us not love with words or speech but with actions and in truth.
1 JOHN 3:18

Many college students go on summer missions trips. But rarely does one come back with plans to rescue a baby. Mallery Thurlow, a student at Cornerstone University in Grand Rapids, went to Haiti to help distribute food. One day a mother showed up at the distribution center with a very sick infant in her arms. The woman was out of options. The baby needed surgery, but no one would perform it. Without intervention, the baby would die. Mallery took baby Rose into her arms—and into her heart.

After returning to the US, Mallery searched for someone to operate on baby Rose. Most doctors held out little hope. Finally, Rose was granted a visa to leave Haiti, and Mallery went back to get her. Detroit Children's Hospital donated the $100,000 surgery, and it was successful. A little life was saved.

It's unlikely that we will have such a dramatic impact on others. Yet challenged by this student's willingness, we can find ways to provide help. She didn't let circumstances, youth, or inconvenience stop her from saving Rose's life.

Like Mallery, we are called to love "with actions and in truth" (1 John 3:18). Who needs you to be God's arms of love today?

DAVE BRANON

Compassion puts love into action.

Bring Them In!

MATTHEW 22:1–10

"Then the master told his servant, 'Go out to the roads and country lanes and compel them to come in, so that my house will be full.'"

LUKE 14:23

I read about an incident in the life of Dwight L. Moody (1837–1899) that occurred when he was only nineteen years old. In his day it was a common practice for people to rent the church pew in which they sat during the worship service. (By doing this, they didn't have to come early to get the "choice" seats.) One Sunday morning young Moody marched down the aisle with a motley crew of society's outcasts trailing behind him. He had rented four pews, and he was determined to fill them with people who were spiritually needy.

Having taken the Savior's "Go" personally (Luke 14:23), he literally "went out into the streets, and gathered all the people [he] could find, the bad as well as the good" (Matthew 22:10). No wonder Moody was so mightily used of the Lord! He recognized that if souls were to be won to Christ, believers would have to go find them.

For some of God's children, Jesus's command to "go" may mean leaving friends and loved ones behind and journeying to a foreign land as a missionary. But for most of us it involves a "home mission" effort like witnessing to our neighbors, giving out salvation tracts, or inviting people to church.

Has the Lord placed a burden on your heart for others who are lost? Then "go" and bring him in!

RICHARD DEHAAN

We must go to the sinner if we expect him to come to the Savior.

Leaving a Legacy

DEUTERONOMY 6:4

Impress them on your children. Talk about them when you sit at home and when you walk along the road, when you lie down and when you get up.
DEUTERONOMY 6:7

One day my grandson Alex accompanied me as I ran errands. Unexpectedly he asked, "So, Grandpa, how did you receive Christ as your Savior?" Touched, I told him about my childhood conversion. Alex was still interested, so I described how his great-grandfather had come to faith. This included a brief overview of how he survived World War II, his initial resistance to the gospel, and how his life changed after becoming a Christian.

Later I was reminded of our conversation when I read a Bible passage that spoke of faith being passed down through the generations. In Deuteronomy, Moses instructed the Israelites to take to heart God's truths and share them with the next generation as a way of life: "These words which I command you today shall be in your heart. You shall teach them diligently to your children, and shall talk of them when you sit in your house, when you walk by the way, when you lie down, and when you rise up" (6:6–7 NKJV).

Biblical parenting is not a guarantee of having godly offspring. But when we see spiritual interest in the next generation, we can cultivate vital conversations about God's Word. This can be one of a parent's, or a grandparent's, greatest legacies.

DENNIS FISHER

The richest legacy a parent can leave a child is a godly example.

Storytime

JOSHUA 2:1–4

When we heard of it, our hearts melted in fear and
everyone's courage failed because of you, for the LORD your God
is God in heaven above and on the earth below.

JOSHUA 2:11

Did you ever wonder why Rahab, the prostitute who lived in the pagan city of Jericho, opened her home to the Israelite spies? And what gave her the courage to name the God of Israel as her own?

This unlikely conversion was prompted by the stories she had heard about the reality and power of God. Though thoroughly steeped in paganism and immorality, her heart was drawn to God. As she told the spies, "We have heard how the LORD dried up the water of the Red Sea for you when you came out of Egypt, and what you did to Sihon and Og, the two kings of the Amorites" (Joshua 2:10).

Under normal circumstances, the highly fortified city of Jericho would have been virtually unconquerable. Yet it became vulnerable because of the compelling stories of God's power. Long before God's people arrived, the self-sufficient pride of this hostile culture dissolved in fear when faced with those who belonged to the God they had heard so much about (v. 11). And inside, one pagan heart turned to receive the God of Israel and played a strategic role in Israel's stunning victory.

Let's boldly tell the stories of God's greatness. You never know whose heart may be ready to respond!

JOE STOWELL

Don't be shy; tell the stories of God's greatness.

By Life or by Death

PHILIPPIANS 1:12–26

I eagerly expect and hope that I will in no way be ashamed,
but will have sufficient courage so that now as always Christ will be exalted
in my body, whether by life or by death.

PHILIPPIANS 1:20

Nineteenth-century British missionary George Atley was killed while serving with the Central African Mission. There were no witnesses, but the evidence indicates that Atley was confronted by a band of hostile tribesmen. He was carrying a fully loaded, ten-chamber Winchester rifle and had to choose either to shoot his attackers and run the risk of negating the work of the mission in that area, or not to defend himself and be killed. When his body was later found, it was evident that he had chosen the latter. Nearby lay his rifle—all ten chambers still loaded. He had made the supreme sacrifice, motivated by his burden for lost souls and his unswerving devotion to his Savior. With the apostle Paul, he wanted Christ to be magnified in his body, "whether by life or by death."

Writing on Philippians 1:20 in *The Bible Knowledge Commentary*, Robert P. Lightner said, "Paul's concern was not what would happen to him but what testimony would be left for his Lord. Release would allow him to continue preaching Christ. But martyrdom would also advance the cause of Christ."

There are those who give of their time, their resources, and their talents. Relatively few people, however, have been willing to give their very lives in service for Christ. How much are we willing to sacrifice for Him?

RICHARD DEHAAN

It is better to suffer for the cause of Christ than for
the cause of Christ to suffer.

The First Face She Ever Saw

REVELATION 22:1–5

They will see his face, and his name will be on their foreheads. There will be no more night. They will not need the light of a lamp or the light of the sun, for the Lord God will give them light. And they will reign for ever and ever.

REVELATION 22:4–5

Although songwriter Fanny Crosby was blinded by an illness at the age of six weeks, she never became bitter. It has been said that when someone remarked that it was too bad she had to suffer blindness, Fanny replied that she would have asked for blindness if she would have had a choice. When she was asked why, she said, "Because when I get to heaven, the first face that shall ever gladden my sight will be that of my Savior!"

One of Miss Crosby's hymns was so personal that for years she kept it to herself. Kenneth Osbeck, author of several books on hymnology, says its revelation to the public came about this way: "One day at a Bible conference in Northfield, Massachusetts, Miss Crosby was asked by Dwight L. Moody to give a personal testimony. At first she hesitated, then quietly rose and said, 'There is one hymn I have written which has never been published. I call it my soul's poem. Sometimes when I am troubled, I repeat it to myself, for it brings comfort to my heart.' She then recited it. 'Someday the silver cord will break, and I no more as now shall sing; but oh, the joy when I shall wake within the palace of the King! And I shall see Him face to face, and tell the story—saved by grace!'" At age of 95, Fanny Crosby passed into glory and saw the face of Jesus.

That's the sure hope of every child of God!

HENRY BOSCH

**Knowing His grace HERE is but a foretaste of seeing
His face over THERE.**

Will You Tell Them?

PROVERBS 24:10-12

"Whoever lives by believing in me will never die. Do you believe this?"
JOHN 11:26

John, a friend of mine, was once addicted to drugs. Several times he nearly died. He was a broken man when he entered the Christian rehabilitation program that my husband and I established. By the end of the program, John had become a Christian.

One day as John strolled along a busy street, he began to see the bustling shoppers as God sees them—dying people. He had learned from God's Word that those who die without Christ will spend eternity separated from Him. With deep concern, John thought, *These people don't have to die*!

We all need to see people as God sees them. But that revelation also brings responsibility. Solomon pleaded, "Rescue those being led away to death; hold back those staggering toward slaughter" (Proverbs 24:11). He also warned that once our eyes are opened we can't pretend we don't know what to do. God, who weighs our hearts and keeps our souls, knows that we know, and He holds us responsible to act (v. 12).

Think of people you know who are without Christ. They don't have to die without Him! Jesus said, "Whoever lives by believing in me will never die" (John 11:26). Will you tell them this good news?

JOANIE YODER

Wanted: Messengers to deliver the good news.

He Lived—and He Died

GENESIS 5:5-20

All the days that Adam lived were nine hundred and thirty years: and he died.
GENESIS 5:5 KJV

A London merchant named Henry Goodear was inclined to scoff at the Bible. But one Sunday, to please his niece, he went to church. She was greatly disappointed when she learned that the pastor's message was based on Genesis 5. As she listened to the monotonous list of names being read, she wondered why God had permitted him to pick such an uninteresting passage. She was afraid her uncle would close his mind to those gloomy verses.

As they walked home, every throb of his heart seemed to repeat the doleful refrain, "And he died! And he died!" The next day he could not concentrate on his work. That night he searched for a half-forgotten family Bible and read once again, "And all the days that Adam lived were nine hundred and thirty years: and he died" (v. 5 KJV). "And all the days of Seth were nine hundred and twelve years: and he died." (v. 8 KJV) "And all the days of Enos were nine hundred and five years: and he died." (v. 11 KJV). The simple story was the same for the good as well as the wicked: "He lived—and he died."

Henry thought, *Now I'm living, but someday I too must die, and then where will I spend eternity?* That very night he trusted Jesus as his Savior. His niece rejoiced when she heard of his conversion. Amazingly, the Holy Spirit can use even the most unlikely passage, such as a genealogical table, to bring conviction to a sinner's heart.

All of us live. And then we die. What then?

HENRY BOSCH

Living without God means dying without hope.

A Surrendered Life

PHILIPPIANS 1:8–21

I eagerly expect and hope that I will in no way be ashamed, but will have sufficient courage so that now as always Christ will be exalted in my body, whether by life or by death.

PHILIPPIANS 1:20

At the age of sixteen C. T. Studd (1860–1931) was already an expert cricket player, and at nineteen he was made captain of his team at Eton, England. Soon he became a world-famous sports personality. But the Lord had different plans for him. A preacher visiting in Studd's home caught him on the way out to play cricket and explained the plan of salvation to him. He dedicated his life to Christ and began witnessing to his teammates.

Sensing God's leading to full-time service, he left England for missionary work in China. While in there, he inherited a sum of money equivalent today to half a million dollars. It wasn't long before he had given the entire inheritance away, investing it in God's work. Later he was forced to go back to England, for his health was failing and his wife was disabled.

But God called him again—this time to the heart of Africa, where he served until his death. His entire adult life was given to tell people in China, India, and Africa about Jesus.

How much have you ever sacrificially given up for Christ? Are you fully surrendered to Jesus?

HENRY BOSCH

**If Jesus Christ be God and died for me,
no sacrifice can be too great for me to make for Him!
—Studd**

True Trust

JOHN 9:1–11

"Neither this man nor his parents sinned," said Jesus, "but this happened so that the works of God might be displayed in him."

JOHN 9:3

If you didn't know him, you might think Nick Vujicic has everything going for him. Nick has never had a sore arm. He's never had knee problems. He's never smashed his finger in a door, stubbed his toe, or banged his shin against a table leg.

But that's because Nick doesn't have a shin. Or a toe. Or a finger. Or a knee. Or an arm. Nick was born with no arms and no legs. Before you begin to feel sorry for Nick, read his words. "God won't let anything happen to us in our life unless He has a good purpose for it all. I completely gave my life to Christ at the age of fifteen after reading John 9. Jesus said that the reason the man was born blind was 'so that the works of God may be revealed through him.' . . . I now see that glory revealed as He is using me just the way I am and in ways others can't be used." Nick travels the world to spread the gospel and love of Jesus.

Nick says, "If I can trust in God with my circumstances, then you can trust in God with your circumstances. . . . The greatest joy of all is having Jesus Christ in my life and living the godly purpose He has for me."

Can we say that? Can we look beyond our limitations and have the same trust in God that transformed a man with no arms or legs into a missionary for Jesus?

DAVE BRANON

Trusting God turns problems into opportunities.

Send the Gospel Light

ACTS 13:42–52

For this is what the Lord has commanded us: "I have made you a light for the Gentiles, that you may bring salvation to the ends of the earth."
ACTS 13:47

A prosperous businessman in Canada returned to the United States to visit his parents, whom he had not seen for many years. The next day they attended church together and heard a sermon on the desperate need for going to other countries with the gospel. Following the service, the businessman's father exclaimed, "I'm sorry you had to listen to such a sermon! I think missions are a waste of men and money." In response, the son told his parents a story.

"Years ago," he said, "a teenager left his father's farm to seek his fortune in Canada. He got into bad company, and one day when he fell down in a drunken stupor, his fair-weather friends deserted him. A missionary came to the aid of that poor derelict. After giving him a warm meal, he spoke to him about his wayward life and eventually led him to the Savior." The son paused and then revealed, "Dad, I was that teenager who went astray. I can't imagine what would have become of me if it hadn't been for that faithful missionary."

In the Sermon on the Mount, Jesus said to His followers, "You are the light of the world" (Matthew 5:14). Then He commanded them to let their light shine so others would see their good works and glorify God (5:16). That is what missions—at home or abroad—is all about. Rescue others with the light of Christ.

HENRY BOSCH

**Here's one thing you cannot do about missions:
get rid of your responsibility.**

"It Never Touched My Heart"

PSALM 41

*The LORD sustains them on their sickbed and restores them
from their bed of illness.*

PSALM 41:3

The Bible does not guarantee us a life free from illness or disability, nor does it assure us that every prayer for recovery will be answered—though many are. But it does promise a spiritual wholeness that is far more desirable than physical health.

This is illustrated by this story of many years ago about a disabled high school student. Although the crutches that helped him get around kept him from being physically active, he excelled in his studies and was well liked by his peers. They saw the problems he had getting around, but for a long time nobody asked him why he had this difficulty. One day, however, his closest friend finally did. "It was polio," answered the student. The friend responded, "How do you keep from becoming bitter about it?" Tapping his chest with his hand, the young man replied with a smile, "Oh, it never touched my heart."

If you are a Christian who is suffering from a long-term illness that God has not seen fit to remove, don't give in to bitterness, rebellion, self-pity, or guilt. When those emotions well up, as they surely will, be honest with God. He understands. Ask Him to make you a channel for His love and power. As long as you keep your life open to Him, your affliction will never touch your heart.

DENNIS DEHAAN

There is nothing suffered by the body from which the soul may not profit.

A Bible for India

ECCLESIASTES 11:1–6

Ship your grain across the sea; after many days you may receive a return.
ECCLESIASTES 11:1

For her seventh birthday Mary's father, who was serving in India, gave her money to purchase an expensive Bible. His letter had so impressed her with the spiritual needs of that foreign country that she made a strange request. She asked her grandmother if it would be all right to buy two cheaper Bibles instead of one fancy edition. "I want one for myself and another for some little girl in India." Before the gift Bible was sent, Mary wrote in it: "From Mary Dillon, who loves the Lord Jesus and wishes with all her heart that whoever reads this will also believe on Him. —John 3:16."

Years later Mary went to India as a missionary. Soon she met a woman who was a very earnest Christian. When the Indian lady heard the missionary's name, a look of glad surprise crossed her face. Hurriedly putting her hand into her pocket, she drew out a tattered Bible and asked Mary to read what was written on the flyleaf. The missionary was thrilled when she saw that it was the one she had sent, and she realized that this believer was the little girl she had been praying for. God had blessed Mary's first piece of missionary work, for through her gift this one in India had been saved. Together the pair knelt and joyfully thanked the Lord for His grace.

The bread of life cast upon the waters had been found!

HENRY BOSCH

Faithfully sow the seed, and God will provide the harvest.

You Can Do Something

JOHN 15:1–8

This is to my Father's glory, that you bear much fruit,
showing yourselves to be my disciples.

JOHN 15:8

John Warr, an eighteenth-century apprentice shoemaker, was determined to be a faithful witness for Christ. Another apprentice was hired, and John repeatedly talked to him about spiritual things. That new worker, however, didn't want to be bothered. Then one day the new worker was caught exchanging a counterfeit shilling for a good one. In his guilty humiliation he asked John for help and prayer. Through the faithful witness of John Warr, that man put his faith in Christ and developed into a committed disciple.

The young apprentice was William Carey, who later became a remarkably fruitful missionary to India. Carey's life and ministry had a tremendous influence on the cause of worldwide gospel outreach in modern times.

Jesus said in John 15:8, "This is to my Father's glory, that you bear much fruit." This could be discouraging to Christians who can't preach, sing, teach, or go to the mission field. They might see themselves as stuck in a situation that makes fruitful service impossible.

If that's how you feel, then take courage from the example of John Warr. His impact on one coworker brought glory to God and untold blessing to multitudes of people around the world.

VERNON GROUNDS

Witness for Christ with your life as well as your lips.

Unable to Sleep

HEBREWS 10:12–22

I, even I, am he who blots out your transgressions, for my own sake,
and remembers your sins no more.

ISAIAH 43:25

William Booth, the founder and commanding general of the Salvation Army, was unable to sleep one night. His son Bramwell, who lived next door, saw that the light was on in his father's home. Thinking something might be wrong, he went to his parents' house. He found his father pacing back and forth with a wet towel wrapped around his head. "Father," he asked, "shouldn't you be asleep?"

"No," William replied, "I am thinking." Seeing the puzzled look that crossed his son's face, he put his hands on Bramwell's shoulders and solemnly said, "I am thinking about people's sins. What will they do with their sins?"

That question should disturb all of us. Sin separates people from a holy God, and it will do so forever unless it is forgiven. There is nothing we can do nor any amount we could pay that could ever atone for our guilt.

But the joyful message of the gospel is that God through His Son's sacrifice on Calvary has made it possible for our sins to be completely forgiven—to take care of our sin problem (Hebrews 10:12–14). That miracle of mercy takes place, however, only when we personally acknowledge in sincere trust that the death of Jesus Christ is our one hope for forgiveness. Have you done that?

VERNON GROUNDS

We are saved by what Christ did, not by what we do.

Life That Matters

1 PETER 5:1–7

Remember your leaders, who spoke the word of God to you. Consider the outcome of their way of life and imitate their faith.

HEBREWS 13:7

Isaac Hann was a little-known pastor who served a small church in Loughwood, England, in the mid-eighteenth century. At the close of his ministry, the membership of the church numbered twenty-six women and seven men. And only four of the men attended with any regularity.

In this age of mass media and mega-churches, who would consider this a successful work? In our world today, Isaac Hann would be considered one of those pastors who never quite "made it." He certainly wouldn't have been invited to speak at pastors' conferences, nor would he have written articles on church growth.

Yet when he died at eighty-eight, his parishioners placed a plaque on the wall of their meeting house that remains to this day. It reads in part:

Few ministers so humble were, yet few so much admired: Ripened for heaven by grace divine, like autumn fruit he fell; Reader think not to live so long, but seek to live as well.

First Peter 5:5–6 comes to mind: "'God opposes the proud but shows favor to the humble.' Humble yourselves, therefore, under God's mighty hand, that he may lift you up in due time." Reverend Isaac Hann "made it big" in a way that matters—humility before God and a reward in heaven. We can too.

DAVID ROPER

Humility is the recipe for success.

The Quiet Place

MATTHEW 14:15–23

One of those days Jesus went out to a mountainside to pray,
and spent the night praying to God.

LUKE 6:12

John G. Paton, missionary to the New Hebrides Islands, wrote a moving account about the way his father communed with God. He said their home was actually a hut, and attached to the living area was a small room called "the closet." "Often throughout a day," says Paton, "we saw our father retire there and shut the door.

"As children we understood by a kind of spiritual instinct that prayers were being poured out for us. We occasionally heard the pathetic echoes of a trembling voice, pleading as for life and we learned to slip in and out past that door on tiptoe, not to disturb the holy fellowship within. The outside world might not know, but we knew where the happy countenance on our father's face came from. It was a reflection from the Divine Presence, in whose consciousness he always lived. Never, in temple or cathedral, in mountain or in glen, can I hope to feel that the Lord God is more near, more visibly walking and talking with men, than under that humble cottage roof of thatch."

Sounds great doesn't it—this kind of fellowship with the Father? It reminds us of the times Jesus spent with the heavenly Father, as in Luke 6:12. Do you have a quiet place of prayer?

HERB VANDER LUGT

Christ's likeness is best developed on the soul in the darkroom of prayer.

Marked by His Name

ACTS 11:19–26

When he found him, he brought him to Antioch. So for a whole year
Barnabas and Saul met with the church and taught great numbers of people.
The disciples were called Christians first at Antioch.

ACTS 11:26

In July 1860, the world's first nursing school opened at St. Thomas Hospital in London. Today that school is part of the King's College, where nursing students are called Nightingales. The school—like modern nursing itself—was established by Florence Nightingale, who revolutionized nursing during the Crimean War. When prospective nurses complete their training, they take the "Nightingale Pledge," a reflection of her ongoing impact on nursing.

Many people, as did Florence Nightingale, have had a significant impact on our world. But no one has had a greater effect than Jesus, whose birth, death, and resurrection have been transforming lives for 2,000 years.

Around the world, Christ's name marks those who are His followers, going back to the earliest days of the church. "When [Barnabas] found [Saul], he brought him to Antioch. So for a whole year Barnabas and Saul met with the church and taught great numbers of people. The disciples were called Christians first at Antioch" (Acts 11:26).

Those who bear Christ's name identify with Him because we have been changed by His love and grace. We declare to the world that He has made an eternal difference in our lives, and we long for that in the hearts of others too.

BILL CROWDER

Followers of Christ—Christians—are marked by His name.

Continuing with Christ

1 KINGS 19:19–21

For whoever wants to save their life will lose it, but whoever loses their life for me will find it.

MATTHEW 16:25

As a child, my favorite week of the summer was the one I spent at a Christian youth camp. At the end of the week, I'd sit elbow-to-elbow with friends in front of an enormous bonfire. There, we would share what we had learned about God and the Bible—then we would sing. One song I still remember was focused on deciding to follow Jesus. The chorus contained an important phrase: "no turning back."

When Elisha decided to follow the prophet Elijah, Elisha did something incredible that made it difficult, impossible really, for him to return to his prior occupation of farming. After going home and having a farewell banquet, Elisha "took his yoke of oxen and slaughtered them" (1 Kings 19:21). Leaving his way of life, he burned up his plowing equipment. He roasted the freshly butchered meat over the blaze and fed everyone present. Then "[Elisha] arose and followed Elijah, and became his servant" (v. 21 NKJV).

Giving ourselves to God, who deserves our devotion, often comes with a price. At times, it means making difficult decisions about relationships, finances, and living arrangements. However, nothing compares with what we gain when we continue on with Christ. Jesus said, "Whoever wants to save their life will lose it, but whoever loses their life for me will find it" (Matthew 16:25).

JENNIFER BENSON SCHULDT

Jesus is looking for fulltime followers.

Disappointment—His Appointment

1 PETER 4:12-19

When my spirit grows faint within me, it is you who watch over my way.
In the path where I walk people have hidden a snare for me.
PSALM 142:3

Sometimes, even as they seek to do God's will, Christians endure difficult trials and encounter baffling, hindering circumstances as they earnestly seek to do God's will. Barnabas Shaw experienced such difficulties. Appointed as a Methodist missionary, he had hoped to serve God in Ceylon. Suddenly there was a change in plans, and he was directed instead to South Africa.

When he arrived at Cape Town, however, the governor forbade him to preach. Shaw and his wife were very disappointed. They wanted so much to serve the Lord, yet twice in a few months their high purposes and plans had been frustrated. With the little money they possessed, they bought a yoke of oxen and a cart, loaded up their goods, and headed toward the interior. On the twenty-seventh day of their journey, they were met by a company of Khoikhoi people who were on their way to Cape Town.

They were searching for a missionary who, they had been told, was being sent to teach them "the great Word of God." That their paths should cross in the dense jungle was nearly incredible. The chief of the Khoikhois led the Shaws two hundred miles farther inland where the faithful missionaries were able to establish a spiritual outpost for Christ. Their disappointments had really been the overruling hand of God directing them into His perfectly appointed way.

HENRY BOSCH

The Lord may sometimes lead you around,
but He will always lead you aright!

The Blessing of Meeting Together

HEBREWS 10:19–25

*Not giving up meeting together, as some are in the habit of doing,
but encouraging one another—and all the more as you see the Day approaching.*
HEBREWS 10:25

Josef Gabor grew up in Czechoslovakia when it was dominated by communism, and religion was despised as weakness. His father taught communist doctrine classes. But Josef's mother, who believed in Jesus Christ, took Josef and his brother with her to church.

They got up early each Sunday morning and took a three-hour train ride to Prague. Then they walked to the church and sat through a two-and-a-half-hour service. After eating lunch in a nearby park, they returned to church for another two-and-a-half-hour meeting. Then they took the three-hour ride home.

Today Josef Gabor is reaching out to his own people in what is now Slovakia and has served a leader for Youth for Christ in that country. When he tells the story about going to church as a child, his eyes fill with tears of gratitude for a mother who cared enough about his spiritual welfare to help him come to know and serve Christ.

Some Christians would do anything to be in church, but for health or other reasons they can't. They know how important it is to worship and fellowship with believers. How great it is to meet together with fellow believers!

DAVID EGNER

Go to church if you want to grow in Christ.

A Winner Either Way

PHILIPPIANS 1:15–26

For to me, to live is Christ and to die is gain.

PHILIPPIANS 1:21

Lois had just undergone cancer surgery and was alone with her thoughts. She had faced death before, but it had always been the death of people she had loved—not her own.

Suddenly she realized that losing someone she loved was more threatening to her than the possibility of losing her own life. She wondered why. She remembered that she had asked herself before her operation, "Am I ready to die?" Her immediate answer had been, and still was, "Yes, I am. Christ is my Lord and Savior."

With her readiness for death assured, she now needed to concentrate on living. Would it be in fear or in faith? Then God seemed to say, "I have saved you from eternal death. I want to save you from living in fear." Isaiah 43:1 came to mind: "Do not fear, for I have redeemed you; I have called you by your name; you are mine" (NKJV).

Now Lois testifies, "Yes, I am His! That reality is more important than doctors telling me I have cancer." And then she adds, "I win either way!"

Lois's insight is a convinced echo of Paul's words: "For to me, to live is Christ and to die is gain." Let's pray that those words will resonate in our heart. That confidence makes us a winner either way.

JOANIE YODER

We can really live when we're ready to die.

Seize the Opportunity

ACTS 8:26–38

Therefore, as we have opportunity, let us do good to all people, especially to those who belong to the family of believers.

GALATIANS 6:10

Heavy rain was falling outside as Marcia, the director of the Jamaican Christian School for the Deaf, spoke to our group. Thirty-four American teenagers and several adults were visiting the school. But one of our students was not distracted by the rain or the children running around the room.

That teenager heard Marcia say, "My dream for these kids is to have a playground." Lauren took that sentence, and through the prompting of the Lord turned it into an idea. Later that day she told me, "We should come back and build them a playground." An opportunity for service was born.

A little over four months later, on another rainy day in Jamaica, we held a celebration in that same room. We had just spent a week assembling a wooden playground—complete with slides, a ladder, climbing bars, swings, forts, and a trapeze. One student had seized an opportunity, and a dream was fulfilled.

How often does God prompt us to take action to meet the needs of others and we let the opportunity go? How many times does the Spirit nudge us to say or do something in Jesus's name and we shake off the nudging? Like Philip in Acts 8 and like Lauren in Jamaica, let's honor the Lord by responding with action. Let's seize each opportunity God gives us to serve others in His name.

DAVE BRANON

When the Spirit prompts, take action.

God's Open Invitation

ISAIAH 55:1–5

The Spirit and the bride say, "Come!" And let the one who hears say,
"Come!" Let the one who is thirsty come; and let the one who wishes
take the free gift of the water of life.

REVELATION 22:17

I read an article about a young woman who told how the Lord brought her to himself. She grew up in Germany, attended church faithfully, and was confirmed at age fourteen, but she knew she needed something more for her soul. She kept asking God to show himself to her.

Then it happened!

As she was watching Billy Graham on a television special, she trusted Jesus Christ as her Lord and Savior. She realized that she had made a giant step, but she also knew she needed help to grow. For four years she prayed that the Lord would somehow direct her to those who could help her. God answered by leading her to an American university where she discovered a Christian campus organization. She joined in Bible studies and is now a stalwart follower of Jesus Christ.

Can you identify with this woman—a moral person troubled with feelings of emptiness? God is speaking to you through those feelings and invites you to receive Jesus as your Savior today. Isaiah put the invitation like this: "Come, all you who are thirsty, come to the waters" (55:1).

When you trust Christ, you will be forgiven, your emptiness will be filled, and the thirst of your soul will be quenched. Say yes to God's invitation.

HERB VANDER LUGT

How can you turn down the greatest invitation ever offered?

Strength out of Weakness

1 CORINTHIANS 2:1–5

But he said to me, "My grace is sufficient for you, for my power is made perfect in weakness." Therefore I will boast all the more gladly about my weaknesses, so that Christ's power may rest on me.

2 CORINTHIANS 12:9

The ministry of missionary David Brainerd (1718–1747) underscores God's promise, "My power is made perfect in weakness" (2 Corinthians 12:9). Brainerd experienced a variety of physical ailments and also suffered from a form of mental neurosis as he sought to reach the Native Americans in what is now New Jersey.

He died at twenty-nine, yet he accomplished great things for the Lord in his brief lifespan. Often desperately ill and all alone, he repeatedly traveled deep into the forest, trying to reach tribes whose language he did not know. At times he spent whole days in prayer, asking the Lord to intervene. Once the only interpreter available was so drunk he could hardly stand up, yet scores were converted through the gospel message. Although Brainerd was extremely weak, God's strength was consistently manifested through him!

The truth that divine power is best displayed against the background of human frailty was emphasized in the life of Paul. He ministered to the Corinthians in "weakness with great fear and trembling" (1 Corinthians 2:3).

What attitude should we take toward our weaknesses? Accept God's loving plan, seek Him in prayer, and serve Him with courage. Our weakness reveals God's strength!

HERB VANDER LUGT

We may face situations beyond our physical reserve but never beyond God's supernatural resources!

A Face that Shines

EXODUS 34:29–35

*When Aaron and all the Israelites saw Moses, his face was radiant,
and they were afraid to come near him.*

EXODUS 34:30

Many years ago, Taylor Smith, a clergyman from England, was invited
to address the Moody Centenary Bible Conference in Chicago. When
he arrived, Smith had lost his voice and couldn't speak above a whisper.
Convinced that he was there in God's will, he spoke at length in spite of
his handicap. His voice carried no farther than the first few rows of the
audience. At the conclusion of the service, a man who had been sitting
up in the balcony came to Smith and said, "I couldn't hear anything you
said, but I watched your face and I want to be a Christian!" Author Ethel
Wilcox commented: "This man's face reflected the glory of the inner life,
the character of Christ."

When we as believers consistently take time to meditate on God's
Word, commune with Him in prayer, and seek to obey His commands,
it will show on our faces. There's a holy serenity, a godly confidence, a
peaceful contentment that belongs only to those who continually live in
the presence of God through the help of the Holy Spirit.

It's true that not everyone with a radiant countenance is a Christian.
But all Christians should reflect the pure light that attracts sinners to
the gospel.

RICHARD DEHAAN

The light of God's Son in your heart will put His sunshine on your face.

Triumph out of Tragedy

2 CORINTHIANS 1:1–7

If we are distressed, it is for your comfort and salvation;
if we are comforted, it is for your comfort, which produces in you patient
endurance of the same sufferings we suffer.

2 CORINTHIANS 1:6

It's easy to be happy and bright when everything goes smoothly, but it takes great faith to rejoice in the Lord in times of darkness and tribulation.

When William Moon of England was a young man, his future looked promising as he began to study to become a minister. Then tragedy struck—he became blind! At first he couldn't accept this trial and exclaimed bitterly, "What are all my abilities worth now that I am shut up here in my room and the whole world is shut out?" Slowly, though, he began to realize that God had a wise purpose in allowing him to be afflicted.

Because his own eyes were sightless, he began to develop a unique system of reproducing the alphabet to assist others in a similar condition. It soon was adapted to fit the languages of many different countries, including remote areas of the world. More than four million blind people were thus enabled to read the Bible. They found that the kind of embossed type he used was easy to learn, even though it required more space on the page than the Braille system that later replaced it. William Moon had become a "minister" in an unusual way and had brought salvation to many. He could rejoice because out of his tragedy had come a great triumph.

How should we react to trials? Perhaps it's best to allow them to help us rise to new heights of usefulness and sanctification.

HENRY BOSCH

Tribulation is designed to refine your gold and redirect your goals.

The Ever-Present Word

PSALM 118:1–8

Keep your lives free from the love of money and be content with what you have, because God has said, "Never will I leave you; never will I forsake you."
_{HEBREWS 13:5}

Many years ago, a missionary had to flee the country where he was serving. As an angry mob gathered—intending to kill him—he hastily boarded a river boat, but his pursuers were right behind him. Realizing he would be captured, he jumped into the water. Although his enemies threw spears at him, he managed to escape unharmed. Later, when he told a Christian friend about this experience, the listener asked, "What Bible verse came to mind as you were ducking beneath the boat to avoid the spears of the murderous mob?" "Verse?" he asked in astonishment. "Why, the Lord himself was with me!"

A similar incident happened to missionary Arthur Mathews as he attempted to escape China before the communists took over. During days of tremendous pressure, while still within that country, he wrote, "In the center of the circle of the will of God I stand,/ Though the universe around me shows small trace of His dear hand./ Yet in darkness as in daylight, in the gloom as sunshine fair,/ I will trust Him for His presence, for I know He's always near!"

Sometimes when we go through a severe time of testing, no Bible verse or special "word" from the Lord fills our heart with peace. That's when we simply rely on the One who is standing with us. He is the ever-present Living Word who has promised, "Never will I leave you; never will I forsake you."

PAUL VAN GORDER

No enemy can come so near that God is not nearer.

Don't Delay

LUKE 9:57–62

Now is the time of God's favor, now is the day of salvation.
2 CORINTHIANS 6:2

For many years I spoke to my distant cousin about our need of a Savior. When he visited me recently and I once again urged him to receive Christ, his immediate response was: "I would like to accept Jesus and join the church, but not yet. I live among people of other faiths. Unless I relocate, I will not be able to practice my faith well." He cited persecution, ridicule, and pressure from his peers as excuses to postpone his decision.

His fears were legitimate, but I assured him that whatever happened, God would not abandon him. I encouraged my cousin not to delay but to trust God for care and protection. He gave up his defenses, acknowledged his need of Christ's forgiveness, and trusted Him as his personal Savior.

When Jesus invited people to follow Him, they too offered excuses— all about being busy with the cares of this world (Luke 9:59–62). The Lord's answer to them (vv. 60–62) urges us not to let excuses deprive us of the most important thing in life: the salvation of our souls.

Do you hear God calling you to commit your life to Him? Do not delay. "Now is the time of God's favor, now is the day of salvation" (2 Corinthians 6:2).

LAWRENCE DARMANI

Today is the day of salvation.

The Best Place to Witness

ACTS 26:19–32

I stand here and testify to small and great alike.
ACTS 26:22

Missionary Doug Nichols and his Filipino coworker Aries went to a Manila garbage dump, asking God how they might effectively reach the poor who scavenged there. Soon an old man approached and asked if they would guard his handful of cans while he hunted for more.

Doug asked the man how old he was, since it's respectful in the Philippines to ask older people their age. "Oh, it's wonderful you asked," replied the man with a big smile. "I'm 78 years old today."

Aries and Doug sang "Happy Birthday," then shook his hand and gave him a hug. "Are you prepared to go to heaven?" asked Doug. When the man indicated that he wasn't sure, Doug shared the gospel. That day the garbage-dump resident trusted Jesus and became a citizen of heaven.

The apostle Paul had an opportunity to witness to a governor, a king, and prominent citizens (Acts 25–26). We don't know the results of his witness, but Paul was faithful where God had placed him.

When you are concerned for the spiritual needs of others and God opens a door of opportunity, any place is the best place to share the gospel—whether it's at a garbage dump or in a king's palace.

DENNIS DEHAAN

Any place can be the right place to witness.

Filling an Empty Heart

ROMANS 10:1–13

For God so loved the world that he gave his one and only Son, that whoever believes in him shall not perish but have eternal life.

JOHN 3:16

"A more vocal man-hater I had never met," said missionary Sophie Jenista. She was describing Erika, a woman she sat next to on a flight from Australia to Singapore. The woman hated men because of an abusive husband.

As they talked, Sophie told her seatmate that God could replace her hard heart with a soft one.

"I don't have a hard heart," Erika replied. "I have an empty heart."

After Sophie shared John 3:16 with her, using her name in the verse: "For God so loved Erika . . . ," she told Erika that God wanted to fill her empty heart with His love.

Just before the plane touched down in Singapore, Erika prayed and asked Jesus to be her Savior. "I feel better already," she told Sophie as they prepared to get off the plane. "What a miracle that we met!"

Do you ever feel that your heart is empty? Do you find yourself bitter about life, feeling helpless to make things work out? Do you try to fill the emptiness in your life with possessions, activities, entertainment, or relationships? Read John 3:16 and put your name in it. Then accept Jesus's offer of forgiveness and eternal life. He'll fill your heart with a joy that is nothing short of miraculous.

DAVE BRANON

Nothing can fill the emptiness in your heart—except God.

Learning from Erin

1 CORINTHIANS 12:21–25

The LORD is gracious and compassionate, slow to anger and rich in love.
PSALM 145:8

Erin's life was so different from that of most eight-year-olds. While other kids were running and playing and eating ice cream, Erin was lying in a bed being fed through a tube—able to see only the brightest lights and hear only the loudest sounds. Her life consisted of needles and nurses and hospital visits as she battled ongoing illnesses and profound disabilities.

Surrounded by a remarkable family who cared for her with compassion and filled her life with love, Erin died before reaching her ninth birthday.

What can be learned from a precious child like Erin—one who never spoke a word or colored a picture or sang a song? A friend of Erin's family put it best: "We are all better for having had Erin in our lives. She taught us compassion, unconditional love, and appreciation for the little things."

Children such as Erin also remind us that this world is not reserved for the perfect, the wealthy, or the athletic. Each person, no matter his or her physical, mental, or emotional condition, is created in the image of God (Genesis 1:26–27) and is of equal value and significance. Our Lord has compassion for the weak, the broken, and all He has made (Psalm 145:8–9), and we should mirror that concern (Ephesians 5:1–2). Is there an "Erin" in your life you can learn from?

DAVE BRANON

Never underestimate the value of one soul.

Mister Rogers

COLOSSIANS 3:22–4:1

Whatever you do, work at it with all your heart, as working for the Lord, not for human masters.

COLOSSIANS 3:23

Fred Rogers (1928–2003), creator and host of the much-loved children's television program *Mister Rogers' Neighborhood*, had a special understanding of his ministry and his work. His widow, Joanne, told a journalist: "I always remind people that he was an ordained Presbyterian minister and this was his ministry. His work was his ministry, and he loved his work; my, did he love his work. That's what makes me sad about losing him. Because I think he would have worked for a long time more if he could have, yet he accepted that with all of his heart and was ready to go to heaven."

We may feel that work is secular, but we view something such as leading a Bible study as spiritual. The Bible draws no such distinction, however. Paul instructed Christians to work "not with eyeservice, as men-pleasers, but in sincerity of heart, fearing God. And whatever you do, do it heartily, as to the Lord and not to men, knowing that from the Lord you will receive the reward of the inheritance; for you serve the Lord Christ" (Colossians 3:22–24 NKJV).

When we honor God and help people, then our work and ministry blend together in pleasing service to the Lord. Mister Rogers showed us how we can do that in our own neighborhood.

DAVID McCASLAND

Daily work done for God takes on eternal value.

Foreign Worship

ACTS 17:16–31

When they heard this, the crowd and the city officials
were thrown into turmoil.

ACTS 17:8

During a trip to the Far East, I visited an unusual shrine made up of hundreds of statues. According to our guide, worshipers would pick the statue that looked the most like an ancestor and pray to it.

A few years ago, I read about a student named Le Thai. An ancestor worshiper, he found great comfort in praying to his deceased grandmother. Because he was praying to someone he knew and loved, he found this to be personal and intimate. But when he came from Vietnam to the US to study, Le Thai was introduced to Christianity. It sounded like a fairy tale based on American thinking. To him, it was the worship of a foreign God (see Acts 17:18).

Then a Christian friend invited him to visit his home on Christmas. He saw a Christian family in action and heard again the story of Jesus. Le Thai listened. He read John 3 about being "born again" and asked questions. He began to feel the pull of the Holy Spirit. Finally, he realized that Christianity was true. He trusted Jesus as his personal Savior.

When a friend sees Christianity as foreign worship, we need to respect their heritage while sharing the gospel graciously and giving them time to explore Christianity. And then trust the Spirit to do His work.

DAVE BRANON

The God of the Bible is the only true God.

God's Embrace

ROMANS 12:3–11

Be devoted to one another in love. Honor one another above yourselves.
ROMANS 12:10

Soon after her family left for the evening, Carol started to think that her hospital room must be the loneliest place in the world. Nighttime had fallen, her fears about her illness were back, and she felt overwhelming despair as she lay there alone.

Closing her eyes, she began to talk to God: "O Lord, I know I am not really alone. You are here with me. Please calm my heart and give me peace. Let me feel Your arms around me, holding me."

As she prayed, Carol felt her fears begin to subside. When she opened her eyes, she looked up to see the warm, sparkling eyes of her friend Marge, who reached out to encircle her in a big hug. Carol felt as if God himself were holding her tightly.

God often uses fellow believers to show us His love. "We, being many, are one body in Christ. . . . Having then gifts differing according to the grace that is given to us, let us use them" (Romans 12:5–6 NKJV). We serve others "with the strength God provides, so that in all things God may be praised through Jesus Christ" (1 Peter 4:11).

When we show love and compassion in simple, practical ways, we are a part of God's ministry to His people.

CINDY HESS KASPER

We show our love for God when we love His family.

You Never Know . . .

ACTS 3:11–4:4

Many who heard the message believed.
ACTS 4:4

The Lord uses the most unexpected situations and unlikely ways to bring people to himself. Our responsibility as Christians is simple and clear: Share the gospel where a lost world can hear it.

Francisco Ramos, a missionary to Europe, is an example of one who was brought to Christ through unusual circumstances. A native of Portugal, he traveled to England to look for work. Because a dangerous aneurysm had been discovered in his father's brain, Francisco had begun asking hard questions about life.

Ramos took a shortcut through Hyde Park in London one day, his heart aching and his mind filled with questions. A young man was preaching about Jesus, and Ramos stopped to listen. In straightforward, unmistakable terms, he heard the plan of salvation. Later that day he encountered another believer selling Christian books. He bought a copy of Billy Graham's *Peace with God*, not knowing what it was. He read the book that night and trusted in Christ as his Savior. Now he and his wife Stephanie are serving the Lord as missionaries in France.

Let's find ways to tell others about Jesus and His love and power to save all who call on Him. We never know what God is doing in someone's heart.

DAVID EGNER

The next person you meet may need to meet Christ.

Jehovah-Jireh

MATTHEW 6:5–15

*Do not be like them, for your Father knows what you need
before you ask him.*

MATTHEW 6:8

In my early years as a pastor, I served in small churches where finances were often tight. Sometimes our family finances felt the weight of that pressure. On one occasion, we were down to the last of our food, and payday was still several days away. While my wife and I fretted about how we would feed our kids in the next few days, our doorbell rang. When we opened the door, we discovered two bags of groceries. We had not told anyone of our plight, yet our provider God had led someone to meet that need.

This reminds me of the Old Testament account of Abraham when he was asked to sacrifice his son Isaac. At just the right moment, God provided a ram instead. Abraham called this place Jehovah-Jireh, "The LORD Will Provide" (Genesis 22:14). He is the One who still cares deeply for His children.

Jesus said, "Your Father knows what you need before you ask him" (Matthew 6:8). He is constantly caring for and seeking the best for us— a reminder that in times of hardship, need, and fear, we have Someone who cares. Peter wrote that we can cast all our cares upon Jesus, because He cares for us (1 Peter 5:7). We can turn to Him in our time of need.

BILL CROWDER

What God promises, God will provide.

Shenandoah

GENESIS 12:1–9

By faith Abraham, when called to go to a place he would later receive as his inheritance, obeyed and went, even though he did not know where he was going.
HEBREWS 11:8

My grandfather grew up on the North American frontier and raised his family on a dairy farm. To pass the time while he worked, he often sang. "Shenandoah" was one a favorite:

> *O Shenandoah, I long to hear you,*
> *Away, you rolling river,*
> *O Shenandoah, I long to hear you,*
> *Away, I'm bound away,*
> *'Cross the wide Missouri.*

That song reflects the love the pioneer songwriter had for the Shenandoah River. Yet he felt compelled to leave its beauty and go west. His love for the familiar rooted him, but the pull of something better won his heart.

When Abraham was called out of Ur to follow God to the Promised Land, he had to leave everything familiar to him (Genesis 12:1). Abraham had probably grown attached to the comfort of his home. But Abraham left the familiar to follow God's leading: "By faith Abraham obeyed when he was called to go" (Hebrews 11:8 NKJV).

When we experience God's call to another place, it may mean leaving behind the people and the things we love. But when we're obedient to God, He will provide something even more fulfilling at our new destination.

DENNIS FISHER

You don't need to see the way if you follow the One who is the Way.

Room 5020

GENESIS 50:15-20

You intended to harm me, but God intended it for good to accomplish what is now being done, the saving of many lives.

GENESIS 50:20

Jay Bufton turned his hospital room into a lighthouse.

The fifty-two-year-old husband, father, high school teacher, and coach was dying of cancer, but his room—Room 5020—became a beacon of hope for friends, family, and hospital workers. Because of his joyful attitude and strong faith, nurses wanted to be assigned to Jay. Some even came to see him during off-hours.

Even as his once-athletic body was wasting away, he greeted anyone and everyone with a smile and encouragement. One friend said, "Every time I visited Jay he was upbeat, positive, and filled with hope. He was, even while looking cancer and death in the face, living out his faith."

At Jay's funeral, one speaker noted that Room 5020 had a special meaning. He pointed to Genesis 50:20, in which Joseph says that although his brothers sold him into slavery, God turned the tables and accomplished something good: "the saving of many lives." Cancer invaded Jay's life, but by recognizing God's hand at work Jay could say that "God intended it for good." That's why Jay could use even the ravages of cancer as an open door to tell others about Jesus.

What a legacy of unwavering trust in our Savior even as death was knocking at the door! What a testimony of confidence in our good and trustworthy God!

DAVE BRANON

By God's grace, we can have our best witness in the worst of times.

The Fault with Faultfinding

MATTHEW 7:1–5

*Therefore let us stop passing judgment on one another.
Instead, make up your mind not to put any stumbling block or
obstacle in the way of a brother or sister.*

ROMANS 14:13

We sometimes criticize others unfairly. We don't know all their circumstances, nor their motives. Only God, who is aware of all the facts, is able to judge people righteously.

John Wesley told of a man he had little respect for because he considered him to be miserly and covetous. One day when this person contributed only a small gift to a worthy charity, Wesley openly criticized him.

After the incident, the man went to Wesley privately and told him he had been living on parsnips and water for several weeks. He explained that before his conversion, he had run up many bills. Now, by skimping on everything and buying nothing for himself he was paying off his creditors one by one. "Christ has made me an honest man," he said, "and so with all these debts to pay, I can give only a few offerings above my tithe. I must settle up with my worldly neighbors and show them what the grace of God can do in the heart of a man who was once dishonest." Wesley then apologized to the man and asked his forgiveness.

Judgmental attitudes spring from pride and are offensive to the Lord. A hypercritical Christian is not operating from the principle of love. That's the real fault with faultfinding!

HENRY BOSCH

Instead of pointing a critical finger, hold out a helping hand.

Feasting on the Word

PSALM 119:97–104

How sweet are your words to my taste, sweeter than honey to my mouth!
PSALM 119:103

Faith in God is a tender plant that needs the Scriptures for its nourishment if it is to grow strong. It withers fast in the dry atmosphere created by a closed Bible. Because "faith comes by hearing, and hearing by the word of God" (Romans 10:17 NKJV), we must have a healthy spiritual appetite for the Bible.

George Müller, who was known for his strong faith, once confided, "The first three years after conversion, I neglected the Word of God. Since I began to search it diligently, the blessing has been wonderful. I have read the Bible through one hundred times and always with increasing delight!"

John Bunyan, who wrote *Pilgrim's Progress*, testified, "Read the Bible, and read it again, and do not despair of help to understand something of the will and mind of God, though you think they are fast locked up from you. Neither trouble yourself, though you may not have commentaries and expositions; pray and read, and read and pray; for a little from God is better than a great deal from man."

These testimonies bear witness to the truths expressed in Psalm 119. As we feast on the Scriptures, we too will learn what Müller and Bunyan learned—that God's words are sweet to the taste and sweeter than honey to the mouth.

HENRY BOSCH

A well-read Bible is a sign of a well-fed soul.

Silent Witness

PHILIPPIANS 1:21–27

Whatever happens, conduct yourselves in a manner worthy of the gospel of Christ. Then, whether I come and see you or only hear about you in my absence, I will know that you stand firm in the one Spirit, striving together as one for the faith of the gospel.

PHILIPPIANS 1:27

On a beautiful, warm January morning, a colleague and I were having breakfast in an outdoor coffee shop at MacRitchie Reservoir Park in Singapore. With a beautiful lake and immaculate gardens surrounding us, the setting was quiet, calm, and lovely with a light breeze blowing across the water.

At a nearby table, a young woman sat quietly reading her Bible. She was absorbed in the text, occasionally looking up to consider what she had read. She never said a word, but her heart and priorities were visible to everyone. It was a gentle, silent witness.

She was not ashamed of Christ or His Book. She neither preached a sermon nor sang a song. She was willing to be identified with the Savior, yet she did not need to announce that allegiance.

In our attempts to share the message of Jesus, we must eventually use words, because ultimately words are needed to present the gospel. But we can also learn from the example of this woman.

There are times when the quietness of our everyday actions speak loudly, revealing our love for the Lord. In our desire to share Christ with a broken world, let's not ignore the power of our silent witness.

BILL CROWDER

Witness for Christ with your life as well as your lips.

Precious in His Sight

MATTHEW 18:1–10

"See that you do not despise one of these little ones. For I tell you that their angels in heaven always see the face of my Father in heaven."

MATTHEW 18:10

It was the late 1700s, and the deacons of a Scottish church realized that few outward results had been seen in recent months. They reluctantly said to their aged minister, "We respect you, Brother, but maybe it's time for you to resign. We haven't had a convert this year."

"You're right," he replied. "It has been a rather fruitless season. Yet I do recall a lad who accepted the Lord. Of course, Robbie Moffat is such a tiny fellow that it's probably not worthwhile to count him." A few years later, that youngster came to the elderly minister and asked, "Do you think I could ever learn to preach? Something deep within tells me I should. I'd be so happy if I could just lead people to Christ." The pastor encouraged him, and later he became a renowned missionary.

When Robert Moffat returned to England from his fifty years of leading people to Jesus in Africa, the king rose to his feet, and Parliament stood to show their esteem. The old preacher was gone and forgotten. But who today would minimize the value of bringing that one little fellow to Jesus?

How vital it is to reach the children! Eternal potential is wrapped up in their lives. Jesus said, "Do not despise one of these little ones." Do we agree?

PAUL VAN GORDER

The flower of youth never appears more beautiful than when it is bent toward the Sun of Righteousness.

Total Giving

MARK 12:41–44

"They all gave out of their wealth; but she, out of her poverty, put in everything—all she had to live on."

MARK 12:44

"Mr. Branon, I have to talk with you about something really important," said the voice on the other end of the line. It was two days before a small group of teens and adults were to leave for Jamaica on a summer missions trip. We had been planning for months to go to a school for deaf children to build a much-needed playground. So when this teen called, I thought, *Oh, no. She can't go.*

But when she, her mom, and I met for lunch that day, I found out how truly special this young lady was. She told me she was donating her entire savings to help pay for the trip—money she had been saving to buy a car. "As I was praying the past couple of nights," she explained, "I felt that God was telling me to give all of my money." That day we had tears of joy with our burgers and fries.

What a picture of how much of ourselves we should offer Him! God wants total sacrifice—as difficult as that can be—not just ten-percent giving. If Jesus is indeed our Lord, we must give our entire being to Him. Our speech. Our time. Our choices. Our resources.

Jesus praised the widow who "out of her poverty, put in everything" (Mark 12:44). Imagine the influence we could have if we practiced giving our all.

DAVE BRANON

Giving is easier when you give yourself to the Lord.

Disaster Diaries

LAMENTATIONS 3:19–33

Because of the LORD's great love we are not consumed, for his compassions never fail. They are new every morning; great is your faithfulness.
LAMENTATIONS 3:22–23

Yves Congar was just ten years old when World War I began, and the French town where he lived was invaded by the German army. His mother encouraged him to keep a diary, and what resulted was a lucid description of a military occupation, complete with written narrative and colored sketches. His diary recorded a disaster from a child's perspective. What he witnessed had such a profound effect on him that he felt called to bring others the hope of Christ.

Centuries earlier the prophet Jeremiah was an eyewitness to the invasion of Jerusalem by Nebuchadnezzar. He wrote down his observations in his "diary"—the book of Lamentations. Despite these distressing times, the prophet found hope in the heart of God. He wrote: "Because of the LORD's great love we are not consumed, for his compassions never fail. They are new every morning; great is your faithfulness" (3:22–23).

At various times, we may experience or witness disasters that feel like hostile forces entering our lives. But these times of trouble do not last forever. Like Jeremiah, our most sustaining hope is to reflect upon the faithfulness and provision of our heavenly Father. The Lord's compassions are new every morning, and His faithfulness is great!

DENNIS FISHER

The best reason for hope is God's faithfulness.

Something More to Give

1 JOHN 1

But if we walk in the light, as he is in the light, we have fellowship with one another, and the blood of Jesus, his Son, purifies us from all sin.

1 JOHN 1:7

When evangelist John Wesley (1703–1791) was returning home from a service one night, he was robbed. The thief, however, found his victim to have only a little money and some Christian literature.

As the bandit was leaving, Wesley called out, "Stop! I have something more to give you." The surprised robber paused. "My friend," said Wesley, "you may live to regret this sort of life. If you ever do, here's something to remember: 'The blood of Jesus Christ cleanses us from all sin!'" The thief hurried away, and Wesley prayed that his words might bear fruit.

Years later, Wesley was greeting people after a Sunday service when he was approached by a stranger. What a surprise to learn that this visitor, now a believer in Christ and a successful businessman, was the one who had robbed him years before! "I owe it all to you," said the transformed man. "Oh no, my friend," Wesley exclaimed, "not to me, but to the precious blood of Christ that cleanses us from all sin!"

John Wesley really did have something more to give the thief that night—the good news of salvation. And we have the same responsibility to share the gospel with those who cross our paths.

HENRY BOSCH

The gospel is a priceless gift to be freely given to others.

Laughter, the Lord, and Little Things

PROVERBS 15:13–31

All the days of the oppressed are wretched,
but the cheerful heart has a continual feast.

PROVERBS 15:15

When Tamer Lee Owens celebrated her 104th birthday, she credited "laughter, the Lord, and the little things" for keeping her going. She still found enjoyment each day in talking with people, taking a walk, and reading the Bible as she had done since childhood. "I don't know how long He'll let me stay here," she said at the time. "I just thank the Lord for what He's given me already."

Most of us won't live 104 years, but we can learn from Tamer Lee how to enjoy each day that we are given.

Laughter—"A happy heart makes the face cheerful, but heartache crushes the spirit" (Proverbs 15:13). True happiness begins deep inside and emerges on our faces.

The Lord—"The fear of the LORD is the instruction of wisdom, and before honor is humility" (v. 33 NKJV). When God is central in our hearts, He can teach us His way through every experience of life.

The Little Things—"Better a small serving of vegetables with love than a fattened calf with hatred" (v. 17). Maintaining loving relationships and enjoying the basic things of life are more important than wealth and success.

Not all of us will live a long time, but we can all live well each day—with laughter, the Lord, and the little things in life.

DAVID McCASLAND

Happiness is not a destination but a day-by-day journey.

What Price for a Book?

JOHN 6:60–69

Simon Peter answered him, "Lord, to whom shall we go?
You have the words of eternal life."
JOHN 6:68

A missionary who worked with Underground Evangelism told a story about a believer in Russia before the collapse of communism. Learning that a friend had acquired a Bible, he asked to borrow it. His friend, however, read the precious Book every evening until 10 p.m. So each night for eight months, from 10 p.m. to 2 a.m., that dedicated believer laboriously copied his friend's Bible. Eventually, when some fellow Christians visited him with Bibles, he exchanged his handwritten labor of love for several copies.

Imagine not having access to a copy of the Bible. What price would you pay to get one? Let's take this question to a deeper level.

When Jesus's teachings began to "offend" those who were following Him, many chose to leave (John 6:60–66). So He asked His disciples, "Do you also want to go away?" (v. 67). Peter replied, "Lord, to whom shall we go? You have the words of eternal life" (v. 68). Peter knew that Jesus was the living Word—God revealed in the flesh. He was willing to forsake everything in this life to pursue the One who is the Way, the Truth, and the Life.

Do we have Peter's commitment? Do we have the devotion of that Russian believer? What price would we pay for the Book? For our Lord?

VERNON GROUNDS

One measure of our love for God is our love for the written Word and our love for the Living Word.

A "Yes" of Love

1 JOHN 3:16–24

Let us not love with words or speech but with actions and in truth.
1 JOHN 3:18

One August day my friend Carissa posted photos on social media of a devastating flood in Louisiana. The next morning she included a note from someone in the flooded area pleading for help. Five hours after that, she and her husband, Bobby, sent out a call for others to join them on a 1,000-mile trip to provide help. Less than twenty-four hours later, thirteen people were on their way to serve those whose homes had been severely damaged.

What motivates people to drop everything and drive seventeen hours to move appliances, do demolition work, and provide hope for people they've never met before? It's love.

Think about this verse, which she posted along with her call for help: "Commit your way to the LORD; trust in him and he will do this" (Psalm 37:5). This is especially true when we follow God's call to help. The apostle John said, "If anyone . . . sees a brother or sister in need but has no pity on them, how can the love of God be in that person?" (1 John 3:17). It may be a daunting task—but we have God's promise of help when we "do what pleases him" (v. 22).

When a need arises, we can honor God by being willing to offer a "yes" of love to what we sense He is asking us to do for others.

DAVE BRANON

We show God's love when we are willing to help others; we show His strength when we take on the task He gives us to do.

Earth Walk

JOHN 1:11–18

The Word became flesh and made his dwelling among us.
We have seen his glory, the glory of the one and only Son,
who came from the Father, full of grace and truth.

JOHN 1:14

After the Apollo 15 mission to the moon in 1971, Colonel James Irwin related some of the high points of his experience. He told of the astronauts' weightless bodies floating free in the space capsule, the rising crescent of the earth as seen from the moon, and the triumphal splashdown before a watching world.

Irwin also spoke of the impact the experience had on his spiritual life. He said that from the lunar surface he sensed both the glory of God and the plight of earthbound man. As he came back to earth, he realized he couldn't content himself with being merely a celebrity. He would have to be a servant, telling his fellowman of a better way to live. Irwin concluded by saying that if we think it is a great event to go to the moon, how much greater is the wonder that God came to earth in the person of Jesus Christ!

Because mankind walked on the moon, science and technology have made tremendous advances. But because God walked on earth, we know both our origin and our destiny. We can know our Creator personally (John 1:1, 14, 18), and we can live in His light (v. 9). Through Jesus's sinless life and sacrificial death, we can know the joy of having our sins forgiven and experience the fullness of an abundant life—all because God walked on the earth.

MART DEHAAN

God made His home with us so that we might
make our home with God.

The Greatest Race

1 CORINTHIANS 13

Love never fails. But where there are prophecies, they will cease; where there are tongues, they will be stilled; where there is knowledge, it will pass away.
1 CORINTHIANS 13:8

Whenever the Summer Olympics roll around again, my thoughts go back to Eric Liddell, a former champion immortalized for his surprising gold medal victory in the 400 meters during the 1924 Games in Paris. A year after his triumph, Liddell went to China, where he spent the last twenty years of his life as a missionary teacher and rural pastor. There he ran the greatest race of his life against opponents we all know—difficult circumstances, war, uncertainty, and disease.

Crowded into a Japanese internment camp with 1,500 other people, Eric lived out the words he had paraphrased from 1 Corinthians 13:6–8: "Love is never glad when others go wrong. Love finds no pleasure in injustice, but rejoices in the truth. Love is always slow to expose, it knows how to be silent. Love is always eager to believe the best about a person. Love is full of hope, full of patient endurance; love never fails."

Eric served the others in camp, whether carrying water for the elderly or refereeing games for the teens. When he died of a brain tumor in February 1945, one internee described him as a man "who lived better than he preached."

In life's most difficult race, Eric Liddell crossed the finish line victorious through love.

DAVID MCCASLAND

**Love enables us to walk fearlessly, to run confidently,
and to live victoriously.**

Hoarding or Helping?

ISAIAH 58:6–12

If you spend yourselves in behalf of the hungry and satisfy the needs of the oppressed, then your light will rise in the darkness, and your night will become like the noonday.

ISAIAH 58:10

In August 1914, when Great Britain entered World War I, Oswald Chambers was forty years old with a wife and a one-year-old daughter. It wasn't long before men were joining the army at the rate of 30,000 a day, people were asked to sell their automobiles and farm horses to the government, and lists of the dead and wounded began appearing in daily newspapers. The nation faced economic uncertainty and peril.

A month into the war, Chambers spoke of the spiritual challenge facing followers of Christ: "We must take heed that in the present calamities, when war and devastation and heart-break are abroad in the world, we do not shut ourselves up in a world of our own and ignore the demand made on us by our Lord and our fellowmen for the service of intercessory prayer and hospitality and care."

God's call to His people rings true in every age: "If you spend yourselves in behalf of the hungry and satisfy the needs of the oppressed, then your light will rise in the darkness, and your night will become like the noonday" (Isaiah 58:10).

Fear causes us to grasp what we have; faith in God opens our hands and hearts to others. We walk in His light when we help others, not hoard for ourselves.

DAVID MCCASLAND

As Christ's love grows in us, His love flows from us.

The Others

HEBREWS 11:32–40

*"Blessed are you when people insult you, persecute you and falsely say
all kinds of evil against you because of me. Rejoice and be glad,
because great is your reward in heaven, for in the same way they
persecuted the prophets who were before you."*

MATTHEW 5:11–12

When I was growing up, I often spent a week each summer with my grandparents. Many afternoons I would lie in the backyard hammock and read books I found in Grandpa's bookcase. One was *Foxe's Book of Martyrs*. It was heavy reading for a young girl, but I was absorbed by the detailed accounts of Christian martyrs, believers who were told to deny their faith in Christ but refused—thus suffering horrific deaths.

Hebrews 11 tells similar stories. After listing the familiar names of those who demonstrated immense faith in God, the chapter tells of the torture and death of people referred to simply as "others" (vv. 35–36). While their names are not mentioned, verse 38 pays them this tribute: "The world was not worthy of them." They died boldly for their faith in Jesus.

Today, we hear of persecuted Christians around the world, yet many of us have not been tested to anything near that extent. When I examine my own faith, I wonder how I would respond to the prospect of martyrdom. I hope I would have the attitude of Paul, who said that although "prison and hardships" awaited him (Acts 20:23), he looked forward to finishing life's race "with joy" (v. 24 NKJV). *Lord, help us face life with that kind of trusting attitude.*

CINDY HESS KASPER

The way to have joy in persecution is to find your joy in Jesus.

Spared from Death

COLOSSIANS 1:24–29

You were bought at a price. Therefore honor God with your bodies.
1 CORINTHIANS 6:20

On August 6, 1945, Kanji Araki, then a toddler, was playing on the floor of his home. Although an air-raid siren had sounded a warning, few paid it any heed since Hiroshima had previously escaped bombing. Then a blinding flash lit up the sky. Superheated air rushed at tremendous speed, knocking down buildings and setting the center of the city ablaze. In the days that followed the nuclear detonation, Kanji's grandmother, brother, and sister died from radiation sickness.

As Kanji grew up, he experienced emotional conflict about those who suffered and died because of the bomb. His parents were Christians, but Kanji adopted a secular view of life. Yet he felt a growing emptiness inside. He began to study the Bible to discover for himself who Jesus is. At a spiritual turning point, Kanji put his trust in Christ, and his empty heart was filled with God's wonderful assurance. When the Lord led him into the ministry, he cited 1 Corinthians 6:20 and said, "I was spared from death so that my life might have a higher purpose in serving God."

The apostle Paul had also been spared to serve God. "I became a minister according to the stewardship from God which was given to me for you," he said (Colossians 1:25 NKJV). What has God entrusted to you?

DENNIS FISHER

**Knowing God gives meaning to life,
and obeying God gives purpose to life.**

Facing Your Enemies

PSALM 27

Though an army besiege me, my heart will not fear; though war break out against me, even then I will be confident.

PSALM 27:3

During the American Civil War, Moorefield, West Virginia, felt the force of the fighting. Because it was close to the North-South border, one day it would be controlled by Union troops; the next, by the Confederates.

In the center of the town an old woman lived alone. According to the testimony of a Presbyterian minister, one morning several enemy soldiers knocked on her door and demanded breakfast. She asked them in and said she would prepare something for them. When the food was ready, she said, "It's my custom to read the Bible and pray before breakfast. I hope you won't mind." They consented, so she took her Bible, opened it at random, and began to read. "The LORD is my light and my salvation; whom shall I fear? The LORD is the strength of my life; of whom shall I be afraid?" She read on through the last verse: "Wait on the LORD; be of good courage, and He shall strengthen your heart" (Psalm 27:1, 14 NKJV). When she finished reading, she said, "Let us pray." While she was praying, she heard sounds of the men moving around in the room. When she said "Amen" and looked up, the soldiers were gone.

If you are facing enemies today, meditate on Psalm 27. God will use His Word to help you face them.

HADDON ROBINSON

No danger can come so near that God is not nearer.

Why Do You Believe?

ISAIAH 50:4–10

*The Sovereign LORD has given me a well-instructed tongue,
to know the word that sustains the weary. He wakens me morning by
morning, wakens my ear to listen like one being instructed.*

ISAIAH 50:4

Francis Collins earned a PhD in physical chemistry at Yale University and then entered medical school. During his training at a North Carolina hospital, a dying woman often talked to him about her faith in Christ. He rejected the existence of God, but he couldn't ignore the woman's serenity. One day she asked, "What do you believe?" Collins was caught off guard, and his face turned red as he stammered, "I'm not really sure." A few days later the woman died.

Curious and uneasy, the young doctor realized that he had rejected God without adequately examining the evidence. He began to read the Bible and the writings of C. S. Lewis. A year later he fell to his knees and gave his life to Jesus Christ. The catalyst? A sincere question from an elderly woman whose physical heart was failing but whose concern for others was strong.

In a prophetic picture of the Messiah, Isaiah 50:4 says, "the Sovereign LORD has given me a well-instructed tongue, to know the word that sustains the weary."

May we be ready with a timely word or a caring question to point others toward our Savior, who offers life and peace to all.

DAVID MCCASLAND

The next person you meet may need to meet Christ.

God Will Make a Way

ACTS 16:16–26

I know that you can do all things; no purpose of yours can be thwarted.
JOB 42:2

Missionary Bill Moore was serving in South Africa, but one day he visited neighboring Zambia to help his mission organization buy some property. The first problem he ran into was that the mission was not recognized by the government, which meant they could not buy any land. And even if they could, they were told registration could take months. Bill and his co-workers prayed, and God provided a contact who helped them secure the needed papers in fifteen minutes.

Next, Bill's group needed permission from the land commissioner to buy the property. This was another months-long process—usually. However, they walked out of the office with approval in minutes. What could have taken a year (if ever)—getting these two documents—took less than an hour! They discovered that God can make a way when it seems there is no way.

Paul and Silas found this out too. While they were praying in prison, God sent an earthquake to free them (Acts 16:26).

Does this mean that we can always expect God to arrange things exactly how we want them? No. But in His sovereignty, He makes a provision for things to get done the way He wants them done. Our job is to pray, to follow His leading, and to trust Him with the results. If He wants it done, God will make a way.

DAVE BRANON

God is greater than our greatest problem.

A Real Savior

1 TIMOTHY 1:12–17

Here is a trustworthy saying that deserves full acceptance: Christ Jesus came into the world to save sinners—of whom I am the worst.

1 TIMOTHY 1:15

Christians who are overly sensitive and introspective can become distraught when they think about their sinfulness. They long for purity, yet they see only defilement within their heart. Guilt dogs their steps, and they begin to doubt their salvation.

Martin Luther (1483–1546) struggled with this problem. When he entered the monastery at Erfurt, Germany, he gave himself wholly to prayers, fasting, and service in an effort to gain relief from the weight of his sins. But the burden remained.

It was the simple testimony of the dean of the theological faculty, John Staupitz, that brought light to his troubled soul. He urged Luther to look away from his dark thoughts and cast himself completely in the Redeemer's arms. "Trust the righteousness of His life and the atonement of His death," he said.

Luther did that and found peace. But a short time later he began doubting. "Oh, my sin, my sin, my sin!" he lamented. With utmost kindness, the dean told him that his great sorrow for his sin was his greatest hope. He said, "Know that Jesus Christ is Savior even of those who are great, real sinners, and deserving of utter condemnation."

Each day let's thank Jesus for dying for us. He is a real Savior for real sinners. Like Martin Luther. And like you and me.

DENNIS DEHAAN

Christ crossed out our sins at Calvary.

When People Pray

ACTS 4:13–31

After they prayed, the place where they were meeting was shaken. And they were all filled with the Holy Spirit and spoke the word of God boldly.
ACTS 4:31

Peter and John faced imminent danger. The religious leaders in Jerusalem who opposed the gospel had warned them to stop their missionary efforts (Acts 4:18). When the apostles reported this to the other believers, they immediately held a prayer meeting.

What happened next is thrilling. The believers first praised God. Then they asked for boldness that they might continue the work. The results were dramatic. The house shook, and the believers were filled with the Holy Spirit. They boldly witnessed, enjoyed spiritual unity, and gave unselfishly to those in need (vv. 31–37).

I've never felt a building shake at a prayer meeting, but I have seen God's power at work. When I've tried to help repair a broken marriage or a divided church, I've asked those involved to pray. Sometimes they refused. Other times, though, they mumbled carefully worded prayers. Those meetings failed.

But occasionally someone would pray in earnest. Almost immediately the atmosphere would change. Confession and forgiveness soon replaced charges and countercharges.

When we pray sincerely, praising God and seeking His glory, great things happen. Prayer must always come from the heart.

HERB VANDER LUGT

Sincere intercession is the key to God's intervention.

God's Little Blessings

PSALM 36:5–10

How priceless is your unfailing love, O God!
People take refuge in the shadow of your wings.

PSALM 36:7

Our family was at Disney World several years ago when God handed us one of His little blessings. Disney World is a huge place—107 acres huge, to be exact. You could walk around for days without seeing someone you know. My wife and I decided to do our own thing while our children sought out the really cool stuff. We parted at 9 a.m. and were planning a rendezvous around 6 p.m.

At about 2 p.m., my wife and I got a craving for tacos. We looked at our map and made our way to a Spanish-sounding place for Mexican food. We had just sat down with our food when we heard, "Hi, Mom. Hi, Dad." Our three amigos had, at the same time, a hankering for a hot burrito.

Ten minutes after they joined us, a violent summer storm ripped through the park with whipping winds, heavy rain, and loud thunder. My wife commented, "I'd be a wreck if the kids weren't with us during this!" It seemed that God had orchestrated our meeting.

Ever notice those blessings from Him? Ever spend time thanking Him for His concern and care? Consider how remarkable it is that the One who created the universe cares enough to intervene in your life. "How priceless is your unfailing love, O God!"

DAVE BRANON

Belonging to God brings boundless blessings.

It's Up to God

1 CORINTHIANS 3:1–9

I planted the seed, Apollos watered it, but God has been making it grow.
1 CORINTHIANS 3:6

Tom Vreman of the Dorcas Society Mission was speaking to our church about the patience required to work on a mission field. He told about a friend and his family who had traveled to the Inner Mongolia region of China to proclaim the gospel.

For the first few years, all they did was get settled and learn the customs of the people. After almost four years, his friend reported with great excitement that he was discipling his first three converts. That's slow progress.

But after another four years, the missionary gave this amazing report: The entire village had turned in faith to Christ. The new Christians began praying for the people in a neighboring town. They sent witnesses, and soon that whole village received Christ. Now the entire region is hearing the gospel—all because one man and his family were willing to plant the seed and trust God for the results.

The apostle Paul gave his life to do God's work. But he knew who was responsible for the success of that work. "Neither he who plants is anything," he wrote, "nor he who waters, but God who gives the increase" (1 Corinthians 3:7 NKJV).

Evangelism calls for patience. We may plant the seed, as Paul did, or we may water, as did Apollos (v. 6). The key is to do our part and leave the results to God.

DAVID EGNER

Faithfulness is God's requirement; fruitfulness is His reward.

Remember and Remind

2 TIMOTHY 2:8–14

Remember Jesus Christ, raised from the dead, descended from David.
This is my gospel. . . . Keep reminding God's people of these things.
Warn them before God against quarreling about words; it is of no value,
and only ruins those who listen.

2 TIMOTHY 2:8, 14

During World War II, Franciszek Gajowniczek was a Nazi prisoner in the Auschwitz prison camp when a fellow inmate escaped. The standard discipline when anyone escaped was to select ten men at random and place them in a cell where they were left to starve to death. When Gajowniczek heard his name read, he sobbed, "My wife and my children." A Franciscan priest and fellow inmate named Kolbe stepped forward and said, "I will die in his place. I have no wife or children." The Commandant granted his request.

For the rest of his life, Gajowniczek went back every year to Auschwitz on August 14 to remember the man who died for him on that date in 1941. And in his yard he has placed a plaque to honor this priest and to remind others of his great sacrifice.

About AD 68, Paul sat in a Roman dungeon awaiting execution. As he thought about Jesus, who had died for him, he wrote his young pastor friend Timothy, reminding him that the Savior's death and resurrection provided hope and the prospect of glory (2 Timothy 2:8–13). He told him to remind others of these truths (v. 14).

We please our Savior when we recall what He did for us and remind others of what He did for them.

HERB VANDER LUGT

**If you want others to know what Christ will do for them,
tell them what He has done for you.**

The Servant Spirit

MATTHEW 20:20–28

For who is greater, the one who is at the table or the one who serves?
Is it not the one who is at the table? But I am among you as one who serves.

LUKE 22:27

To be effective in the Lord's service we must willingly take the role of a servant. The disciples of Jesus had a hard time learning this, and so do we. Even the most godly people sometimes rebel when called upon to do something they feel is beneath their dignity.

Samuel L. Brengle (1860–1936), a brilliant orator and highly successful pastor, was so burdened by the plight of the inner-city poor that he resigned his church and joined the Salvation Army in London. Soon after being inducted, he was given the task of cleaning a pile of muddy boots. This was too much! Inwardly he rebelled. But then he thought about how Jesus washed the feet of His disciples. He asked the Lord for a servant spirit, cleaned the boots, and went on to a fruitful ministry among the disadvantaged.

A young pastor refused to help set up tables for a church banquet, saying, "I didn't go to seminary to do this kind of work." But he soon learned that his pride destroyed his effectiveness. Since then, he has learned to be a servant.

This attitude does wonders! It frees us from the hurt feelings, animosities, jealousies, and resentment that cause us so much misery and cripple us spiritually.

Ask Jesus to help you have a servant spirit. It will change your life.

HERB VANDER LUGT

If you are too big to do little things, you are too little to do big things.

Touched by a Stranger

ROMANS 12:3–16

Be devoted to one another in love. Honor one another above yourselves.
ROMANS 12:10

Marsha Burgess was a complete stranger to us, so we were touched by the note she sent. She knew my husband Carl's mom, who had recently died. She had often seen her when visiting her own mother at a local nursing home.

So when Carl lost his mother, Marsha took the time to share her memories with us. She closed her note with these words: "Your mom always had a big smile on her face and was happy to see us. How wonderful to have such precious memories! We just loved your mom. We'll never forget her." Marsha is a Christian, and her words brought comfort in our grief. They reminded us of the joy of being part of Christ's body (Romans 12:5).

Every believer has been given a specific gift or gifts by God to use in building up others—ministering, teaching, exhorting, giving, leading, and showing mercy (vv. 6–8). But all of us are to "be kindly affectionate to one another with brotherly love" (v. 10 NKJV) and to "rejoice with those who rejoice; mourn with those who mourn" (v. 15).

Sometimes we hesitate to reach out to someone we don't know. We wonder if it is appropriate or if it will mean anything to the person. But that note from Marsha reminds us how much it means to be touched by a stranger.

ANNE CETAS

Opportunities to be kind are never hard to find.

Expect Great Things

HEBREWS 11:32–40

Who through faith conquered kingdoms, administered justice, and gained what was promised; who shut the mouths of lions, quenched the fury of the flames, and escaped the edge of the sword; whose weakness was turned to strength; and who became powerful in battle and routed foreign armies.

HEBREWS 11:33–34

William Carey (1761–1834) was an ordinary man with an extraordinary faith. Born into a working-class family, Carey made his living as a shoemaker. While crafting shoes, Carey read theology and journals of explorers. God used His Word and the stories of the discovery of new people groups to burden him for global evangelism.

He went to India as a missionary, where he was both an evangelist and a Bible translator. Carey's passion for missions is expressed by his words: "Expect great things from God; attempt great things for God." Carey lived out this maxim, and thousands have been inspired to do missionary service by his example.

The Bible tells of many whose faith in God produced amazing results. Hebrews tells of those "who through faith conquered kingdoms, administered justice, and gained what was promised; who shut up the mouths of lions, quenched the fury of the flames, and escaped the edge of the sword; whose weakness was turned to strength" (11:33–34).

The list of heroes of the faith has grown through the ages, and we can be a part of that list. Because of God's power and faithfulness, we can attempt great things for God and expect great things from God.

DENNIS FISHER

When God is your partner, you can make your plans large!

Shoes

PSALM 146

Blessed are those whose help is the God of Jacob,
whose hope is in the LORD their God.

PSALM 146:5

Shoes. Nobody had thought about shoes. The hectic pace of another summer week was suddenly upon our family, and it was time for Julie to begin her week at basketball camp. Just a few minutes before she was to leave, it suddenly dawned on my wife, Sue, that Julie didn't have any decent basketball shoes.

We weren't prepared for a $40 surprise like that. Furthermore, it was too late to do anything about it. So Julie would have to show up at the gym wearing an old pair of ill-fitting shoes that weren't meant for competitive sports. But when Sue opened the door to go out to the car, there stood Connie, our next-door neighbor. And what was in her hands? Shoes. Basketball shoes. Too small for her Erin, but just right for our Julie. Although we had not thought about shoes, Someone had.

Did you ever read through the list of reasons to praise the Lord in Psalm 146? It mentions many ways in which God has demonstrated His providential care for those who live by faith in Him. The almighty Creator of the world lovingly cares for the needs of His people.

The Lord provides what we need today too. Things like shoes. Things that keep giving us one more reason to praise Him.

DAVE BRANON

God keeps giving us more reasons to praise Him.

Praying on Target

MATTHEW 14:22–31

When he saw the wind, he was afraid and, beginning to sink,
cried out, "Lord, save me!"

MATTHEW 14:30

"Lord, save me!" Peter's three little words make up one of the shortest prayers recorded in the Bible. Although the apostle cried out in desperation, his plea points out a vital aspect of effective communication with God—praying on target.

George Sweeting, longtime president of Moody Bible Institute (1971–1987), cites an instance of a pointed petition. In an article entitled "Harnessing Your Prayer Power," he tells of a missionary who was evacuated by a freighter from a South Pacific island during World War II. The vessel had to zig-zag through hostile waters to avoid detection by submarines. One day a periscope appeared above the surface of the ocean. "That's when I learned to pray specifically," said the missionary. "While the enemy was looking our ship over (probably trying to decide whether or not to sink us), we cried, 'Lord, stop his motors! Jam his torpedo tubes! Break his rudder!'"

Most of our heaven-directed words do not arise out of pressing circumstances. Yet we should always strive to make our requests as clear and sharp as if they did. "Lord, control my tongue," for example, is more pointed than, "Help me be a better Christian." The more specific our requests, the more definite His response. Let's pray on target.

DENNIS DeHAAN

In praying, if you aim at nothing, you're bound to hit it.

Re-Creation

2 CORINTHIANS 5:12–21

Therefore, if anyone is in Christ, the new creation has come:
The old has gone, the new is here!

2 CORINTHIANS 5:17

Chris Simpson's life used to be consumed by hate. After he and his wife lost their first child, he was confused and angry. He directed that anger toward various ethnic groups and covered his body with hate-filled tattoos.

Many years later, after listening to his son mimic his hatred, though, Simpson knew he needed to change. He watched a Christian movie about courage and began attending church. One month later he was baptized as a follower of Jesus Christ. Simpson is now a new person and is leaving the hate behind him, which includes the painful and expensive process of having his tattoos removed.

The apostle Paul knew something about this kind of deep transformation. He hated Jesus and persecuted His followers (Acts 22:4–5; 1 Corinthians 15:9). But a personal encounter and spiritual union with Christ (Acts 9:1–20) changed all of that, causing him to reevaluate his life in light of what Jesus accomplished on the cross. This union with Christ made Paul a new person. The old order of sin, death, and selfishness was gone and a new beginning, a new covenant, a new perspective and way of living had come.

Following Jesus is not turning over a new leaf; it is beginning a new life under a new Master.

MARVIN WILLIAMS

Being in Christ is not rehabilitation, it's re-creation.

Where Have You Been?

ROMANS 10:11–15

How, then, can they call on the one they have not believed in?
And how can they believe in the one of whom they have not heard?
And how can they hear without someone preaching to them?

ROMANS 10:14

Missionary Egerton Ryerson Young served the Salteaux tribe in Canada in the 1700s. The chief of the tribe thanked Young for bringing the good news of Christ to them, noting that he was hearing it for the first time in his old age. Since he knew that God was Young's heavenly Father, the chief asked, "Does that mean He is my Father too?" When the missionary answered, "Yes," the crowd that had gathered around burst into cheers.

The chief was not finished, however. "Well," said the chief, "I do not want to be rude, but it does seem to me . . . that it took a long time for you to . . . tell it to your brother in the woods." It was a remark that Young never forgot.

Many times I've been frustrated by the zigs and zags of my life, thinking of the people I could reach "if only." Then God reminds me to look around right where I am, and I discover many who have never heard of Jesus. In that moment, I'm reminded that I have a story to tell wherever I go, "for the same Lord over all is rich to all who call upon Him. For 'whoever calls on the name of the LORD shall be saved'" (Romans 10:12–13 NKJV).

Remember, we don't have just any story to tell—it's the best story that has ever been told.

RANDY KILGORE

Sharing the good news is one beggar telling another beggar where to find bread.

How Can I Forgive?

MATTHEW 18:21–35

But if you do not forgive others their sins, your Father will not forgive your sins.
MATTHEW 6:15

Some of life's hurts are so deep and painful that to forgive the people who caused them seems impossible. Yet Jesus says that we can't experience His forgiveness if we have an unforgiving spirit.

In World War II, Corrie ten Boom and her sister Betsie were arrested for concealing Jews and were sent to a German concentration camp. Betsie died a slow and terrible death as a result of the cruel treatment.

Then, after the war, in 1947, Corrie spoke about God's forgiveness to a church in Munich. Afterward, a man sought her out. She recognized him as one of the guards who had mistreated her and Betsie. He told her that he had become a Christian, and with extended hand he asked for her forgiveness. Corrie struggled with her feelings, but when she recalled the words of Jesus in Matthew 6:15, she knew she had to forgive. She silently prayed, "Jesus, help me!" and thrust her hand into the hand of her former tormentor.

Someone has said, "Forgiveness is not a case of 'holy amnesia' that wipes out the past. Instead, it is the experience of healing that drains the poison from the wound."

God asks us to do for others what He has done for us through Jesus Christ. He'll give us strength to forgive.

DENNIS DEHAAN

Since we all need forgiveness, we should always be forgiving.

A Child's Wonder

PSALM 78:1–8

So the next generation would know them, even the children yet to be born, and they in turn would tell their children. Then they would put their trust in God and would not forget his deeds but would keep his commands.

PSALM 78:6–7

In nineteenth-century Scotland, a young mother observed her three-year-old son's inquisitive nature. It seemed he was curious about everything that moved or made a noise. James Clerk Maxwell would carry his boyhood wonder with him into a remarkable career in science. He went on to do groundbreaking work in electricity and magnetism. Years later, Albert Einstein would say of Maxwell's work that it was "the most fruitful that physics has experienced since the time of Newton."

From early childhood, religion touched all aspects of Maxwell's life. As a committed Christian, he prayed: "Teach us to study the works of Thy hands . . . and strengthen our reason for Thy service." The boyhood cultivation of Maxwell's spiritual life and curiosity resulted in a lifetime of using science in service to the Creator.

The community of faith has always had the responsibility to nurture the talent of the younger generation and to orient their lives to the Lord, "that they may arise and declare [God's law] to their children, that they may set their hope in God" (Psalm 78:6–7 NKJV).

Finding ways to encourage children's love for learning while establishing them in the faith is an important investment in the future.

DENNIS FISHER

We shape tomorrow's world by what we teach our children today.

Just Watch

1 CORINTHIANS 4:14–17

Follow my example, as I follow the example of Christ.
1 CORINTHIANS 11:1

The young boy looked up at his grandfather and wondered aloud, "Grandpa, how do you live for Jesus?" The respected grandfather stooped down and quietly told the boy, "Just watch."

As the years went by, the grandfather lived as an example to the boy of how to follow Jesus. He stayed rock-steady in living for Him—always proclaiming Jesus to others in a ministry in his profession. Yet the grandson often lived in a way that was not pleasing to God.

One day the young man visited his grandfather for what both knew would be the last time. As the older man lay dying, his grandson leaned over the bed and heard his grandpa whisper, "Did you watch?"

That was the turning point in the boy's life. He understood that when his grandpa had said, "Just watch," he meant, "Follow my example, as I follow the example of Christ" (1 Corinthians 11:1). He vowed that from then on he would live as his grandfather did—striving to please Jesus. And he has.

He had watched, and now he knew how to live.

DAVE BRANON

There is no better sermon than a good example.

"Dear Jesus, Take Care of Me"

PSALM 23

Abishai son of Zeruiah came to David's rescue; he struck the Philistine down and killed him. Then David's men swore to him, saying, "Never again will you go out with us to battle, so that the lamp of Israel will not be extinguished."

2 SAMUEL 21:17

Years ago a young girl named Jenny was taken to a hospital in New Mexico to receive treatment for rheumatic fever. This eleven-year-old loved the Lord. Although physically weak, she was always cheerful to the people who attended her. In fact, the head nurse often said Jenny seemed too sweet for this evil world.

Despite her hospitalization, Jenny's health didn't improve. She continued to lose weight—partly because of a severe case of tonsillitis. Surgery was dangerous, but it was obvious that doctors would have to operate. Jenny was not afraid. Just before losing consciousness from the anesthetic, she whispered quietly, "Dear Jesus, take care of me."

Later the head nurse said, "We'll never forget those words, for they were the last she ever spoke. After the surgery was completed and they were about to wheel Jenny back to her room, she stopped breathing. There was no struggle; the Lord just took her to heaven. Everyone was heartbroken. At her funeral when her little friends sang, 'Safe in the Arms of Jesus,' we realized that her prayers had been answered, for Jesus was taking care of her in a most glorious way!"

As we repeat her simple prayer, "Dear Jesus, take care of me," we can be reminded that the faith of this young girl guaranteed that God would do just that in His own way.

HENRY BOSCH

Faith keeps the sails of life filled with the breath of heaven.

Learning to Love

1 CORINTHIANS 13:4–13

Love is patient, love is kind. It does not envy, it does not boast, it is not proud.
1 CORINTHIANS 13:4

When Hans Egede went to Greenland as a missionary in 1721, he didn't know the Inuit language. His temperament was often overbearing, and he struggled to be kind to the people.

In 1733, a smallpox epidemic swept through Greenland, wiping out almost two-thirds of the Inuit people—and claiming Egede's wife as well. This shared suffering melted Egede's harsh demeanor, and he began to tirelessly labor to care for the people physically and spiritually. Because his life now better represented the stories he told them of God's love, the Inuits could at last grasp His desire to love them. Even in suffering, their hearts turned to God.

Perhaps you are like the Inuits in this story, and you are unable to see God in the people around you. Or perhaps you are like Hans Egede, who struggled to express love in a way that taught people about God. Knowing we are weak and needy people, God showed us what love is like. He sent His Son, Jesus Christ, to die for our sins (John 3:16). That's how much God loves you and me.

Jesus is the perfect example of the love that is described in 1 Corinthians 13. As we look to Him, we learn that we are loved and we learn how to love in turn.

RANDY KILGORE

May I never be the barrier that blocks one's view of God.

A Clear Call

1 SAMUEL 3:1–10

The LORD came and stood there, calling as at the other times, "Samuel! Samuel!" Then Samuel said, "Speak, for your servant is listening."

1 SAMUEL 3:10

When George Washington Carver was a student at Iowa Agricultural College (now Iowa State University), he and a friend planned to go as missionaries to Africa. But as his agricultural studies progressed, Carver, a devout Christian, began to sense a different calling from God.

When Booker T. Washington asked him to join the faculty of Tuskegee Institute in Alabama, Carver made it a matter of earnest prayer. In 1896, Carver wrote to Washington: "It has been the one ideal of my life to be of the greatest good to the greatest number of my people possible, and to this end I have been preparing myself for these many years." He pledged to do all he could through the power of Christ to better the conditions of African Americans in the racially segregated South.

Carver's sensitive heart and willing obedience to God bring to mind the experience of Samuel. Under the guidance of Eli the priest, Samuel responded to God's voice by saying, "Speak, for your servant is listening" (1 Samuel 3:10).

During a lifetime of service, the distinguished scientist George Washington Carver honored God by obeying His call. He has left a rich legacy and lasting example for us all.

DAVID MCCASLAND

A life lived for God leaves a lasting legacy.

No Unkind Words

EPHESIANS 4:29–32

Do not let any unwholesome talk come out of your mouths,
but only what is helpful for building others up according to their needs,
that it may benefit those who listen.

EPHESIANS 4:29

One of the greatest honors ever offered to me came during one of life's saddest times.

I was heartbroken in the late summer of 2003 when my good friend and coworker Kurt DeHaan died suddenly while out on his regular lunchtime run. Kurt was managing editor of *Our Daily Bread* from 1989 until the time of his death. Losing him was a huge blow to each of us at our ministry, but his wife Mary and their four children were suffering the worst pain.

A couple of days before the funeral, I got a call from Mary, who asked if I would share a eulogy of Kurt. I was overwhelmed with this bittersweet privilege.

As I reflected on Kurt's life, one trait continued to surface. It was a remarkable characteristic, and it was something that I focused on in my eulogy. In the twenty-two years I had known him, worked with him, and talked with him, I never once heard Kurt say a negative word about any other person.

What a remarkable legacy of a true Christian heart! Kurt lived up to the standard of Ephesians 4:29–32. He sought to build up others, showing kindness, good humor, and tenderheartedness instead of bitterness and malice.

Will others be able to say the same about us?

DAVE BRANON

A kind word is the oil that takes the friction out of life.

Sacrificial Giving

MARK 10:23-31

Peter spoke up, "We have left everything to follow you!"
MARK 10:28

Some teenage girls formed a "do without" club to raise money for missions—adding to their fund by sacrificial giving. Many were well-to-do and easily found ways to contribute. But for Margie it was more difficult. One day she asked the Lord to show her something she could do without. As she prayed, her pet spaniel licked her hands.

Suddenly she remembered that the family doctor had offered to buy him. "Oh Bright, I couldn't think of parting with you!" she exclaimed through tears. Then she thought of John 3:16, "God so loved the world that he gave his one and only Son."

So she sold her dog to the doctor for $50. Even though she missed Bright, she was still happy because she had been able to put all of the money into the mission fund.

The doctor was pleased with the dog, but he wondered why she had parted with him. So he stopped by to talk with Margie. After he heard her story, he recalled that in his life of abundance he had never denied himself anything. The next morning Margie found Bright scratching at her bedroom door. A note was fastened to his collar: "Your practical Christianity has done more for me than any sermon I've ever heard. Last night I offered my life to God. I'd like to join your club, and I begin by doing without Bright."

To be dedicated to God involves self-sacrifice. Can we say with Peter, "We have left everything to follow [Jesus]"?

HENRY BOSCH

Love is never afraid of giving too much.

Does Your Faith Show?

HEBREWS 11:30–40

By faith the people passed through the Red Sea as on dry land;
but when the Egyptians tried to do so, they were drowned.
HEBREWS 11:29

The faith of Arthur and Wilda Matthews, missionaries in northern China, was on the line. They had been taken captive by the communists, and they realized that this was their opportunity to put into practice what they had been telling the Chinese people for years—that God is faithful and can be trusted. They knew that how they responded during this ordeal would either confirm or deny their spoken testimony.

After a time in captivity, they were set free. When they returned to their people, they discovered that their steadfastness in the midst of confinement and deprivation had borne an even more effective witness than everything they had said before. The Christians of that region of China saw clearly that the Matthews' faith was real. What had come from their lips had been verified by their life.

For us to be a fruitful witness for God, it's vital to realize that we must not only talk about Jesus but also trust Him in life's trials. Nothing demonstrates the truthfulness of our verbal witness for Christ more than a life in which the fruit of the Spirit—the very character of Jesus—can be seen. Our response to the problems that confront us, and our loving, caring concern can have an amazing impact on the people whose lives we touch. If a godly life backs up our words of witness, our faith will show.

PAUL VAN GORDER

People may doubt what you say, but they will believe what you do.

Servants Anonymous

MATTHEW 20:17–28

Whoever wants to be first must be your slave.
MATTHEW 20:27

A truly humble person will want to do things for others without calling attention to himself or to his deeds.

Jean Frederic Oberlin, a minister in eighteenth-century Germany, was traveling by foot in winter when he was caught in a severe snowstorm. He soon lost his way in the blowing snow and feared he would freeze to death. In despair he sat down, not knowing which way to turn. Just then, a man came along in a wagon and rescued Oberlin. He took him to the next village and made sure he would be cared for.

As the man prepared to journey on, Oberlin said, "Tell me your name so I may at least have you in grateful remembrance before God." The man, who by now had recognized Oberlin, replied, "You are a minister. Please tell me the name of the Good Samaritan." Oberlin said, "I cannot do that, for it is not given in the Scriptures." His benefactor responded, "Until you can tell me his name, please permit me to withhold mine."

Jesus is our example. He did not come to be praised and served, but to serve others unselfishly (Matthew 20:28). That same quality should mark our service as well.

It doesn't matter whether people know our name or not as long as the kindness we show reminds them of Jesus.

PAUL VAN GORDER

When we forget about ourselves, we do things others will remember.

A Useful "Note"

JAMES 2:14–20

In the same way, faith by itself, if it is not accompanied by action, is dead.
JAMES 2:17

The genuineness of our faith in Christ is proven by our works. The apostle Paul spoke of "faith expressing itself through love" (Galatians 5:6). We indicate what we believe not only by what we say but also by what we do.

Samuel Bradburn (1751–1816), an associate of English theologian John Wesley, was highly respected by his friends and used by God as an effective preacher. On one occasion he was in desperate financial need. When Wesley learned of his circumstances, he sent him the following letter: "Dear Sammy: 'Trust in the Lord, and do good; so shalt thou dwell in the land, and verily thou shalt be fed.' Yours affectionately, John Wesley." Attached to the letter was a five-pound note (then worth about $10).

Bradburn's reply was prompt. "Reverend and Dear Sir: I have often been struck with the beauty of the passage of Scripture quoted in your letter, but I must confess that I never saw such a useful 'expository note' on it before."

Someone has said, "Pious talk can't take the place of helpfulness." To profess faith in Christ as Savior and Lord while ignoring the needs of fellow believers is inconsistent. James said that true faith translates into compassion in action (James 2:15, 16).

Let's learn from Wesley and from James by turning our faith into action every day.

PAUL VAN GORDER

A good commentary on faith is action.

A Child's Last Prayer

MATTHEW 18:1–6

When Jesus saw this, he was indignant. He said to them,
"Let the little children come to me, and do not hinder them,
for the kingdom of God belongs to such as these."
MARK 10:14

Two missionaries from the Philippines, Bernard and Eleanor Bancroft, relate this touching story: "In our work among the children, we contacted a little girl who came from an unsaved family. Shortly after attending our meetings, she was taken to the Cuyo Hospital on the island of Palawan, dying of typhoid. It was expected that she would be delirious, but she lay perfectly still. The brokenhearted parents stood by her bed weeping.

"Then Rosa's head stirred and her lips moved. Everyone came closer, hoping to hear her last words. Feebly, yet with meaning, she began to sing, 'Into my heart, into my heart, come into my heart, Lord Jesus.' For hours she drifted in and out of consciousness, but her tiny voice kept on, haltingly repeating those same lines. Then she was gone, and the doctor gently covered the small face."

Eleanor remembered the bright-eyed tot gazing intently at the flannelgraphs used in illustrating Bible stories, and she wondered if she fully understood. She recalled, "Whenever we begin to doubt the value of repeating the glad news of salvation to the little folk, we hear again the echo of that faint voice whispering: 'Come into my heart, Lord Jesus!'"

Would anyone dare to say that Rosa's simple, childish prayer went unanswered?

HENRY BOSCH

Jesus invites children to come to Him, knowing that
little folk have large faith!

Multiplied Love

1 JOHN 4:20–5:5

This commandment we have from Him:
that he who loves God must love his brother also.

1 JOHN 4:21 NKJV

When a woman in Karen's church was diagnosed with ALS (amyotrophic lateral sclerosis, also known as Lou Gehrig's disease), things looked bad. This cruel disease affects nerves and muscles, eventually leading to paralysis. The family's insurance wouldn't cover home care, and the stricken woman's husband couldn't bear the thought of putting her in a nursing home.

As a nurse, Karen had the expertise to help, so she began going to the woman's home to care for her. But she soon realized she couldn't take care of her own family while meeting the needs of her friend, so she started teaching others in the church to help. As the disease ran its course over the next seven years, Karen trained thirty-one additional volunteers who surrounded that family with love, prayer, and practical assistance.

Those who love God "must also love their brother and sister," said John the disciple (1 John 4:21). Karen gives us a shining example of that kind of love. She had the skills, compassion, and vision to rally a church family around a hurting friend. Her love for one person in need became a multiplied love lived out by many.

TIM GUSTAFSON

Love your neighbor as yourself.
—Jesus

"He Also Sent a Doll!"

JAMES 5:13–18

The LORD is far from the wicked, but he hears the prayer of the righteous.
PROVERBS 15:29

Truly the Lord "hears the prayer of the righteous"! Hannah asked God for a child, and Samuel was born. Daniel prayed for protection, and the lions left him alone.

Dr. Helen Roseveare (1925–2016), missionary to what is now the Democratic Republic of Congo in Central Africa, told this story: "A mother at our mission station died after giving birth to a premature baby. We tried to improvise an incubator for the newborn, but our only hot water bottle was damaged. During devotions that morning we asked the children of our mission station to pray for the baby and her sister, who were now orphans. One girl responded, 'Dear God, please send a hot water bottle today. Tomorrow will be too late. And please send a doll for her sister so she won't feel so lonely.'"

That afternoon a large package arrived from England. Eagerly the children watched as we opened it. Surprisingly, under some clothing was a hot water bottle! Immediately the girl who had prayed started to dig deeper, exclaiming, "If God sent that, I'm sure He also sent a doll." And she was right! God knew in advance of the child's sincere requests, and five months before, He had led a ladies' group to include both of those specific articles in the package they were sending to Africa.

Not all of our prayers are answered so dramatically, but God always sends what is best. Praise Him for His loving responses to our needs.

HENRY BOSCH

God's help is only a prayer away.

Losing and Finding Our Lives in Him

LUKE 9:18–27

For whoever wants to save their life will lose it, but whoever loses their life for me will save it.

LUKE 9:24

When Mother Teresa died in 1997, people marveled again at her example of humble service to Christ and to people in great need. She had spent fifty years ministering to the poor, sick, orphaned, and dying through the Missionaries of Charity in Calcutta, India.

After extensive interviews with her, British journalist Malcolm Muggeridge wrote: "There is much talk today about discovering an identity, as though it were something to be looked for, like a winning number in a lottery; then, once found, to be hoarded and treasured. Actually, . . . the more it is spent the richer it becomes. So, with Mother Teresa, in effacing herself, she becomes herself. I never met anyone more memorable."

I suspect that many of us may be afraid of what will happen if we obey Jesus's words: "If anyone desires to come after Me, let him deny himself, and take up his cross daily, and follow Me. For whoever desires to save his life will lose it, but whoever loses his life for My sake will save it" (Luke 9:23–24 NKJV).

Our Savior reminded His followers that He came to give us life abundantly (John 10:10). We are called to lose our lives for Christ, and in so doing discover the fullness of life in Him.

DAVID MCCASLAND

As we lose our lives for Christ, we find fullness of life in Him.

Look What Jesus Has Done

LUKE 8:1–8

But since you excel in everything—in faith, in speech, in knowledge,
in complete earnestness and in the love we have kindled in you—
see that you also excel in this grace of giving.

2 CORINTHIANS 8:7

The little boy was only eight when he announced to his parents' friend Wally, "I love Jesus and want to serve God overseas someday." During the next ten years or so, Wally prayed for him as he watched him grow up. When this young man later applied with a mission agency to go to Mali in West Africa, Wally told him, "It's about time! When I heard what you wanted to do, I invested some money and have been saving it for you, waiting for this exciting news." Wally has a heart for others and for getting God's good news to people.

Jesus and His disciples needed financial support as they traveled from one town and village to another, telling the good news of His kingdom (Luke 8:1–3). A group of women who had been cured of evil spirits and diseases helped to support them "out of their own means" (v. 3). One was Mary Magdalene, who had been freed from the presence of seven demons. Another was Joanna, the wife of an official in Herod's court. Nothing is known about Susanna and "many others" (v. 3), but we know that Jesus had met their spiritual needs. Now they were helping Him and His disciples financially.

When we consider what Jesus has done for us, His heart for others becomes our own. Let's ask God how He wants to use us.

ANNE CETAS

Jesus gave His all; He deserves our all.

The Supreme Sacrifice

ACTS 21:1–14

*Then Paul answered, "Why are you weeping and breaking my heart?
I am ready not only to be bound, but also to die in Jerusalem
for the name of the Lord Jesus."*

ACTS 21:13

Since the church began, thousands of men and women have died for their Christian testimony. They chose to die rather than to renounce their faith in Christ.

Polycarp (69–155), one of the early church fathers was put on trial because of his faith in Christ. When the Roman proconsul told him to deny his faith, Polycarp answered, "For eighty-six years I have served Him, and He has never wronged me. How can I blaspheme my King, who has saved me?"

The proconsul then threatened to cast him in with wild beasts, but Polycarp answered, "Call them!" He was then warned that he might be burned at the stake. Even that failed to move him. He responded, "You threaten me with fire which burns only for a moment, but you are ignorant of the fire of eternal punishment, reserved for the ungodly."

These are Polycarp's final words: "O Father of Thy beloved and blessed Son, Jesus Christ! I bless Thee that Thou hast counted me worthy of this day, and of this hour, to receive my portion in the number of the martyrs, in the cup of Christ."

What would we have done in a situation like his? How strong is our loyalty to Christ? Would we be willing to make the supreme sacrifice? Are we willing to suffer ridicule or even death for Him?

RICHARD DEHAAN

You're not ready to live until you're ready to die.

Storm Before the Calm

MATTHEW 6:9–15

*For if you forgive other people when they sin against you,
your heavenly Father will also forgive you.*
MATTHEW 6:14

The small church was struggling, and everyone knew why. Two elderly church members had a conflict, and the people had divided their loyalties between them, which made any kind of progress impossible. They blatantly disregarded Jesus's clear instructions on forgiving others (Matthew 6:14).

A new pastor came to the church and spent several weeks teaching about forgiveness and trust. For a while, the people stuck to their divided loyalties and continued to slog along in their stagnant pool of distrust.

After much prayer, the pastor felt directed by the Lord to take action. So during a morning service, he called on the two men to stand and then asked them to forgive each other. He knew that if the church were ever to have peace again, a storm of confrontation had to occur. The men faced off, paused, and then embraced. Tears ran down their faces as each begged the other for forgiveness. Forty-five minutes later, the crying and hugging and forgiving throughout the congregation finally stopped. The church was revitalized to serve together as a loving community for the glory of God.

Forgiveness is a powerful thing, bringing a comforting calmness. With it, we can enjoy harmony with God's people; without it, the storm continues.

DAVE BRANON

Forgiveness is Christianity in action.

"Aim Day Co"

PSALM 1

As surely as I live, declares the Sovereign Lord, I take no pleasure in the death of the wicked, but rather that they turn from their ways and live. . . . Whether you turn to the right or to the left, your ears will hear a voice behind you, saying, "This is the way; walk in it."

EZEKIEL 33:11, ISAIAH 30:21

Jesus pointed out that only two directions are open to us in this world of sin. One is the narrow way that leads to life eternal with God, and the other is the broad way that leads to destruction and a godless eternity (Matthew 7:13–14). Jesus declared that He is "the way" (John 14:6). His way offers forgiveness of sin, eternal life, and the assurance of an everlasting kingdom of peace. We have a duty to proclaim this truth.

Many years ago, *The Sunday School Times* (now *The Gospel Herald and the Sunday School Times*) carried the story of Miss Reside, a missionary to the Kiowa tribe of Native Americans who live in Oklahoma. After she had lived with them long enough for them to know what it meant to be a Christian, they gave her a new name: "AIM DAY CO." Chief Bigtree explained, "When we Kiowas see anyone on the wrong trail, we call out, 'Aim day co,' which means 'Turn this way.' Our sister came to us and found us on the wrong path and in great danger. She called to us, 'Turn this way,' and then she showed us the Jesus road. God bless Miss Aim Day Co."

We as Christians can point others to Jesus, crying, "Aim day co! Turn this way!"

HENRY BOSCH

Christ is the only way to heaven—all other ways are detours to doom.

Being Mary and Martha

LUKE 10:38–42

But Martha was distracted by all the preparations that had to be made.
She came to him and asked, "Lord, don't you care that my sister has left me
to do the work by myself? Tell her to help me!"

LUKE 10:40

While Martha served Jesus unsparingly, her sister Mary sat at His feet, listening and learning. British preacher Charles H. Spurgeon believed that Martha's mistake wasn't her serving, but rather that she allowed it to distract her attention from Jesus. Spurgeon said that we should be Martha and Mary in one. He wrote, "We should do much service and have much communion at the same time. For this we need great grace. It is easier to serve than to commune."

I once met a young mother who found the grace to do both. She hungered after God and His Word but was unavoidably immersed in family life each day. Then an idea came to her. In each room she placed paper and a pencil on a high surface, away from tiny hands. As she served the Lord in household responsibilities, she also kept herself open to God. Whenever a Scripture came to mind, or something to confess, to correct, or to pray about, she jotted it on the nearest pad of paper. In the evening after the children were asleep, she gathered her pieces of paper and pondered them prayerfully over her open Bible.

This woman found a way to be Martha and Mary. May we too discover ways to serve God and commune with Him—both at the same time.

JOANIE YODER

To keep your life in balance, lean on the Lord.

Songs in the Night

PSALM 42

By day the LORD directs his love, at night his song is with me—
a prayer to the God of my life.

PSALM 42:8

Seventeenth-century German pastor and songwriter Paul Gerhardt faced many trials. In one incident during the Thirty Years' War (1618–1648), Gerhardt and his family were forced to flee their home. As he worried about what might happen to his wife and children during this ordeal, he was filled with distress. One night as they stayed in a small village inn, homeless and afraid, his wife wept openly in despair. To comfort her, Gerhardt reminded her of Scripture promises about God's provision and keeping. Then he went out to a garden where he too burst into tears.

Not long afterward, he sensed anew the presence of the Lord. He took a pen and began to write a hymn that is still used in hymnals today. The last lines read: "Give to the winds thy fears, and be thou undismayed; God hears thy sighs and counts thy tears—God shall lift up thy head." Gerhardt had been given a song in the night! A short time later, God delivered the family from danger.

Often it is in the darkest times of life that God makes His presence known most clearly to us.

Are you facing struggles right now? Take heart. In the midst of suffering, put your life in God's hands. He still gives songs in the night.

PAUL VAN GORDER

When troubles call on you, call on God.

Walking with the Lord

PSALM 37:23–31

The LORD makes firm the steps of the one who delights in him.
PSALM 37:23

A small pamphlet I received from a friend was titled *An Attempt to Share the Story of 86 Years of Relationship with the Lord.* In it, Al Ackenheil noted key people and events in his journey of faith over nearly nine decades. What seemed to be ordinary choices at the time—memorizing Bible verses, meeting for prayer with others, telling his neighbors about Jesus—became turning points that changed the direction of his life. It was fascinating to read how God's hand guided and encouraged Al.

The psalmist wrote, "The LORD makes firm the steps of the one who delights in him" (Psalm 37:23). The passage continues with a beautiful description of God's faithful care for all who want to walk with Him. "The law of their God is in their heart; their feet do not slip" (v. 31).

All who are believers in Jesus could create a record of God's leading and faithfulness, reflecting on God's guidance—the people, places, and experiences that are landmarks on our pathway of faith. Every remembrance of the Lord's goodness encourages us to keep walking with Him and to thank someone who influenced us for good.

The Lord guides and guards all who walk with Him.

DAVID MCCASLAND

You are headed in the right direction when you walk with God.

The Victory of Faith

GALATIANS 6:6–10

Without faith it is impossible to please God, because anyone who comes to him must believe that he exists and that he rewards those who earnestly seek him.

HEBREWS 11:6

For ten years Robert and Mary Moffat labored faithfully in the British Protectorate of Bechuanaland (now the Republic of Botswana) without one ray of encouragement to brighten their way. They could not report a single convert. The directors of their mission board began to question the wisdom of continuing the work. The thought of leaving their post, however, brought great grief to this devoted couple, for they felt sure they would see people turn to Christ eventually. They stayed, and for a while, darkness reigned.

Then one day a friend in England sent word to the Moffats that she wanted to mail them a gift, and she asked what they would like. Looking ahead, Mrs. Moffat replied, "Send us a communion set; I am sure it will soon be needed." God honored her faith. The Holy Spirit moved upon the hearts of the villagers, and soon a little group of six converts was united to form the first Christian church in that land. The communion set from England was delayed in the mail, but on the day before the first commemoration of the Lord's Supper in Bechuanaland, it arrived.

Has your faith been tested for a long time? Do not despair. If you are in the center of God's leading, His "rewards" will surely come. The victory of faith will be that much sweeter because of the delays your heart has faithfully endured.

HENRY BOSCH

Faith is never surprised at success—it expects it.

Be a Star

MATTHEW 2:1–12

Those who are wise will shine like the brightness of the heavens, and those who lead many to righteousness, like the stars for ever and ever.

DANIEL 12:3

Many today seek stardom by trying to get into the media spotlight. But a young Jewish captive achieved "stardom" in a better way.

When Daniel and his friends were taken captive by a ruthless invading nation, it was unlikely that they would be heard from again. But the godly young men soon distinguished themselves as intelligent and trustworthy.

When the king had a dream that his wise men could not repeat nor interpret, he condemned them to death. After a night of prayer with his friends, Daniel received from God the content of the dream and its interpretation. As a result, the king promoted Daniel to be his chief advisor (see Daniel 2).

If the story ended there, it would be remarkable enough. But some scholars believe that Daniel's influence in Babylon made people aware of messianic prophecies about a Savior who would be born in Bethlehem. Daniel's teaching may have been the reason that 500 years later wise men from the East followed a star to a remote and unfamiliar part of the world to find an infant King, worship Him, and return to their country with the good news of God's incredible journey to earth (Matthew 2:1–12).

By turning others to righteousness, we, like Daniel, can become a star that will shine forever.

JULIE ACKERMAN LINK

You can attract people to Jesus when you have His light in your life.

Bad Things—Good Results

PHILIPPIANS 1:1-14

Now I want you to know, brothers and sisters, that what has happened to me has actually served to advance the gospel.

PHILIPPIANS 1:12

Prison is not pleasant, but it can bring good results. In fact, I know some men who trusted Jesus because of this experience.

The apostle Paul didn't like being detained for preaching the gospel, but even in prison he was grateful. Officials and guards were hearing and believing the gospel. His example was challenging many believers to a new zeal and fearlessness in proclaiming Christ.

And think of John Bunyan. He was in prison when he wrote *Pilgrim's Progress*.

Over and over God transforms unpleasant and painful situations into something beneficial. Think of Joni Eareckson Tada! As a vibrant, active teenager, a diving accident left her a paraplegic. But now, more than fifty years later, she continues to carry on a unique and helpful ministry to the Christian community. And I'm sure you know of others who faced difficult circumstances and still "served to advance the gospel" (Philippians 1:12).

If you are hemmed in by bad circumstances, don't give in to despair, self-pity, or bitterness. Instead, trust the Lord for strength. Thousands can testify that their bad times changed their lives for the good.

Yes, for a child of God, bad things can produce good results.

HERB VANDER LUGT

The difficulties of life are intended to make us better—not bitter.

Witnessing Smarter

ACTS 13:44-52

The word of the Lord spread through the whole region.
ACTS 13:49

An art teacher from Mustang, Oklahoma, had a burden for the spiritual welfare of the 600 students she taught in the public school. So while on a trip to the Holy Land, she purchased 600 tiny wooden crosses. But when she discovered that she would not be allowed to give the crosses to her students in the classroom, her witnessing opportunity seemed doomed.

Instead of giving up, this teacher embarked on an ambitious project. Armed with her crosses and gospel tracts, she visited every one of her students in their homes—all 600 of them! "Many parents were moved to tears that I cared for their child," she said of her visits.

The life of the apostle Paul points out that witnessing for Jesus Christ is neither easy nor popular. In his case, he was sometimes told by city officials or opposing groups to get out of town. Yet Paul still found a way to tell the story of Jesus—even at the loss of his freedom.

A world trying to eliminate Christianity is one that needs Jesus Christ more than ever. As we face obstacles in our efforts to tell others about our faith, let's look for new ways to spread the gospel. We may need to witness smarter.

DAVE BRANON

The rewards of witnessing are worth the risks.

He Will Provide

GENESIS 22:1–4

Abraham answered, "God himself will provide the lamb for the burnt offering, my son." And the two of them went on together.
GENESIS 22:8

Pastor Roy S. Nicholson told of a time when he had no money to buy food. Determined to trust God for his needs and not tell anyone, he and his wife presented their case to the Lord in prayer.

The next morning he set the table for breakfast, confident that the Lord would provide something to eat. Just then a boy from their Sunday school came to the house with a sack of flour and some milk. Tears welled up in the pastor's eyes. No sooner had he left than Granny Turner appeared at the door carrying a large serving tray loaded with Virginia ham, eggs, grits and gravy, hot biscuits, butter, jelly, and coffee. Nicholson was filled with praise to God.

Abraham faced an even more serious test of faith. God had told him he would become the father of a great nation, but then God asked him to sacrifice his promised son Isaac on the altar. How could Abraham do such a thing? Many years of trusting God for his long-awaited son had taught him that his confidence in God would be fully rewarded. "God himself will provide the lamb," he told Isaac (Genesis 22:8).

Faith like that is not born in a day. It's the result of years of seeing God's faithfulness to His promises, and it grows as we daily choose to believe what He says.

DENNIS DeHAAN

Man's poverty is never a strain on God's provision.

Brown Bag Witness

1 THESSALONIANS 1

*The Lord's message rang out . . . [and] your faith in God has
become known everywhere.*

1 THESSALONIANS 1:8

Ivan was a brilliant engineer, highly respected by his coworkers. But sometimes they called him "Deacon" or "Parson" because he had a deep religious faith, and he didn't hide it. Every day at lunch, for example, Ivan would bow his head over a little brown bag and thank God for his food.

Jean Zeiler, who worked with Ivan, was intrigued by his consistent testimony. She wanted to find out what made him so different. She found her answer in a book Ivan told her about—the Bible. After buying one and reading it three times, she came to know Jesus in a personal way.

Ivan told Jean, "I used to wonder if I would ever lead anyone to Christ." But his quiet witness was not only the key to Jean's salvation but it also challenges thousands as she travels throughout the world and gives her testimony.

The apostle Paul reminded the persecuted Thessalonian believers that their "faith in God" was touching lives in far-off places (1 Thessalonians 1:8). This must have encouraged them to remain faithful to the Savior.

We should never underestimate the impact we can have for Christ. When we live for Him in our workplace or neighborhood, we will send forth a quiet message that will be heard. *Lord, help us to be consistent witnesses for you.*

DENNIS DEHAAN

A quiet testimony is more convincing than a loud sermon.

A Passion for Souls

ROMANS 10:1–13

Brothers and sisters, my heart's desire and prayer to God for the Israelites is that they may be saved.

ROMANS 10:1

In Raymond C. Ortlund's book *Lord, Make My Life a Miracle*, there's a story about A. B. Simpson, founder of the Christian and Missionary Alliance. A guest in Simpson's home arose early one morning and walked down the hall to the study. There he saw a sight that deeply moved and impressed him. Simpson sat alone at his desk with his arms encircling a globe of the world. Tears were running down his cheeks. He was weeping for a world lost in sin.

The apostle Paul was greatly burdened for the salvation of his own Jewish people. He expressed the depth of his feelings in Romans 9: "I speak the truth in Christ—I am not lying, my conscience confirms it through the Holy Spirit—I have great sorrow and unceasing anguish in my heart. For I could wish that I myself were cursed and cut off from Christ for the sake of my people, those of my own race" (vv. 1–3). And in Romans 10:1, we read Paul's words: "my heart's desire and prayer to God for the Israelites is that they may be saved."

How much do we care about a world estranged from God? Enough to witness? Enough to give of our means? Enough to give ourselves? Enough to die? How is our passion for souls?

RICHARD DeHaan

A passion for Jesus soon becomes a passion for telling others about Jesus.

Much Speaking

MATTHEW 6:1–8

*When you pray, do not keep on babbling like pagans, for they think
they will be heard because of their many words.*

MATTHEW 6:7

You may have heard the story about the great evangelist Dwight L. Moody, who was quite perturbed when a man who had been asked to pray at one of his meetings continued to pray on and on and on. The man became so lost in his own words that people in the audience began to grow restless.

Moody saw no end in sight, so he suddenly stood up and said, "While our brother is finishing his prayer, let us sing hymn number 75." This seemed quite rude and brusque, and Moody was criticized for it later, but few know the rest of the story.

In the audience was a medical student who was so bored with the long-winded supplication that he reached for his hat and was ready to leave. When Moody suddenly switched the audience from trying to follow the tedious prayer to singing a song of grace and blessing, the young man's attention was arrested by the music. He put his hat down and remained in the service. At the close, he was among those who came forward to put his faith in Jesus Christ as Savior. That new Christian later became a world-renowned missionary—Sir William Grenfell!

God uses a variety of ways to reach people with the message of the gospel—song, message, prayer, and even interruptions. It is His Word that makes a difference, not ours.

HENRY BOSCH

**Our prayer depends on God's heart of love,
not our words of eloquence.**

Our Great Deliverer

ACTS 5:17–32

*During the night an angel of the Lord opened the doors
of the jail and brought them out.*

ACTS 5:19

Margaret Nikol was born into a pastor's family in Bulgaria. Her mother and father were murdered for their faith by the communists in the 1960s. Margaret was a brilliant violinist, and in spite of opposition she got an excellent education. She achieved fame throughout Europe and became concertmaster of the Dresden Symphony. But because of her faith in Christ, she was subjected to physical and emotional cruelty. Eventually, she was given a prison sentence—to begin as soon as the concert season was over.

But God had other plans. Margaret was invited to play in Vienna at an Easter concert in 1982. The communists repeatedly denied permission, but finally, because of outside pressure, they relented. "God was faster than they were," testifies Margaret. In Vienna she requested political asylum, and no less than five free nations offered it! Today, Margaret Nikol still travels all over the world to spread her powerful testimony of faith through her music.

The same God who delivered Margaret from communist oppression and who sent an angel to free the apostles from prison (Acts 5:19) can also rescue us from whatever is holding us captive—physically or spiritually. We must never give up hope! God is our great deliverer.

DAVID EGNER

The God who holds the universe is the God who is holding you.

A God-Given Opportunity

ACTS 8:26–38

Then Philip began with that very passage of Scripture and told him the good news about Jesus.

ACTS 8:35

Former Cedarville University president Paul Dixon tells the story of a high school girl who was in the audience several years ago when he was speaking about the need to tell others about Christ. As she listened, she decided she wanted to make a difference in her high school. She asked God to give her an opportunity.

The next day at school, one of her teachers, who was fed up with the way things were going, walked into his classroom and said, "I've had it. I'm tired of the hassle of teaching kids who don't have any respect. If any of you can tell me what life is all about and what our purpose is, go ahead."

Surprised, the girl raised her hand and explained that she had found answers to those questions in Jesus Christ. The teacher, who was an agnostic, invited her to stay after class and explain her beliefs. When she suggested that he attend an evangelistic meeting, he agreed. That Friday night he put his trust in Jesus as Savior, and today he's active in Christian service.

She had seized a God-given opportunity—like Philip did with the Ethiopian official (Acts 8:29–30).

We may have sweaty palms and cottonmouth as we witness to unbelievers. But when the Lord gives us the opportunity to talk about Him, let's seize it.

DAVE BRANON

Any place can be the right place to witness for Christ.

A Secure Environment

PSALM 121

The angel of the LORD encamps around those who fear him,
and he delivers them.

PSALM 34:7

The Christian is guarded on all sides. We have God before us (Isaiah 48:17), behind us (Isaiah 30:21), on our right (Psalm 16:8), to our left (Job 23:9), and above us (Psalm 36:7). God is our true environment. What protection!

An Australian missionary told of God's special care for him as he made a lonely, dangerous journey on foot. He had no problem getting to his destination, but he was uneasy on the return trip because he carried a large sum of money. Unbeknown to the missionary, a man was waiting at a lonely spot, planning to rob and kill whoever passed by. As the missionary walked, concerned about his safety, he prayed aloud for protection.

Before the bandit saw him, he heard him talking, and immediately he thought there must be two men, so he decided not to attack. Later, he told someone what he had intended to do that day, and the news got around. When the missionary heard it, he realized that God's Spirit had prompted him to pray aloud. His heart rejoiced as he thought of the Lord's protection from harm.

Although we as believers are not insulated from all danger and accident, we are nonetheless surrounded by God's care every moment of the day. Wherever we are and whatever may happen, we know that He is with us. And "if God is for us, who can be against us?" (Romans 8:31). Yes, we have a most secure environment.

HENRY BOSCH

No danger can come so near the Christian that God is not nearer.

Taste and Say!

PSALM 34

Taste and see that the LORD is good; blessed is the one who takes refuge in him.
PSALM 34:8

Do you believe God is good, even when life isn't? Mary did, and I gasped with amazement the day I heard her pastor share her story at her funeral. She, being dead, yet speaks!

Mary had been a widow, very poor, and totally housebound because of her ailments in old age. But like the psalmist, she had learned to praise God amid her hardships. She had come to develop deep gratitude for every good thing He sent her way.

Her pastor said he occasionally would visit her at home. Because of her crippling pain, it took her a long time to inch her way to the door to let him in. So he would call on the phone and tell her he was on his way, and he gave her an estimated time he would get there. Mary would then begin the slow, arduous journey to the door, reaching it about the time he arrived. Without fail, he could count on her greeting him with these triumphant words: "God is good!"

I've observed that those who speak most often about God's goodness are usually those with the most trials. They choose to focus on the Lord's mercy and grace rather than on their troubles, and in so doing they taste His goodness.

Mary challenges us—not only us to taste and *see* but also to taste and *say* that the Lord is good. Even when life isn't.

JOANIE YODER

Those who bless God in their trials will be blessed by God through their trials.

Believing Prayer

MARK 11:20–24

*Whatever you ask for in prayer, believe that you have received it,
and it will be yours.*

MARK 11:24

This story by Charles H. Spurgeon reminds me of the kind of faith we must exercise when we pray: "A small boy once attended a prayer meeting at church. At the conclusion he went to the man in charge and said, 'Sir, when you meet again, could you ask the people to pray that my sister will begin reading the Bible? I'm sure if she does, she will be saved.' The following week the leader shared the boy's request with the group. As they began to pray, the lad got up and left. The next day the leader saw him and asked, 'Why did you leave last night?' 'Oh, Sir,' came the reply. 'I just wanted to get home as soon as possible so I could see my sister reading her Bible for the first time.'" He was confident that God would answer their prayer.

Peter's friends could have learned from this boy. They were praying for their friend's release from prison, but then they doubted that he could be the one knocking at the gate after the Lord had freed him (Acts 12:5–17).

For the Christian whose trust is centered in God, who delights to do the impossible, believing prayer should not be the exception but the rule!

PAUL VAN GORDER

When we pray, we can rely on God's reply.

"I Dare You"

PSALM 119:41–48

Never take your word of truth from my mouth, for I have put my hope in your laws. I will always obey your law, for ever and ever.

PSALM 119:43–44

I heard a story of a little church that was having a reunion. A former member who attended the celebration had worked hard and had become a millionaire. When he testified about how he had grown in the faith, he related an incident from his childhood.

He said that when he earned his first dollar as a boy, he decided to keep it for the rest of his life. But then a guest missionary preached about the urgent need on the mission fields. He struggled about giving his dollar. "However, the Lord won," the man said proudly, "and I put my treasured dollar in the offering basket. And I am convinced that the reason God has blessed me so much is that when I was a little boy I gave Him everything I possessed." The congregation was awestruck by the testimony—until a little old lady in front piped up, "I dare you to do it again!"

There's a vital truth behind that humorous story. We must not let past attainments stop our spiritual growth. The psalmist said, "I will obey your law, for ever and ever." He knew he needed to keep his commitment fresh every day.

As Christians, we cannot rest on past achievements. We must give the Lord our full devotion now. Then no one will be able to say to us, "I dare you to do it again!"

DAVID EGNER

Use the past as a springboard, not as a sofa.

The Strength of Our Bridge

JUDE 20–25

To him who is able to keep you from stumbling and to present you before his glorious presence without fault and with great joy—to the only God our Savior be glory, majesty, power and authority, through Jesus Christ our Lord, before all ages, now and forevermore! Amen.

JUDE 24–25

Robert Lewis Dabney (1820–1898) was an outstanding Presbyterian theologian. He served as a minister, as a chaplain, as chief of staff to General Stonewall Jackson, and as a seminary professor. He also helped establish a seminary in Austin, Texas.

As he aged, Dabney began to worry about his impending death, and he expressed his fears in a letter to a former student and fellow theologian, C. R. Vaughan. Dabney wondered about his ability to die honorably and to hold on to his Christian faith.

Vaughan replied: "Dear friend, let me advise you now as you often have me. If you were about to cross a deep chasm, and there were a bridge over it, would you stand there looking in at yourself, wondering if you trusted enough in bridges to be able to cross? Or would you not rather go and examine the beams and timbers of the bridge and the quality of its construction, and determine whether the bridge were trustworthy, and then pass over it in confidence? Our faith is in Christ; spend yourself focusing on Him and His sufficiency, rather than on yourself."

Do you have doubts about dying? Remember, God "is able to keep you from stumbling and to present you before his glorious presence without fault" (Jude 24–25).

HADDON ROBINSON

Faith focuses on God instead of the problem.

A "Handful of Thorns"

PSALM 105:1–5

*Let them give thanks to the LORD for his unfailing love
and his wonderful deeds for mankind.*

PSALM 107:21

Jeremy Taylor (1613–1667) was an English clergyman who was severely persecuted for his faith. Although his house was plundered, his family was left destitute, and his property was confiscated, he continued to count the blessings he could not lose.

He wrote: "They have not taken away my merry countenance, my cheerful spirit, and a good conscience; they have still left me with the providence of God, and all His promises . . . my hopes of heaven, and my charity to them, too, and still I sleep and digest, I eat and drink, I read and meditate. And he that hath so many causes of joy, and so great should never choose to sit down upon his little handful of thorns."

Although we may not be afflicted with the grievous difficulties that Jeremy Taylor endured, all of us face trials and troubles. Are we grumbling? Or do we refuse to let our "little handful of thorns," our troubles, obscure the overwhelming abundance of our blessings?

When we feel like complaining, let's remember God's faithfulness and "give praise to the LORD, proclaim his name; make known among the nations what he has done. . . . Remember the wonders he has done" (Psalm 105:1, 5).

VERNON GROUNDS

Spend your time counting your blessings, not airing your complaints.

Only the Best

JOHN 3:9–21

For God so loved the world that he gave his one and only Son, that whoever believes in him shall not perish but have eternal life."
JOHN 3:16

A poignant story is told about children of Untouchables in a Christian school in India before World War II. Each year the students received Christmas presents from children in England. The girls got a doll, and the boys a toy.

On one occasion, the doctor from a nearby mission hospital was asked to distribute the gifts. In the course of his visit, he told the youngsters about a village where the boys and girls had never heard of Jesus. He suggested that maybe they would like to give them some of their old toys as presents. They liked the idea and readily agreed.

A week later, the doctor returned to collect the gifts. The sight was unforgettable. One by one the children filed by and handed the doctor a doll or a toy. To his great surprise, they all gave the new present they had received a few days earlier. When he asked why, a girl spoke up, "Think what God did by giving us His only Son. Could we give less than our best?"

The beloved Son of God was the costliest gift the heavenly Father could have given to a world of ruined sinners. When we think of that, how can we withhold anything from Him?

Let's renew our commitment to God, who gave His Son, and to the Savior who gave His all.

PAUL VAN GORDER

God's highest gift calls for our deepest gratitude.

The Voice

JOHN 1:19–34

John saw Jesus coming toward him and said, "Look, the Lamb of God, who takes away the sin of the world!"
JOHN 1:29

Bicycling down a street in an English village, George Cutting, author of a Christian book called *Safety, Certainty, and Enjoyment*, passed a certain cottage and felt compelled by the Holy Spirit to call out, "Behold the Lamb of God which taketh away the sin of the world!" Then he repeated it.

Six months later, Cutting was evangelizing that area, visiting from house to house. He came to one cottage and asked the woman who came to the door if she was saved. Joyfully she replied, "Oh, yes! Six months ago, I was in great distress about the salvation of my soul. I pleaded for God's help. Then a voice cried, 'Behold the Lamb of God which taketh away the sin of the world.' I asked God to repeat what He had said, and the voice came again." George Cutting had been that voice! Because he had been sensitive and obedient to the Holy Spirit's urging, God used him as an instrument through which to speak His Word to that needy heart.

God will probably never lead us to witness that way. He has many different methods for us. But we all meet sin-burdened people who need to know the Savior.

Let's be "the voice" that tells them the story of Jesus, the Lamb of God who can take away their sins.

PAUL VAN GORDER

When God speaks to you about others, be sure you speak to others about God.

He's Been There

PHILIPPIANS 2:1–8

The Word became flesh and made his dwelling among us. We have seen his glory, the glory of the one and only Son, who came from the Father, full of grace and truth.

JOHN 1:14

Corrie ten Boom was not looking forward to her turn to speak. She and the others in her ministry team had gone to a prison to talk to the inmates about Christ. They had set up their equipment at one end of a long corridor lined with cells. The men peered through the bars to see the visitors.

First, a woman sang, and the prisoners tried to drown her out. Then, when a young man stood to pray, the noise grew worse. Finally, it was Corrie's turn. Shouting to be heard, she said, "When I was alone in a cell for four months . . ." Suddenly, the corridor grew quiet. With those few words, Corrie established a bond with the prisoners. They realized that she knew what they were going through. Her time in a World War II prison camp made her one of them. They listened, and six of them responded to her invitation to receive Christ.

This incident reminds us of something important about Jesus's coming to this earth. When He "became flesh and made his dwelling among us," He *became* one of us. Therefore, He understands our suffering. He knows what we are going through.

Do you think no one gets it? Turn to Jesus. He knows Your need. He's been there.

DAVE BRANON

**When you think no one has problems like yours,
remember what Jesus endured.**

Confident Hope

PHILIPPIANS 1:19–26

I am torn between the two: I desire to depart and be with Christ, which is better by far; but it is more necessary for you that I remain in the body.

PHILIPPIANS 1:23–24

Dr. William Wallace was serving as a missionary surgeon in Wuzhou, China, in the 1940s when Japan attacked China. Wallace, who was in charge of Stout Memorial Hospital at the time, ordered the hospital to load his equipment on barges and continue to function as a hospital while floating up and down rivers to avoid infantry attacks.

During dangerous times, Philippians 1:21—one of Wallace's favorite verses—reminded him that if he lived, he had work to do for the Savior; but if he died, he had the promise of eternity with Christ. The verse took on special meaning when he died while falsely imprisoned in 1951.

Paul's writing reflects a deep devotion we can aspire to as followers of Jesus. It enables us to face trials and even danger for His sake. It is devotion empowered by the Holy Spirit and the prayers of others (v. 19). It's also a promise. Even when we surrender ourselves to continued service under difficult circumstances, it is with this reminder: when our life and work end here, we still have the joy of eternity with Jesus ahead of us.

In our hardest moments, with hearts committed to walking with Christ now, and with our eyes firmly fixed on the promise of eternity with Him, may our days and our acts bless others with the love of God.

RANDY KILGORE

Sacrifices offered to God are opportunities to showcase His love.

The Peacemaker's Reward

LUKE 6:27–35

*When the LORD takes pleasure in anyone's way,
he causes their enemies to make peace with them.*
PROVERBS 16:7

As Christians, we must be gracious to people who mistreat us. If we yield to the Holy Spirit's control and obey God, in time even our enemies can be at peace with us.

The conduct of missionary Nathatus Stach illustrates the impact of a life guided by our Lord's peacemaking principles. For twenty years he labored in Greenland, where he encountered fierce opposition. He says, "My every move was misunderstood. My efforts to win these people whom I loved were repulsed by scoffing, but I knew that God who had called me was faithful and that He would eventually conquer the hearts of my vindictive critics. After two decades of weary toil, I sat one day reading aloud from John 3. Unknown to me, my chief persecutor was listening intently to every word.

"Suddenly, he burst into my hut and demanded that I read it again. As I repeated the gracious words, this former enemy began to tremble. He asked me to show him the way of salvation. The Holy Spirit then began to work in the hearts of others, and soon many were led to Christ. One after another, those who had been antagonistic came to me and pleaded for pardon. My foes became my friends."

Believer, if you desire to win the love of your enemies, be sure your ways truly "please the Lord," and you will experience the peacemaker's reward!

HENRY BOSCH

**The most glorious victory you can have over an enemy
is to turn him into a friend!**

A Shiny Face

PSALM 51:7–13

Nehemiah said, "Go and enjoy choice food and sweet drinks, and send some to those who have nothing prepared. This day is holy to our Lord. Do not grieve, for the joy of the LORD is your strength."

NEHEMIAH 8:10

One of the results of the Holy Spirit's presence is "joy." The contentment that comes with the forgiveness of sins and the assurance of the Spirit's guidance provides us with inner strength to meet earth's trials. This joy, generated by God's Spirit, gives the believer an optimistic outlook on life that soon becomes obvious to the unsaved.

A man in India once asked a missionary, "What do you put on your face to make it shine?" With surprise he answered, "I don't put anything on it!" His questioner replied, "Yes, you do! All of you who believe in Jesus seem to have it. I've seen it in the towns of Agra and Surat, and even in the city of Bombay." Suddenly, the Christian understood. "Now I know what you mean, and I will tell you the secret. It's not something we put on from the outside but something that comes from within. It's the reflection of the light of God in our hearts."

Those who don't know the Savior may experience superficial happiness, but only the redeemed soul can know the invigorating power of the abiding joy of the Lord.

If you will let the Holy Spirit take full control of you, the peace He gives will indicate to them that "the joy of the LORD is your strength!"

HENRY BOSCH

God's song of joy in your heart should show itself in your face.

Take What Nobody Wants

COLOSSIANS 3:12–17

Therefore, as God's chosen people, holy and dearly loved, clothe yourselves with compassion, kindness, humility, gentleness and patience.

COLOSSIANS 3:12

What a joy it is to meet a child of God who gives evidence of genuine humility! That's what Paul was calling for when he exhorted Christians not to think of themselves more highly than they ought to think (Romans 12:3).

Several years ago, I read the story of Sammy Morris, a devoted Christian from Africa who came to America to go to school. Although his pathway to service for Christ was not easy, his difficulties never deterred him. Perhaps this was because he had learned genuine humility. One incident that showed this occurred when he arrived at Taylor University in Upland, Indiana. He was asked by the school's president what room he wanted. Sammy replied, "If there is a room nobody wants, give it to me." Later the president commented, "I turned away, for my eyes were full of tears. I was asking myself whether I was willing to take what nobody else wanted."

Today we are bombarded with the philosophy of "I'm Number 1" and the concept of self-love—even in religious circles. We need to clothe ourselves with "humility" (Colossians 3:12). Paul said, "Let this mind be in you which was also in Christ Jesus, who . . . made Himself of no reputation" (Philippians 2:5–7 NKJV). If we do this, we can, like Sammy Morris, be willing to take what nobody else wants. That's genuine humility. That's the mind of Christ.

PAUL VAN GORDER

The smaller we become the more room God has to work.

"Something Different"

ROMANS 5:1–5

Hope does not put us to shame, because God's love has been poured out into our hearts through the Holy Spirit, who has been given to us.

ROMANS 5:5

Salvation enables us to rejoice in our sufferings, because God's love is "poured out into our hearts." This can make our lives attractively different to others, especially in times of trial.

Karol had just graduated from Moody Bible Institute, so she packed her car, thinking she would head for home the next morning. But during the night her car was stolen. Later the next day, the Chicago police recovered it. Her belongings were still inside, but the car was completely stripped. What would have been a harrowing experience of frustration and anxiety for most people became a unique opportunity for Karol to witness of her faith in Christ. As the officer who was conducting the investigation proceeded through his inquiry, he noticed a quiet composure about Karol that baffled him. Curious, he said, "There is something different about you. Most people go all to pieces about these things. I don't have what you have." Sensing that the Holy Spirit had prepared his heart, Karol led the officer to a saving knowledge of Jesus Christ.

How do we react when trouble changes our plans? Let's remember that the God of our salvation provides peace, grace, glory, and patience. When we manifest these traits, others will see God's love in us. It's a difference that can lead them to the Savior.

DAVE BRANON

Sinners will be attracted to Christ when you have His sunshine in your life.

Is Everything in Order?

LUKE 12:35–40

*You also must be ready, because the Son of Man will come at
an hour when you do not expect him.*

LUKE 12:40

How often do we think about the possibility of Jesus's second coming? Could it be that we have built our "nests" so strong here that we are no longer watching eagerly for the return of the Lord as the early Christians did? Or maybe we don't like the thought of having our plans interrupted by the Savior's return. Perhaps we hope he waits to come until He is just in time to rescue us from a painful death.

Several years ago, *Moody* magazine related the story of a six-year-old, golden-haired child who had a strong, simple faith in Jesus, and who took seriously what she heard in Sunday school. She seemed especially impressed by the thought of the Lord's return. One morning a guest in her home found the youngster carefully arranging the things in her bedroom. He remarked, "You sure keep your room nice and neat!" Looking up with a smile, she replied, "I'm putting everything in order, 'cause Jesus might come today."

If we are dreading the Savior's return, we're not as holy or happy as we should be. Let's make sure that everything in our lives is in good order. Then we will be able to serve the Lord with joyous anticipation, ready to meet Him face to face.

HENRY BOSCH

Test the depth of your spirituality by this: are you looking forward to
Christ's return or dreading it?

Which Way?

1 CORINTHIANS 1:18–31

For the message of the cross is foolishness to those who are perishing,
but to us who are being saved it is the power of God.

1 CORINTHIANS 1:18

Every night, Howard and Mel frequented the cheap bars in Grand Rapids, Michigan, hoping to drown away another miserable day. Finally, the pain of a wasted life became too much, so Mel hopped a train for Chicago, where he hoped to end it all.

But as he walked barefoot through a Chicago snowstorm in 1897, heading for a self-imposed demise in Lake Michigan, he was stopped by a worker from the Pacific Garden Mission. Mel went inside, heard the gospel, and accepted Christ as his Savior.

Later, Mel went back to Grand Rapids to start a mission. Howard heard that he was saved and sober. But instead of trusting Jesus, Howard just laughed at "Old Mel." To him, "the message of the cross [was] foolishness" (1 Corinthians 1:18). Finally, the drinking took its toll on Howard, and he committed suicide.

More than 120 years later, Mel Trotter Ministries still welcomes people who need a place to stay and who need Jesus. And 120 years later, our family is still saddened by Howard's demise. He was my wife's grandfather.

Like Mel and Howard, we have a choice. "Whoever believes in the Son has eternal life, but whoever rejects the Son will not see life, for God's wrath remains on them" (John 3:36). What do you choose? Life or hopelessness?

DAVE BRANON

To choose Christ now is a choice for eternity.

A Common Language

MATTHEW 26:17–29

*While they were eating, Jesus took bread, and when he had given thanks,
he broke it and gave it to his disciples, saying, "Take and eat; this is my body."
". . . This is my blood of the covenant, which is poured out for many
for the forgiveness of sins."*

MATTHEW 26:26, 28

A young Russian woman had been sent to a hospital in Japan for a rare, life-saving procedure. After she arrived she couldn't stop crying. The doctors and nurses, who didn't speak Russian, were unable to console her. Finally, they decided to call an American missionary in their town to see if he could help her.

The missionary came to the hospital and tried to comfort her, but he didn't know Russian either. When the patient saw his Bible and the communion wafers and juice he had brought with him, however, she smiled and nodded to indicate her approval. Then, with no verbal communication at all, this American man and Russian woman shared a common bond in Christ. He later learned that this fellow believer was encouraged and strengthened as they shared in remembering the Lord's death.

I'm not surprised. This experience illustrates the unity we have as believers in Christ. We celebrate that oneness as together we remember His death and the forgiveness and new life He has given to us.

Sometimes, as in the case of the American man and the Russian woman, Christian unity transcends language barriers. Followers of Christ will always experience a common bond in Him.

DAVID EGNER

Christian unity begins at the cross.

The Prayer Remedy

JAMES 5:13-20

The prayer offered in faith will make the sick person well; the Lord will raise them up. If they have sinned, they will be forgiven.

JAMES 5:15

Louis Banks relates the story of a veteran missionary who returned to China after a long absence. On the day of his return, he was met by a former convert and six other Chinese nationals. These six, as the missionary later learned, had received Christ while living in the dark shadows and pain of opium addiction.

Amazed by their good health, the missionary asked his former convert what remedy he had used in their deliverance. The man answered by pointing to his knees. He had prayed for them, and when the men came to him for help he encouraged them to pray for themselves. When they came back saying it did them no good, the man of faith sent them back to their knees. He did this again and again until they stood before him clean, sound in body and mind. Through prayer, their cruel chains had been broken, and they had new songs of joy and praise on their lips.

James 5:15, which speaks about the "prayer offered in faith" saving the sick poses some difficult questions for Bible scholars. But one thing is clear—we must not neglect to call on the Lord. And when we get no immediate answer, we must not stop waiting on God. This doesn't imply that we shouldn't use other means of help, but it says that whatever help we seek, nothing must replace the role of prayer.

MART DEHAAN

Time spent in prayer is always time well spent.

Springs of Living Water

JOHN 4:5–15

"Whoever believes in me, as the Scripture has said, rivers of living water will flow from within them."

JOHN 7:38

In 1896, Sherwood Eddy enthusiastically began his ministry as a missionary to India. But after just a year he was ready to quit—his energy depleted, his spirit broken.

One morning after a sleepless night he begged God for help. Then he remembered the promise of Jesus to the woman at Jacob's well, "The water that I shall give him will become in him a fountain of water springing up into everlasting life" (John 4:14 NKJV).

Eddy wrote, "I resolved to stop drawing on myself so constantly and begin instead drawing on God." From then on he daily set aside time for prayerfully drinking from the well that never runs dry—the inexhaustible, soul-renewing wellspring of God's grace. "Since that day," Eddy said, "I have known not one hour of darkness and despair. The eternal God has been my refuge, and underneath me I have felt the everlasting arms."

No matter how much energy or talent we have, sooner or later we discover that the well of our personal resources is running dry. But when Christ, the source of living water, indwells our lives, we aren't locked into the drudgery of drawing on our human abilities. Jesus becomes our unfailing source of spiritual renewal. We find that when we have nothing left, He is the well that never runs dry.

VERNON GROUNDS

You may have to lose everything to find that God is everything you need.

The Borrowed Bible

PSALM 119:49–56

My comfort in my suffering is this: Your promise preserves my life.
PSALM 119:50

Syeed was a Bengali guard hired by missionary Tom McDonald to protect the property of a Christian hospital under construction in Bangladesh. As Jay Walsh tells the story in his book *Ripe Mangoes*, Syeed noticed another worker, Monindra, reading an unfamiliar book.

One day Syeed visited Monindra to ask what he was reading. "That's a Christian Bible," he replied. The Bible was so precious to Monindra that when Syeed asked to see it, he refused. But Syeed would not be denied. For nearly a week he would sneak into Monindra's quarters, take the Bible to a secluded place to read, and then return it unnoticed.

Then one day Syeed could not be found. After a short search, he was discovered kneeling before that Bible, calling out, "Lord Jesus, save me!" As the months and years passed, Syeed suffered severe persecution for his beliefs, yet he never backed down from the decision he made that day while reading a "borrowed" Bible.

The Word of God is indeed powerful. It did for Syeed what it did for the author of Psalm 119. It gave him life, comfort, and courage (vv. 50–53).

How has the power of God's Word revolutionized your life?

DAVE BRANON

Many books can inform, but only the Bible can transform.

Every Moment Matters

PHILIPPIANS 1:12–24

For to me, to live is Christ and to die is gain.
PHILIPPIANS 1:21

When I met Ada, she had outlived her entire group of friends and family and was living in a nursing home. "It's the hardest part of getting old," she told me. "Watching everyone else move on and leave you behind." One day I asked Ada what kept her interest and how she spent her time. She answered me with a Scripture passage from the apostle Paul (Philippians 1:21): "For to me, to live is Christ and to die is gain." Then she said, "While I'm still around, I have work to do. On my good days, I get to talk to the people here about Jesus; on the hard days, I can still pray."

Significantly, Paul wrote Philippians while in prison. And he acknowledged a reality many Christians understand as they face their mortality: Even though heaven seems so inviting, the time we have left on Earth matters to God.

Like Paul, Ada recognized that every breath she took was an opportunity to serve and glorify God. So Ada spent her days loving others and introducing them to her Savior.

Even in our darkest moments, Christians can hold on to the promise of permanent joy in the company of God. And while we live, we enjoy relationship with Him. He fills all our moments with significance.

RANDY KILGORE

When God comes to call us home, may He find us serving Him.

Be a Friend!

MARK 2:1–12

A friend loves at all times, and a brother is born for a time of adversity.
PROVERBS 17:17

Every time I read the story of the paralytic man in Mark 2, I am challenged. This incident says to me, "Be a Christian friend." You see, if it hadn't been for those four friends of the crippled man, he probably would not have experienced physical and spiritual healing that day. But they cared enough to lift him to the roof of the building where Jesus was speaking and lower him through a hole to the room below.

If we fully realized what being a friend could mean to the aged, to the ill, and to the lonely, we would more readily reach out to them. An aged man recently expressed his gratitude for the friendship of a young couple. He said that he and his wife were lonely—just waiting to die—until these lovely young Christians started showing an interest in them. Now they eagerly look forward to the weekly visit, which includes a table game, Bible study, and prayer. The kind attention of a caring Christian is often the best therapy for those who are elderly, sick, or alone.

Look around! Many people are hurting. Ask the Lord to give you compassion. Then find someone who needs you. Be ready to give yourself— a warm smile, a friendly word, and a helping hand. Be a Christian friend!

HERB VANDER LUGT

**A friend is the first person who comes in
when the whole world has gone out.**

Counting the Change

ROMANS 12:9–21

*Do not repay anyone evil for evil. Be careful to do what is right
in the eyes of everyone.*
ROMANS 12:17

A young Christian businessman from Nashville was invited to speak at a local church. He chose for his text, "Thou shalt not steal," and he spoke unswervingly on the topic.

The next morning he boarded a city bus for the ride to work. He handed a dollar bill to the driver and received some change, which he counted as he proceeded down the aisle of the bus. Before he reached his seat, he realized he had been given a dime too much. His first thought was that the transit company would never miss it. But deep inside he knew he should return it. So he went back to the driver and said, "You gave me too much change, sir."

To the businessman's amazement, the driver replied, "I know, a dime too much. I gave it to you on purpose. Then I watched you in my mirror as you counted your change. You see, I heard you speak yesterday, and if you had kept the dime, I would have had no confidence in what you said."

If we consider that bus driver's dime an insignificant matter, we need to meditate carefully on today's Scripture text and others like it. Paul said in 2 Corinthians 4:2 that we should renounce "the hidden things of dishonesty, . . . commending ourselves to every man's conscience in the sight of God" (KJV). Let's never forget that people are watching us "count the change," and so is God.

PAUL VAN GORDER

No one knows of your honesty unless you give out some samples.

Jesus's Very Own Peace

MATTHEW 16:21–23

Peace I leave with you; my peace I give you. I do not give to you as the world gives. Do not let your hearts be troubled and do not be afraid.

JOHN 14:27

On the night before the execution of Christian martyr Nicholas Ridley (1500–1555), his brother offered to stay with him in prison to be of comfort. Ridley declined, saying that he planned to sleep as soundly as usual. Because he knew the peace of Jesus, he could rest in his Lord.

The next morning, Ridley told a fellow Christian who was also being executed, "Be of good heart, brother, for God will either assuage the fury of the flame or else strengthen us to abide it." Then they knelt and prayed by the stake, and after a brief conversation, they were burned to death for their faith.

Jesus had given Nicholas Ridley His peace (John 14:27). But what kind of peace did Jesus have? In Matthew 16:21–23, we see His peace in His determination to go to Jerusalem even though He knew He would suffer and die (see Luke 9:51). Peter rebuked Him, but Jesus trusted His Father and went to the cross. His purpose for living was to die.

Amy Carmichael once said, "The peace of Jesus stood every sort of test, every strain, and it never broke. It is this, His very own peace, which He says 'I give.'"

No matter how big or small our trials may be, we can trust Jesus to give us His very own peace in the midst of them.

ANNE CETAS

When Jesus rules the heart, peace reigns.

God Is Alive!

PSALM 30

My heart may sing your praises and not be silent.
LORD my God, I will praise you forever.

PSALM 30:12

The great sixteenth-century theologian Martin Luther once experienced a long period of worry and despondency. One day his wife dressed in black mourning clothes.

"Who has died?" asked Luther.

"God," said his wife.

"God!" said Luther, horrified. "How can you say such a thing?"

She replied, "I'm only saying what you are living."

Luther realized that he indeed was living as if God were no longer alive and watching over his family in love. He then changed his outlook from gloom to gratitude.

Occasionally we too live as if God were dead. When we are discouraged, though, we can turn to the Psalms. Some of the writers faced bleak and barren times, but they had one habit in common that kept them from being soured: giving thanks to God. For example, David wrote, "You turned my wailing into dancing. . . . LORD my God, I will praise you forever" (Psalm 30:11–12).

Meeting each situation with thanksgiving isn't a denial of trouble. It helps us see situations from God's perspective—opportunities to discover His power and love. Every time we express gratitude to God in a difficult situation, we're declaring, "God is alive!"

JOANIE YODER

Instead of complaining about the thorns on roses,
be thankful for the roses among the thorns.

Beginning from the End

JOB 3:20-26

*"May the day of my birth perish, and the night that said,
'A boy is conceived!'"*

JOB 3:3

At age thirty she was ready to give up. She wrote in her diary, "My God, what will become of me? I have no desire but to die." But the dark clouds of despair gave way to the light, and in time she discovered a new purpose for living. When she died at age ninety, she had left her mark on history. Some believe that she and others who introduced antiseptics and chloroform to medicine did more than anyone to relieve human suffering in the nineteenth century.

Her name was Florence Nightingale (1820–1910), founder of the nursing profession.

Job went so far as to wish he had never been born (3:1–3). But thank God, he didn't end his life. Just as Florence Nightingale came out of her depression and found ways to help others, so too Job lived through his grief, and his experience has become a source of endless comfort to suffering souls.

Maybe you're at the point of not wanting to go on. Being God's child intensifies your desperation, for you wonder how a believer could feel so alone and forsaken. Don't give up. Coming to the end of yourself emotionally could be the most painful experience you've ever encountered. But take courage. Cling to the Lord in faith and start all over. God can use this kind of "beginning from the end."

MART DEHAAN

In Christ, the hopeless find hope.

Service and Witness

2 CORINTHIANS 4:1–12

*For what we preach is not ourselves, but Jesus Christ as Lord,
and ourselves as your servants for Jesus' sake.*
2 CORINTHIANS 4:5

While serving as a maid in London, England, in the early part of the twentieth century, Gladys Aylward had other dreams. Her goal was to be a missionary to China. Having been rejected by a Christian missionary organization as "unqualified," Gladys decided to go there on her own. At the age of twenty-eight, she used her life savings to purchase a one-way ticket to Yangcheng, a remote village in China. There she established an inn for trade caravans where she shared Bible stories. Gladys served in other villages as well and became known as Ai-weh-deh, Chinese for "virtuous one."

The apostle Paul also spread the gospel to distant regions of the world. He extended himself as a servant to meet the needs of others (2 Corinthians 11:16–29). He wrote this about serving: "We do not preach ourselves, but Christ Jesus the Lord, and ourselves your bondservants for Jesus' sake" (4:5 NKJV).

Not all of us are called to endure hardship to spread the gospel in distant lands. But each of us is responsible as a servant of God to share Christ with people in our sphere of influence. It's our privilege to help our neighbors, friends, and relatives. Ask God for openings to serve and to talk about Jesus, who gave himself for us.

DENNIS FISHER

We serve God by sharing His Word with others.

Charlie's List

PSALM 119:9-16

Let the message of Christ dwell among you richly as you teach and admonish one another with all wisdom through psalms, hymns, and songs from the Spirit, singing to God with gratitude in your hearts.

COLOSSIANS 3:16

When Charles Hayward died at the age of eighty-seven, he left a legacy for his children and grandchildren. He and his wife Virginia had faithfully served as missionaries for many years both in India and South Africa. But at age seventy-three, he began to select and memorize portions of Scripture so he would "finish well" with his mind full of God's truth.

He called his project "The Whole Bible Memorization Plan." His children call it "Charlie's List." Charles chose a theme verse (Colossians 3:16), at least one verse from each Old Testament book, at least one from each New Testament narrative book, and a verse or verses from each chapter of the New Testament Epistles. He began with Genesis 15:6, "Abram believed the LORD, and he credited it to him as righteousness" and ended with Revelation 22:17, "Let the one who is thirsty come; and let the one who wishes take the free gift of the water of life."

Charles committed 239 verses to memory. He reminds me of the psalmist who wrote: "I have hidden your word in my heart that I might not sin against you" (119:11). Like Charles, the psalmist meditated and delighted in God's Word (vv. 15–16). What better goal could any of us have than to fill our minds with God's truth?

CINDY HESS KASPER

**Memorizing God's Word is like planting seeds
that bear the fruit of a righteous life.**

Doctor Jesus

HEBREWS 13:1–9

Keep your lives free from the love of money and be content with what you have, because God has said, "Never will I leave you; never will I forsake you."
HEBREWS 13:5

Om Seng was an elderly Cambodian widow who had been separated from her children by a long and bitter war. When she walked into the emergency room of a missionary hospital in a Thai refugee camp, she asked to see "Doctor Jesus." She was having terrible pain in her eyes and was haunted by nightmarish memories of cruelty and death.

Although the woman was dressed in the white robes of a Buddhist nun, she was deeply troubled about what would happen to her when she died. The doctors diagnosed her eye condition and cured her. When doctors then told her about this Doctor Jesus she was asking about, she put her trust in Him and found inner healing also.

Om Seng became a shining witness in that refugee camp and formed a church that met in her bamboo-and-thatch house. When it was time for her to return to Cambodia, thirty-seven new believers in Jesus had been baptized. Seng was thankful for everything God had done, but she was apprehensive about what it would be like back in her own country. Would she be free to worship God, or would there be persecution? Her fear turned into peace when she realized that Doctor Jesus would be going back with her.

Jesus is always at our side as Savior, Protector, and Helper. What a wonderful reality!

HERB VANDER LUGT

You need not be afraid of where you're going when you know that God's going with you.

Undeterred Determination

2 CORINTHIANS 5:16–21

*All this is from God, who reconciled us to himself through Christ
and gave us the ministry of reconciliation.*

2 CORINTHIANS 5:18

One of the great privileges of serving as president of both Moody Bible Institute and Cornerstone University was hearing about graduates who impacted the world for Christ. Their stories of sacrifice, perseverance, and passion for the gospel are inspiring.

In the late nineteenth century, Mary McLeod Bethune spent two years studying at Moody in Chicago, training to become a missionary in Africa. But after she graduated, no mission board would give her the opportunity, as an African American woman, to serve on the mission field. Unable to fulfill her dream to go to Africa, she didn't give up on her calling to serve Jesus. Undaunted, she started a small school for African American girls in Florida that would eventually blossom into Bethune-Cookman College. She became a powerful force for change in the status of women.

Mary's legacy was forged by her determination to serve Jesus even in the face of shattered dreams. She knew that God had entrusted to her "the ministry of reconciliation" (2 Corinthians 5:18)—and she wouldn't give up.

That wasn't just a mandate for Mary McLeod Bethune alone. Telling people they can be reconciled to God through Christ is a calling given to all of us. Look for a way to make a difference for Jesus today—right where you are!

JOE STOWELL

**One of the qualities God looks for in His people is a heart
that is willing to serve Him.**

Goats for Jesus

1 JOHN 3:16–20

If anyone has material possessions and sees a brother or sister in need but has no pity on them, how can the love of God be in that person?

1 JOHN 3:17

When Dave and Joy Mueller felt God prompting them to move to Sudan as missionaries, all they knew was that they would be helping to build a hospital in that war-ravaged land. How could they know that goats would be in their future?

As Joy began working with the women there, she discovered that many were widows because of the devastating civil war and had no way to earn a living. So Joy had an idea. If she could provide just one pregnant goat to a woman, that person would have milk and a source of income. To keep the program going, the woman would give the newborn kid back to Joy—but all other products from the goat would be used to support the woman's family. The baby goat would eventually go to another family. The gift of goats given in Jesus's name would change the life of numerous Sudanese women—and open the door for Joy to explain the gospel.

What is your equivalent to goats? What can you give a neighbor, a friend, or even someone you don't know? Is it a ride? An offer to do yardwork? A gift of material resources?

As believers in Christ, we have the responsibility to care for the needs of others (1 John 3:17). Our acts of love reveal that Jesus resides in our hearts, and giving to those in need may help us tell others about Him.

DAVE BRANON

God gives us all we need, so let's give to others in their need.

Turning Pain into Praise

2 CORINTHIANS 1:7–11

No temptation has overtaken you except what is common to mankind. And God is faithful; he will not let you be tempted beyond what you can bear. But when you are tempted, he will also provide a way out so that you can endure it.

1 CORINTHIANS 10:13

After years of a remarkable and fruitful ministry in India, Amy Carmichael became a bedridden sufferer. As the courageous founder and dynamic heart of the Dohnavour Fellowship, she had been instrumental in rescuing hundreds of girls and boys from a terrible life of sexual servitude. All the while she carried on that rescue operation of bringing young people into spiritual freedom through faith in Jesus Christ, she was writing books and especially poems that continue to bless readers around the world.

Then arthritis wracked Amy's body with pain and disabled her. Did she bemoan her affliction or question God? No. Amy was still the guiding inspiration of Dohnavour, and she still kept on writing. Her meditations, letters, and poems are full of praise to God and encouragement to her fellow pilgrims.

When affliction strikes us, how do we react? Are we embittered, or do we trustfully appropriate God's sustaining grace? (1 Corinthians 10:13). And do we prayerfully encourage those around us by our Spirit-enabled cheerfulness, our courage, and our confidence in God?

As we rely on the Lord, He can help us to turn pain into praise.

VERNON GROUNDS

**When you're up to your neck in hot water,
be like a teapot and start to sing.**

Remain Faithful

1 PETER 4:12–19

So then, those who suffer according to God's will should commit themselves to their faithful Creator and continue to do good.

1 PETER 4:19

During the uprisings in Zaire in 1964, the rebels were treating all outsiders with suspicion. Americans and Belgians were particularly despised because their nations were backing the government in power. The day came when the rebel forces rounded up many foreigners, including Al Larson, his wife, and their fellow missionaries.

Al was thrown into a little building with nine other men. Only three were believers, and they made an important decision: They were in Zaire to proclaim Christ and serve Him, and they would continue to do that.

The days that followed were far from pleasant. They lived in constant fear. On two occasions the men were loaded into vehicles and told they were going to be executed.

The Christians continued to witness and serve. Finally, they were dramatically rescued. When those ten men left that little shack for the last time, all of them were believers in Jesus Christ!

Times getting rough? Being persecuted? Under extreme stress? Scared? Make the same decision those believers did, and continue to serve Christ. Even if you are discouraged and feel like quitting, decide that throughout the ordeal you are going to remain faithful.

DAVID EGNER

What we call adversity God calls opportunity.

Unlikely Giants

MATTHEW 3

"I tell you, among those born of women there is no one greater than John;
yet the one who is least in the kingdom of God is greater than he."
LUKE 7:28

Dwight L. Moody was greatly moved by a lay preacher's statement that the world has yet to see what God can do through a person fully yielded to Him. Because an attitude of submission is far more important than outward appearance, some unlikely people have become spiritual giants.

The first time I met Pete, he had a two-day growth of stubble, a missing front tooth, and a suit that looked as if he had slept in it. But I discovered that God was using him in an unusual way to reach disadvantaged people.

And there's Bill Leslie, who Philip Yancey described as "disheveled," "disorganized," and one who "laughed uproariously at his own [bad] jokes." But Yancey pointed out that as pastor of the LaSalle Street Church in Chicago, this man had led many people to Christ and brought great social and economic changes to that part of the city. This unlikely spiritual giant died at age sixty after three decades of work in the inner city.

Pete and Bill remind me of John the Baptist. Although he lived as a recluse and wore a rough, camel's-hair garment, he had a ministry to thousands. Jesus called him the greatest of the prophets (Luke 7:28).

God uses ordinary people, and He wants to use you. Serve Him humbly, zealously, and expectantly.

HERB VANDER LUGT

God uses those who are small in their own eyes.

Road to Blessing

EXODUS 15:22–27

Then Moses cried out to the LORD, and the LORD showed him a piece of wood. He threw it into the water, and the water became fit to drink. There the LORD issued a ruling and instruction for them and put them to the test.

EXODUS 15:25

Robyn and Steve have a counseling ministry that provides very little income. A few years ago, a family crisis forced them to take a 5,000-mile round trip in their well-used minivan. After attending to the crisis, they started back to Michigan. While about 2,000 miles from home, their van began to sputter and stall. A mechanic looked at it and told them, "It's done. You need a new engine."

Unable to afford one, they had no choice but to coax the van home. Three days, a case of oil, and a lot of prayers later, they miraculously limped into their driveway. Then they heard of a "car missionary" who assisted people in ministry. Amazed that the van had made it, he offered to replace the engine free of charge. If Steve had gotten the van fixed en route, it would have cost him thousands of dollars he didn't have.

In Exodus 15, the Israelites were led by God into the desert. Three days into their trip, they ran out of water and had no way to get it. But God knew about the problem. In fact, a solution awaited them in Marah (v. 25) and Elim (v. 27). God not only fixed their water problem but also provided a place to rest.

Even when our situation looks difficult, we can trust that God is leading. He already knows what we'll need when we get there.

DAVE BRANON

Facing an impossibility gives us the opportunity to trust God.

His Highest Blessing

PSALM 23

But he brought his people out like a flock; he led them like sheep through the wilderness. He guided them safely, so they were unafraid; but the sea engulfed their enemies.

PSALM 78:52–53

When John Henry Jowett (1863–1923) was young, he was so intent on pursuing a law career that he didn't ask the Lord what He wanted him to do with his life. One day he met his old Sunday school teacher, who asked him what he was going to do with his many talents. Jowett replied that he was studying to be a lawyer. Disappointed, his friend said, "I've prayed for years that you would go into the ministry."

This startled the brilliant young student and set him to thinking seriously about entering the ministry. Later Jowett, who became an influential British preacher and writer, said, "I then sought God's will and reverently obeyed His call. Now, after thirty-five years in His service, I can say I've never regretted my choice."

Instead of charting our own future, let's seek God's direction. Because His will is based on His infinite love and wisdom, we can be sure that our highest joy and greatest fulfillment will be found in doing what He wants us to do.

If we surrender to God, He will guide us into the place of His special choosing. He always leads us to the calling of greatest usefulness.

As we follow the Lord, life becomes a beautiful adventure. He'll direct our steps along the paths of His highest blessing.

HENRY BOSCH

God may lead you around, but He'll always lead you aright.

Never Alone

MATTHEW 28:16–20

*"[Teach] them to obey everything I have commanded you.
And surely I am with you always, to the very end of the age."*
MATTHEW 28:20

When the famous missionary David Livingstone made his first trip to Africa, some friends accompanied him to the ship to bid him farewell. They loved him deeply and were greatly concerned for his safety in that faraway land. In fact, one of them pleaded with him not to go.

Livingstone, however, was convinced that he was doing God's will. Opening his Bible, he read to his concerned friend Jesus's words, "Lo, I am with you always, even unto the end of the age" (Matthew 28:20 KJV). Then he said, "That, my friend, is the word of a gentleman. So let us be going."

Many years later Livingstone was invited to speak at the University of Glasgow. He posed this question to his audience, "Would you like me to tell you what supported me through all the years of exile among a people whose language I could not understand, and whose attitude toward me was always uncertain and often hostile? It was this: 'Lo, I am with you always, even unto the end of the age.' On these words I staked everything, and they have never failed."

As you serve the Lord, do you sometimes feel neglected, helpless, and alone? Remember the Savior's promise, "I am with you always." With Christ as your companion, you are never alone!

RICHARD DeHAAN

He is not alone who is alone with Jesus.

A Remarkable Life

EPHESIANS 2:1–10

*It is by grace you have been saved, through faith—and this is not
from yourselves, it is the gift of God.*

EPHESIANS 2:8

This is the story of a man with whom I worked. David Haaksma was a remarkable person. Remarkable in his steady demeanor through thirty-three years of service with the same ministry. Remarkable in his gentle, caring love for his wife of thirty years. Remarkable in his unwavering dedication to his children—through triumph and trouble. Remarkable in the respect he earned from coworkers and acquaintances. Remarkable in that when he died too suddenly and too soon at age fifty-six, no one had anything bad to say about him. Remarkable!

Yet as friends and family sat in solemn silence at the funeral, David's pastor put his life in perspective. Family members had extolled David's character and comforted everyone with the assurance that he was in heaven. Then the pastor said, "None of the good things David did earned him one second in heaven. He is there because he accepted God's salvation through Christ."

It's true. No matter how remarkable our lives are, we cannot earn heaven. It's a gift.

Examine your life. As religious and well-loved as you may be, you won't go to heaven unless you accept God's gift of eternal life. Ask Jesus Christ to forgive your sins. That will make your life truly remarkable.

DAVE BRANON

The most exemplary life is nothing without Christ.

How to Be Unpopular

JEREMIAH 23:16–23

*"Woe to the shepherds who are destroying and scattering the sheep
of my pasture!" declares the LORD.*

JEREMIAH 23:1

In 1517, Martin Luther nailed his Ninety-Five Theses to the door of the castle church in Wittenberg, Germany. Luther became known as a reformer, and we remember his bold stand as a turning point in church history.

The fiery priest demonstrated great courage in expressing outrage at the church's practice of selling forgiveness through indulgences, which allowed the people to sin intentionally in exchange for money. Luther's passion to stop these practices did not make him popular with the religious authorities of his day. In fact, his efforts resulted in a series of attempts to silence him.

Long before Luther, the prophet Jeremiah felt the power of God's Word in his heart "like a fire, a fire shut up in my bones. I am weary of holding it in; indeed, I cannot" (Jeremiah 20:9). Jeremiah and Luther refused to allow God's truth to be compromised.

Living for God is about grace and forgiveness, but it's also about boldly standing for the truth. Having God's Word in our heart doesn't always result in warm, pleasant feelings. Sometimes His truth becomes a blazing fire that causes us to challenge corruption—even though we may be attacked for it.

JULIE ACKERMAN LINK

**It's better to declare the truth and be rejected than to
withhold it just to be accepted.**

A Life That Shined

MATTHEW 5:3–16

*In the same way, let your light shine before others, that they may
see your good deeds and glorify your Father in heaven.*
MATTHEW 5:16

According to the International Basketball Federation, basketball is the
world's second-most popular sport, with an estimated 450 million followers
in countries around the globe. In the US, the annual NCAA tournament in
March often brings mention of legendary coach John Wooden. During his
twenty-seven years at UCLA, Wooden's teams won an unprecedented ten
national championship titles. Yet today John Wooden, who died in 2010, is
remembered not just for what he accomplished but for the person he was.

Wooden lived out his Christian faith and his genuine concern for others
in an environment often obsessed with winning. In his autobiography, *They
Call Me Coach*, he wrote, "I always tried to make it clear that basketball is
not the ultimate. It is of small importance in comparison to the total life
we live. There is only one kind of life that truly wins, and that is the one
that places faith in the hands of the Savior. Until that is done, we are on
an aimless course that runs in circles and goes nowhere."

John Wooden honored God in all he did, and his example challenges us
to do the same. Jesus said, "Let your light shine before others, that they may
see your good deeds and glorify your Father in heaven" (Matthew 5:16).

DAVID MCCASLAND

**Let your light shine—whether you're a candle in a corner
or a lighthouse on a hill.**

Mighty in the Scriptures

ACTS 18:24–28

A Jew named Apollos, a native of Alexandria, came to Ephesus.
He was a learned man, with a thorough knowledge of the Scriptures.

ACTS 18:24

Apollos was "an eloquent man, and mighty in the scriptures" (Acts 18:24 KJV). He convinced the Jews by teaching "about Jesus accurately." He was skillful in using God's Word to benefit others.

In a *Moody* magazine article, theologian Wilbur M. Smith (1894–1976) included an interesting story about John A. Broadus, an outstanding scholar, teacher, and preacher of the nineteenth century. Written by a former student, this story describes an incident that took place just nine days before that beloved professor died. The young man remembered that as Broadus was lecturing his class, he paused and said, "Young students, if this were the last time I should ever be permitted to address you, I would feel amply repaid for consuming the whole hour endeavoring to impress upon you these two things: true piety, and, like Apollos, to be men 'mighty in the scriptures.'" The student went on to say that Broadus then paused and stood for a moment with his piercing eyes fixed upon the class. Over and over he repeated in that slow but wonderfully impressive style that was distinctly his, "mighty in the scriptures, mighty in the scriptures." The whole class seemed to be lifted through him into a sacred nearness to the Master.

You may not be an aspiring student, but you should desire to reach the lofty goal spoken of by that godly teacher. Do you long to be mighty in the Scriptures?

RICHARD DEHAAN

Apply yourself wholly to the Scriptures and
the Scriptures wholly to yourself.

When Things Don't Go Well

ROMANS 8:28–30

We know that in all things God works for the good of those who love him,
who have been called according to his purpose.

ROMANS 8:28

The first words that many people like to quote when misfortune hits are: "We know that in all things God works for the good of those who love him, who have been called according to his purpose" (Romans 8:28). But that's hard to believe in hard times. I once sat with a man who had lost his third son in a row, and I listened as he lamented, "How can this tragedy work for my good?" I had no answer but to sit silently and mourn with him.

Tough as Romans 8:28 may be to understand, countless testimonies give credence to the truth of it. The story of hymn writer Fanny Crosby is a classic example. The world is the beneficiary of her memorable hymns, yet what worked together for good was born out of her personal tragedy, for she became blind when she was an infant. At age eight, she began to write poetry and hymns. Writing more than 8,000 sacred songs and hymns, she blessed the world with such popular songs as "Blessed Assurance," "Safe in the Arms of Jesus," and "Pass Me Not, O Gentle Savior." God used her difficulty to bring good for her and us and glory for Him.

When tragedy befalls us, it's hard to understand how anything good can come from it, and we won't always see it in this life. But God, who has good purposes in mind, will always remain with us.

LAWRENCE DARMANI

God always has good purposes for our trials.

Inspired by a Child's Giving

2 CORINTHIANS 9:1–7

Each of you should give what you have decided in your heart to give,
not reluctantly or under compulsion, for God loves a cheerful giver.

2 CORINTHIANS 9:7

One Sunday morning Pastor Larry Browning told his small congregation in Mississippi that the church faced an urgent need for a $1,000 missionary offering. Just before the plates were passed, six-year-old John Jordan leaned over to his mother and said, "Mom, I feel God wants me to give $100." His mother was surprised and at first didn't know what to say. That amount seemed far too much for a young boy to give. Besides, she had already decided to make a sacrificial contribution herself.

When she realized that the youngster was not about to change his mind, she asked the pastor if she could say something. Standing to her feet, she told the congregation what her son wanted to do. The announcement electrified the audience. John's father quickly offered to provide the $100, but the boy shook his head. He said he had saved up that exact amount and wanted to give it to the missionaries so others could find out about Jesus. His words convicted many hearts. Wallets and purses were reopened. When the offering was received and counted, the goal of $1,000 was easily surpassed. The boy's generous spirit had inspired the people to new heights of Christian stewardship.

Open-hearted financial support of the church and its missionary outreach honors the Lord. He loves sacrificial, cheerful givers.

HENRY BOSCH

When love governs the heart, it also guides the hand to the pocketbook.

Great Expectations

PHILIPPIANS 1:12–21

I eagerly expect and hope that I will in no way be ashamed,
but will have sufficient courage so that now as always Christ will be
exalted in my body, whether by life or by death.

PHILIPPIANS 1:20

I once asked a counselor what the major issues were that brought people to him. Without hesitation he said, "The root of many problems is broken expectations; if not dealt with, they mature into anger and bitterness." In our best moments, it's easy to expect that we will find ourselves in a good place surrounded by good people who like and affirm us. But life has a way of breaking those expectations. What then?

Stuck in jail and beset by fellow believers in Rome who didn't like him (Philippians 1:15–16), Paul remained surprisingly upbeat. As he saw it, God had given him a new mission field. While under house arrest, he witnessed to the guards about Christ, an action that sent the gospel into Caesar's house. And even though those opposing him were preaching the gospel from wrong motives, Christ was being preached, so even in that Paul rejoiced (v. 18).

Paul never expected to be in a great place or to be well liked. His only expectation was that "Christ will be exalted" through him (v. 20). He wasn't disappointed.

If our expectation is to make Christ visible to those around us, we will find those expectations met and even exceeded. Christ will be exalted.

JOE STOWELL

Make it your only expectation to magnify Christ wherever you are
and whoever you are with.

Where the Battle Lies

PSALM 40:1–8

"I have brought you glory on earth by finishing the work you gave me to do."
JOHN 17:4

Miriam Booth, daughter of the founder of the Salvation Army, was a brilliant and cultured woman who began her Christian work with great promise and unusual success. Very soon, however, disease brought her to the point of death. A friend told her it seemed a pity that a woman of her capabilities should be hindered by sickness from doing the Lord's work. With deep insight and gentle grace, Miriam replied, "It's wonderful to do the Lord's work, but it's greater still to do the Lord's will!"

Commenting on John 17:4, blind minister and hymn writer George Matheson said, "Was the work of the Master indeed done? Was not His heaviest task yet to come? He had not yet met the dread hour of death. Why did He say, then, that His work was done? It was because He knew that when the will is given, the battle is ended! . . . The cup which our Father gives us to drink is a cup of the will. It is easy for the lips to drain it when once the heart has accepted it. . . . The act is easy after the choice."

Yes, that is where the battle lies. If, like Jesus, we delight to do the Father's will, then the work He assigns will be done with grace and without hesitation, no matter what the personal sacrifice may be.

HENRY BOSCH

The best way to know God's will is to say "I will" to God.

Still Say "Hallelujah"

PSALM 34:1–10, 19

I will extol the LORD at all times; his praise will always be on my lips.
PSALM 34:1

This story from the childhood of a missionary named Mary D. Kimbrough warmed my heart. It was during the Great Depression in America, and money was scarce. When winter came, Mary's family was concerned because her father, who was employed in a local bakery, had been injured and was unable to work. Their money was soon gone, and their flour bin was empty.

Her devout mother never lost faith, however, that God would supply their needs. She had determined with the psalmist to bless "the LORD at all times" (34:1); so she said, "Who still has faith to say 'hallelujah' although we have an empty flour bin?" Without exception, they all praised the Lord and said, "Hallelujah!"

A few minutes later the phone rang. It was the baker. "A batch of bread was burned," he said. "Could you folks use some?" "Could we!" Mary and her two little sisters were dancing about with joy when the bread man arrived and began piling golden brown loaves of bread, buns, and cookies on their kitchen table. Recalls Mary, "They weren't burned—just a bit too brown to sell—but they were delicious to our family who had fully trusted God for our daily bread."

Have you ever stood facing an "empty bin" when earthly resources seemed at an end and the prospects for the future were dim? Did you have the grace then to turn it all over to the Lord without murmuring? You will find He will never let you down if you just have faith to say "hallelujah" anyway!

HENRY BOSCH

**Praise in desperate straits is faith at work—
and such faith can move mountains!**

Looking for Good Fruit

MATTHEW 12:33–45

A good man brings good things out of the good stored up in him, and an evil man brings evil things out of the evil stored up in him.

MATTHEW 12:35

Many years ago, I saw the Lord transform a notorious drunkard in the town where I was pastoring a church.

Before that, though, whenever I tried to interact with him, he was rude to me. He was also crude in the way he criticized the Christian people of his community.

But for some reason he started attending our church, and it wasn't long before he trusted Christ as his Savior. As a result of his conversion, he was miraculously delivered from his drinking habit. I recall meeting a man in a store who asked me, "Pastor, what did you do to Joe? The change in him is unbelievable." Several others called me to give me names of people for whom they were burdened.

Although Joe was a babe in Christ he had become "a good man." And out of his life began to come "good things." He was a living example of the fact that if you make a tree good it produces good fruit.

If you are concerned about whether or not your faith is real, take a look at your life. Are you bearing good fruit? Has your faith made you a better person? If it isn't doing this, acknowledge your spiritual need, confess your sin, and receive Jesus Christ as your Savior. Let Him produce "good fruit" through a transformed life.

HERB VANDER LUGT

Man needs more than a new start—he needs a new heart.

How Can We Keep from Singing?

PSALM 146

I will praise the LORD all my life; I will sing praise to my God as long as I live.
PSALM 146:2

Robert Lowry (1826–1899) felt that preaching would be his greatest contribution in life. However, this pastor is best remembered for his gospel music and hymns. Lowry composed words or music for more than 500 songs, including "Christ Arose," "I Need Thee Every Hour," and "Shall We Gather at the River?"

In 1860, as the United States teetered on the brink of civil war, Lowry wrote these enduring words that focus not on threatening circumstances but on the unchanging Christ:

> *What though my joys and comforts die?*
> *The Lord my Savior liveth;*
> *What though the darkness gather round!*
> *Songs in the night He giveth:*
> *No storm can shake my inmost calm*
> *While to that refuge clinging;*
> *Since Christ is Lord of Heav'n and earth,*
> *How can I keep from singing?*

Lowry's confidence in God during difficult times echoes the psalmist's words: "Do not put your trust in princes, in human beings, who cannot save. . . . Blessed are those whose help is the God of Jacob, whose hope is in the LORD their God" (Psalm 146:3–5).

Whether we react to life with faith or fear depends on our focus. Knowing that "the LORD reigns forever" (v. 10), how can we keep from singing?

DAVID McCASLAND

If you keep in tune with Christ, you can sing even in the dark.

Dying for Justice

DEUTERONOMY 24:14–22

Remember that you were slaves in Egypt and the LORD your God redeemed you from there. That is why I command you to do this.
DEUTERONOMY 24:18

When Presbyterian clergyman Elijah Lovejoy (1802–1837) left the pulpit, he returned to the printing presses in order to reach more people. After witnessing a lynching, Lovejoy committed to fighting the injustice of slavery. His life was threatened by hateful mobs, but this did not stop him: "If by compromise is meant that I should cease from my duty, I cannot make it. I fear God more than I fear man. Crush me if you will, but I shall die at my post." Four days after these words, he was killed at the hands of another angry mob.

Concern about justice for the oppressed is evident throughout Scripture. It was especially clear when God established the rules for His covenant people after they were released from Egyptian bondage (Deuteronomy 24:18–22). Moses emphasized concern for the underprivileged (Exodus 22:22–27; 23:6–9; Leviticus 19:9–10). Repeatedly, the Israelites were reminded that they had been slaves in Egypt and should deal justly with the underprivileged in their community. They were to love strangers ("foreigners") because God loves them, and the Israelites had themselves been foreigners in Egypt (Exodus 23:9; Leviticus 19:34; Deuteronomy 10:17–19).

God desires that His people affirm the supreme worth of every individual by fighting against injustice.

MARVIN WILLIAMS

Standing for justice means fighting against injustice.

Caught in the Darkness

COLOSSIANS 2:1–10

See to it that no one takes you captive through hollow and deceptive philosophy, which depends on human tradition and the elemental spiritual forces of this world rather than on Christ.

COLOSSIANS 2:8

Marolyn Wragg knew she should be attending church, but she found excuses not to. She had professed faith in Christ years before, but she never read her Bible. Therefore, when a couple of cult missionaries came to her door, she was easy prey for their teachings. For five years she was part of their group, which taught that to be saved a person had to depend on its complex system of salvation—not on Christ alone.

But God kept working on Marolyn, and eventually she left the cult. She had been invited to a Bible-believing church, where she discovered major differences between the teachings of the cult and the teachings of Scripture. When she asked Christ to forgive her waywardness, she "felt once again the peace and joy that comes from trusting fully in Jesus." In recounting her story, she commented, "I know now the importance of regular attendance in a Bible-teaching church, and of diligent Bible study."

Many Christians are swept away by crafty religionists who profess to have answers not based on God's Word. But they lead people into the darkness of man-made traditions that are "not according to Christ" (Colossians 2:8 NKJV).

Be on guard. If you have accepted Christ as your Savior, you are complete in Him. You don't need any other gospel. Don't let anyone confuse you.

DAVE BRANON

Christ is the only way to heaven; all other paths are detours to doom.

The Heat of Our Desire

PSALM 42

As the deer pants for streams of water, so my soul pants for you, my God.
PSALM 42:1

Pastor A. W. Tozer (1897–1963) read the great Christian theologians until he could write about them with ease. He challenges us: "Come near to the holy men and women of the past and you will soon feel the heat of their desire after God. They mourned for Him, they prayed and wrestled and sought for Him day and night, in season and out, and when they had found Him the finding was all the sweeter for the long seeking."

The writer of Psalm 42 had the kind of longing for the Lord that Tozer wrote about. Feeling separated from God, the psalmist used the simile of a deer panting with thirst to express his deep yearning for a taste of the presence of God. "As the deer pants for streams of water, so my soul pants for you, my God. My soul thirsts for God, for the living God" (vv. 1–2). The heat of his desire for the Lord was so great and his sorrow so intense, he did more weeping than eating (v. 3). But the psalmist's longing was satisfied when he placed his hope in God and praised Him for His presence and help (vv. 5–8).

Oh that we would have a longing and thirsting for God that is so intense others would feel the heat of our desire for Him!

MARVIN WILLIAMS

Only Jesus, the Living Water, can satisfy the thirsty soul.

"The Man Behind the Church"

ROMANS 16:1–16

I commend to you our sister Phoebe, a deacon of the church in Cenchreae.
ROMANS 16:1

Pastor Clint Eastman, writing in *Decision* magazine, told of an experience he had in Jamaica. He was there with others from Massachusetts to help erect a small cement-block church building.

One day a sudden storm interrupted the work, and he and a Jamaican man named Daniel sought shelter together. As they watched the rain, Eastman asked, "Are you an officer in the church?" "No," Daniel replied. "I'm the man behind the church." He meant he was not one to be up front in the church—pastor, teacher, board member—but one who stayed in the background, doing all sorts of things to keep the church functioning.

In our Scripture reading today, Paul commended many people like Phoebe, who worked hard in their congregations. In my home church, George Monroe was one of those kinds of people. "Let George do it," we joked whenever we needed a window replaced, a cabinet built, or a leak fixed.

No service we do for the Lord is unimportant. So, if you're the Daniel or George or the Phoebe behind your church, be encouraged. And if you have people like this in your congregation, be grateful—your church is truly blessed of God. And be sure to thank them every once in a while. They're invaluable!

DAVID EGNER

Service for Christ is never insignificant.

The Prayers of a Little Girl

MATTHEW 5:43–48

I tell you, love your enemies and pray for those who persecute you.
MATTHEW 5:44

The prayers of Christians should extend beyond the circle of family, friends, and missionaries. We are also to pray for those we don't get along with, for people on the fringe areas of our lives, and even for our enemies.

In *Christianity Today*, psychiatrist Robert Cole told an amazing story of a girl who had learned to pray for those who were hostile to her. Cole was in New Orleans in 1960 when a federal judge ruled that the city schools must be integrated. A six-year-old girl, Ruby Bridges, was the only black child to attend the William T. Franz School. Every day for weeks as she entered and left the building, a mob would be standing outside to scream at her and threaten her. They shook their fists, shouted obscenities, and threatened to kill her. One day her teacher saw her lips moving as she walked through the crowd, flanked by burly federal marshals. When the teacher told Cole about it, he asked Ruby if she was talking to the people. "I wasn't talking to them," she replied. "I was just saying a prayer for them." Cole asked her why, she said, "Because they need praying for."

This little first-grader gave us a stirring example of the fact that it is possible to pray for our enemies.

Like Ruby Bridges, we can learn to pray for those who persecute us.

DAVID EGNER

Nothing makes us love our enemies so much as praying for them.

Jailed to Free Others

HEBREWS 11:1-6, 32-40

As the body without the spirit is dead, so faith without deeds is dead.
JAMES 2:26

The missionary had been in jail for more than two weeks. He was stuck behind bars in a Kosovo prison because he had tried to tell others about Jesus Christ.

Other missionaries tried to negotiate for his freedom, but day after day they were turned down. Eventually they received the good news that their friend would soon be released, so they went to the jail to tell him.

The missionaries discovered that their friend had been witnessing to his fellow inmates, and when they told him that he was about to be let out of jail, he said, "No, not yet. Give me another week. I need more time to share the gospel with these people."

What does it take for a person to be so burdened for others that he is willing to stay locked up so he can continue to proclaim the gospel? First, it takes an unwavering faith that Jesus Christ is the only way to heaven (John 14:6; Hebrews 11:1–6) and that life without Him leads to a hopeless future. Second, it takes a faith that God is in control and that He can be trusted with our lives when we are not in control at all (Proverbs 3:5–6; Hebrews 11:32–40). And third, it takes a faith that results in action—not just thoughts and words (James 2:26).

Do we have that kind of faith?

DAVE BRANON

True faith produces a life full of actions, not a head full of facts.

No Greater Joy

3 JOHN 1:1–8

I have no greater joy than to hear that my children are walking in the truth.

3 JOHN 1:4

Bob and Evon Potter were a fun-loving couple with three young sons when their life took a new direction. In 1956 they attended a Billy Graham Crusade in Oklahoma City and gave their lives to Christ. Before long, they wanted to reach out to others to share their faith and the truth about Christ, so they opened their home every Saturday night to high school and college students who had a desire to study the Bible. A friend invited me, and I became a regular at the Potters' house.

This was a serious Bible study that included lesson preparation and memorizing Scripture. Surrounded by an atmosphere of friendship, joy, and laughter, we challenged each other, and the Lord changed our lives during those days.

I stayed in touch with the Potters over the years and received many cards and letters from Bob, who always signed them with these words: "I have no greater joy than to hear that my children are walking in the truth" (3 John 1:4). Like John writing to his "dear friend Gaius" (v. 1), Bob encouraged everyone who crossed his path to keep walking with the Lord.

A few years ago, I attended Bob's memorial service. It was a joyful occasion filled with people still walking the road of faith—all because of a young couple who opened their home and their hearts to help others find the Lord.

DAVID McCASLAND

Be a voice of encouragement to someone today.

When Did We See You Sick?

MATTHEW 25:31–40

*"The King will reply, 'Truly I tell you, whatever you did for one of the least
of these brothers and sisters of mine, you did for me.'"*
MATTHEW 25:40

When Ana first entered the hospital in Madrid, Spain, missionary Rose Anne Thornburgh offered to come and visit her and do whatever she could to ease her suffering. Little did Rose Anne realize how much time and energy would be required. You see, she didn't know that Ana was not going to get better. She had AIDS.

This made no difference to Rose Anne, however. Every day for months she faithfully visited the Madrid hospital where Ana lay. She would rub Ana's arms and back when they hurt. She would read the Bible to her. She would pray. Sometimes she would just hold Ana in her arms and comfort her. Day after day after day, Rose Anne continued her mission of love.

Matthew 25:40 sets forth the principle that Jesus identifies with those who are deprived and oppressed. And people who minister to the hungry, the thirsty, the stranger, the naked, the sick, and the prisoner are actually serving Him. Although the passage refers to events just prior to His return to earth, the truth applies today.

Like Rose Anne, are we willing to offer our help, even before we know the whole story? Would our commitment be any different if it were Jesus himself who needed our assistance? Remember what Jesus said in Matthew 25:40.

DAVE BRANON

If you would live for Christ, live for others.

Witnessing with Grace and Power

ACTS 20:16–27

*With great power the apostles continued to testify to the resurrection of the
Lord Jesus. And God's grace was so powerfully at work in them all.*

ACTS 4:33

Under the control of the Holy Spirit the apostles witnessed with great
power. As a result, great grace was the wondrous experience of all who
assembled with them. Still today we need zealous teachers and Spirit-
filled people who will proclaim the story of Jesus's redeeming sacrifice and
transforming love to a needy world.

Whenever we need an example of a Christ-centered witness, we can
always turn to Paul. No matter what the personal cost, he never shrank
from hardship or peril.

A missionary who reminds me of Paul's dedication was John Geddie
(1815–1872), a Canadian missionary to an island in the South Pacific.
Although in constant peril of his life, he won the confidence of the people
who inhabited the island. After studying their language, he developed
an alphabet for them and translated into their dialect the entire New
Testament and a number of hymns. One by one those who came to his
little mission station to be taught by him turned from superstition to Jesus.
Several churches were built, and by 1854 more than half of the 4,000
people had become Christians. Many of them set out for the neighboring
islands to give the good news to others.

It wasn't easy, but John Geddie witnessed about the gospel "with great
power."

HENRY BOSCH

**Don't be afraid to go out on a limb for God—
that's where the fruit is!**

Are You Struggling?

HEBREWS 12:1–17

Therefore, since we are surrounded by such a great cloud of witnesses,
let us throw off everything that hinders and the sin that so easily entangles.
And let us run with perseverance the race marked out for us.

HEBREWS 12:1

I was in my second year of widowhood and I was struggling. Morning after morning my prayer life consisted of one daily sigh: "Lord, I shouldn't be struggling like this!" One morning, His still, small voice asked me from within: "And why not?"

Then the answer came—unrecognized pride! Somehow I had thought that a person of my spiritual maturity should be beyond such struggle. What a ridiculous thought, since I had never been a widow before and needed the freedom to be a true learner, even a struggling learner.

At the same time, I was reminded of the story of a man who took home a cocoon so he could watch the emperor moth emerge. As the moth struggled to get through the tiny opening, the man enlarged it with the snip of his scissors. The moth emerged easily—but its wings were shriveled. The struggle through the narrow opening is God's way to force fluid from its body into its wings. The "merciful" snip, in reality, was cruel.

Hebrews 12 describes the Christian life as an effort that involves discipline, correction, and training in righteousness. Surely such a race could not be run without a holy striving against self and sin. Sometimes the struggle is exactly what we need.

JOANIE YODER

God's chastening is compassionate, never cruel.

Times and Seasons

ECCLESIASTES 3:1–8

There is a time for everything, and a season for every activity under the heavens.
ECCLESIASTES 3:1

The Rev. Gardner Taylor has been called "the dean of American preaching." Born in Louisiana in 1918, the grandson of slaves, he overcame the segregation of his youth to become the pastor of a large New York congregation and a leader in the struggle for racial equality. For six decades he traveled the world as a much sought-after preacher.

But at age eighty-nine, Rev. Taylor's health gave way, and he could no longer accept speaking engagements. He told Rachel Zoll of the Associated Press: "I at first felt rather crestfallen." But then he spoke of his belief that "there are seasons and eras, and we have to see what they are as best as we can, and to find what is positive in them."

In an effort to face the challenges of life, we often turn to Solomon's words: "There is a time for everything, and a season for every activity under the heavens" (Ecclesiastes 3:1). But we readily admit that we would rather laugh than weep, dance than mourn, and gain than lose (vv. 4, 6).

We know, however, that as we embrace the lessons and opportunities of every season that comes to us, we find that "God is our refuge and strength" (Psalm 46:1).

Whatever season we're in, it's always the season to trust in Him.

DAVID MCCASLAND

Whatever the season of life, attitude makes all the difference.

Say So

ROMANS 10:1–13

*Through Jesus, therefore, let us continually offer to God a sacrifice of praise—
the fruit of lips that openly profess his name.*

HEBREWS 13:15

Mel Trotter was a drunken barber whose salvation changed the lives of thousands. He was saved in 1897 in Chicago at the Pacific Garden Mission and was soon named director of the City Rescue Mission in Grand Rapids (Now Mel Trotter Ministries).

Thirty-five years later, at a meeting at the mission, Mel was conducting "Say-So" time. He asked people in the crowd to testify how Jesus had saved them. That night, a fourteen-year-old boy stood up and said simply, "I'm glad Jesus saved me. Amen." Trotter remarked, "That's the finest testimony I ever heard." Encouraged by those words from such an important leader, that teenager, Mel Johnson, went on to become a Christian leader in his own right. Today the Mel Johnson Media Center on the campus of the University of Northwestern in St. Paul, Minnesota, stands as a testament to his efforts in communicating the gospel. Young Mel was encouraged to say so, and he did. Six little words, followed by an encouraging comment led to a life of service for God.

Let's look for opportunities to offer "the fruit of [our] lips," to tell others that Jesus is Lord and that He saved us. Tell your own salvation story, and ask others to share theirs as well—as a "sacrifice of praise" (Hebrews 13:15). Whether we are children, teens, or adults, we who belong to Jesus Christ need to stand up and "say so."

DAVE BRANON

The more you love Jesus, the more you'll talk about Him.

Arranging Your Mind

PHILIPPIANS 4:4–9

Rejoice in the Lord always. I will say it again: Rejoice!
PHILIPPIANS 4:4

Several years ago, I read a story about a ninety-two-year-old Christian woman who was legally blind. In spite of her limitation, she was always neatly dressed, with her hair carefully brushed and her makeup tastefully applied. Each morning she would meet the new day with eagerness.

After her husband of seventy years died, it became necessary for her to go to a nursing home where she could receive proper care. On the day of the move, a helpful neighbor drove her there and guided her into the lobby. Her room wasn't ready, so she waited patiently in the lobby for several hours.

When an attendant finally came for her, she smiled sweetly as she maneuvered her walker to the elevator. The staff member described her room to her, including the new curtains that had been hung on the windows. "I love it," she declared. "But Mrs. Jones, you haven't seen your room yet," the attendant replied. "That doesn't have anything to do with it," she said. "Happiness is something you choose. Whether I like my room or not doesn't depend on how it's arranged. It's how I arrange my mind."

The Bible says, "Rejoice in the Lord" (Philippians 4:4). Remind yourself often of all that Jesus has given to you and be thankful. That's how to arrange your mind.

DAVID ROPER

The happiness of your life depends on the quality of your thoughts.

The Lord Will Provide

PSALM 37:16−26

My God will meet all your needs according to the riches of his glory in Christ Jesus.
PHILIPPIANS 4:19

A needy widow in Chicago lived by the motto: "The Lord will provide." Even when severely tested, Mrs. Hokanson never lost her ready smile and triumphant faith. Casting her care on God (1 Peter 5:7), she found that He always took the burden and supplied the needed blessing.

Mrs. Hokanson was the sole support for her disabled son. Eventually, chronic arthritis confined her to bed. When a church youth group went to Mrs. Hokanson's house to cheer her up, they were amazed to discover that she was not depressed. They inquired, "Now what will you and Arthur do?" She gave her usual quiet, confident response, "The Lord will provide."

When Mrs. Hokanson died, many people wondered what would happen to her son. But when friends and neighbors went home with Arthur after the funeral, he proudly showed them his collection of stamps. Instead of tearing the stamps off the envelopes, he had intercepted and kept scores of letters intended for his mother and left them unopened. Many contained substantial gifts—enough to care for the boy for the rest of his life.

When we cast all our cares on the Lord, we'll be amazed at the wondrous way He provides!

HENRY BOSCH

Our needs can never exhaust God's supply.

Working on the Inside

2 CORINTHIANS 4:8–18

*Therefore we do not lose heart. Though outwardly we are wasting away,
yet inwardly we are being renewed day by day.*

2 CORINTHIANS 4:16

It was a typical summer Sunday evening service. People were scattered throughout the five-hundred-seat auditorium. There was a testimony time, and several people spoke up, sharing from their hearts what God had done.

Then Buddy stood and talked. He was grateful he could be in church. When he told us that even though he didn't have a ride he was glad he was able to walk the mile or so to church, you could hear the others respond in surprise. On this Sunday night when so many had found reasons to stay away from church, Buddy had come alone, one dark step at a time. Buddy is blind.

We can learn a lot from him. He struggles to do things we can do with little effort, but often neglect. He is more aware perhaps than those of us without physical disabilities that "outwardly we are wasting away" (2 Corinthians 4:16), so he works hard at feeding his "inward man" by meeting with other believers. He knows what the apostle Paul knew: It is only through a strong reliance on the Lord that we can succeed in our Christian life.

Buddy did not lose heart when he had to walk to church in his blindness. May his example help us to stop letting outward things halt our inner growth.

DAVE BRANON

Discipleship requires discipline.

A Good Man

ROMANS 3:10-18

*For it is by grace you have been saved, through faith—
and this is not from yourselves, it is the gift of God.*
EPHESIANS 2:8

"Jerry was a good man," the pastor said at Jerald Stevens's memorial service. "He loved his family. He was faithful to his wife. He served his country in the armed services. He was an excellent dad and grandfather. He was a great friend."

But then the pastor went on to tell the friends and family gathered that Jerry's good life and good deeds were not enough to assure him a place in heaven. And that Jerry himself would have been the first to tell them that!

Jerry believed these words from the Bible: "All have sinned and fall short of the glory of God" (Romans 3:23) and "the wages of sin is death" (6:23). Jerry's final and eternal destination in life's journey was not determined by whether he lived a really good life but entirely by Jesus dying in his place to pay sin's penalty. He believed that each of us must personally accept the free gift of God, which is "eternal life in Christ Jesus our Lord" (6:23).

Jerry was a good man, but he could never be "good enough." And neither can we. It is only by grace that we can be saved through faith. And that has absolutely nothing to do with our human efforts. "It is the gift of God" (Ephesians 2:8).

"Thanks be to God for his indescribable gift!" (2 Corinthians 9:15).

CINDY HESS KASPER

We are not saved by good works, but by God's work.

The River of God

PSALM 65

*The streams of God are filled with water to provide the people with grain,
for so you have ordained it.*

PSALM 65:9

When I was fifteen, I heard a story from missionary pioneer Johanna Veenstra, and it encouraged me the rest of my life.

I recall that she spoke about the terrible droughts that often visited a certain section of the territory she lived in while ministering in Sudan, Africa. But she also mentioned a stream that ran from the springs in the hills to her village. It never ran dry, even when all the rest of the country was parched.

She told of the joy of the local people who were able to glean the drinking water necessary for their survival because this crystal tributary flowed from the higher plateaus. Here is the application to that story, an application that I've never forgotten: "In this world," she said, "our pleasures often dry up, and we live in the arid country of sorrow and disappointment; but praise the Lord, 'the river of God' is 'full of water!' In our trials we can always go to Him and find the refreshment for our soul we so sorely need. When the nether springs dry up, the river of His pleasure and blessing is still available to us."

If you are experiencing spiritual drought in your Christian life, drink from the "streams of God." Find there the comfort and reviving of spirit you so desperately need. Never forget that "the streams of God are filled with water!"

HENRY BOSCH

**The promises of God put a rainbow of hope in every cloud
and an oasis of refreshment in every desert.**

Looking for Hope

PSALM 42:5–11

Why, my soul, are you downcast? Why so disturbed within me? Put your hope in God, for I will yet praise him, my Savior and my God.

PSALM 42:5

A missionary in India lay burning with the fever of malaria. As the disease sapped her strength, a feeling of depression dragged her into the depths of despair. She felt so overwhelmed that she asked God to take her to heaven. But one day, while enclosed in this cocoon of discouragement, the sounds of music drifted into her room from another part of the house. A group of Indian young people were having a worship service. She heard them sing in their dialect, "I have decided to follow Jesus; no turning back, no turning back." The song touched her heart and she began praying. Soon prayer graduated to praise, and God lifted her discouragement. Not long afterward, her health returned. For many years after that, she continued to spread God's hope to others.

Can you relate to her experience? Have you known discouragement so deep that it can make you want to give up? Have you felt such a burden of depression that you have raised David's question, "Why, my soul, are you downcast? Why so disturbed within me?" (Psalm 42:11).

David had not only the problem but also the solution. "Hope in God," he said. The encouragement of God's presence will bring praise to your heart and renewed faithfulness to your walk. Sing from your deepest being, "I have decided to follow Jesus; no turning back, no turning back." When you trust Jesus, you'll find hope.

PAUL VAN GORDER

If you're having trouble coping, try hoping—in God.

Ascended!

2 CORINTHIANS 5:1–8

*We are confident, I say, and would prefer to be away from the body
and at home with the Lord.*

2 CORINTHIANS 5:8

Joseph Parker (1830–1902) was a beloved English preacher in the Congregational denomination. When his wife died, he didn't have the customary wording inscribed on her gravestone. Instead of the word *Died* followed by the date of her death, he chose the word *Ascended*.

Joseph Parker found great comfort in being reminded that though his wife's body had been placed in the grave, the "real" Mrs. Parker had been transported to heaven—into the presence of her Savior. When Parker himself died, it's no wonder that his friends made sure his gravestone read: "Ascended November 28, 1902."

When a loved one dies in the Lord, or when we face dying ourselves, there's great comfort in the fact that "to be away from the body" is to be "at home with the Lord." Death for us is not a dark journey into the unknown. It is not a lonely walk into a strange and friendless place. Rather, it is a glorious transition from the trials of earth into the joys of heaven, where we will be reunited with our loved ones in Christ who have gone before. Best of all, we will enjoy the presence of our Lord forever.

When a believer dies, the body is buried but not the soul. It has ascended!

RICHARD DeHAAN

For the Christian, death is the doorway to glory.

Rainbow of Promise

GENESIS 9:8–17

*Let us hold unswervingly to the hope we profess,
for he who promised is faithful.*
HEBREWS 10:23

In the years after the great flood, Noah must have felt amazing confidence and assurance every time he saw a rainbow in the sky. The bow was a reminder from God of His covenant with Noah. Even today we think of the rainbow as a sign that God keeps His promises. That thought can brighten the darkened sky of our trials and testings!

A widowed missionary was returning by plane to the jungles of Irian Jaya where her husband had died. As the small plane made its way to the remote outpost where she planned to continue her service to God, it flew between mountains and over dense jungle valleys. As it did, she suddenly began to ask herself, "Why am I here?" The death of her husband, the increased responsibility for her family, the resumption of demanding labor among people in an undeveloped country—all of this and more troubled her. As they neared her mission outpost, the pilot said, "Look!" Below them she saw a full circle rainbow with the dark, tiny outline of her little village in the center of that circle. "Thank you, Lord," she prayed. "I'm in the center of your rainbow of promise."

When you face life's difficulties—whether a sudden squall of testing or a prolonged storm of trial—try this: Repeat all of the promises from God's Word that relate to your difficulty. As you do, every problem becomes an opportunity for the Lord to ring the sullen sky with His "rainbow of promise."

PAUL VAN GORDER

The believer's future is as bright as the promises of God.

Be Specific

JAMES 5:13–18

Elijah was a human being, even as we are. He prayed earnestly that it would not rain, and it did not rain on the land for three and a half years.

JAMES 5:17

If you've ever bought ice cream for a group of youngsters, you know they will request as many varieties as there are children. "I want raspberry!" "Make mine vanilla!" "I like mint chocolate chip!"

When we pray, we often fail to be that specific. We say, "Lord, bless my friends. Help the missionaries." In some cases, of course, it may be difficult to know the exact need, and we must rely on God's Spirit to help us pray in the Father's will (Romans 8:26). Yet God's Word tells us to ask specifically (Matthew 7:7–11).

Eighteen-year-old Hudson wandered into his father's library and read a gospel tract. He couldn't shake off its message. Finally, falling to his knees, he accepted Christ as his Savior. Later, his mother, who had been away for an extended time, returned home. When Hudson told her the good news, she said, "I already know. Ten days ago, the very date on which you told me you read that tract, I spent the entire afternoon in prayer for you until the Lord assured me that my wayward son had been brought into the fold." So the specific prayer was answered for Hudson Taylor, who would become one of the greatest missionaries of the nineteenth century.

Such experiences may not be the norm, but when God gives a particular burden He wants us to ask for a definite answer. Be specific.

HENRY BOSCH

The best prayers are specific requests, not vague generalities.

Grey Power

JOSHUA 14:6–12

*I am still as strong today as the day Moses sent me out; I'm just as vigorous
to go out to battle now as I was then.*

JOSHUA 14:11

Dutch artist Yoni Lefevre created a project called "Grey Power" to show the vitality of the aging generation in the Netherlands. She asked local schoolchildren to sketch their grandparents. Lefevre wanted to show an "honest and pure view" of older people, and she believed children could help supply this. The youngsters' drawings reflected a fresh and lively perspective of their elders—grandmas and grandpas were shown playing tennis, gardening, painting, and more!

Caleb of ancient Israel was vital into his senior years. As a young man, he infiltrated the Promised Land before the Israelites conquered it. He believed God would help his nation defeat the Canaanites, but the other spies disagreed (Joshua 14:8). Because of Caleb's faith, God miraculously sustained his life for forty-five years so he could enter the Promised Land. When it was finally time to enter Canaan, eighty-five-year-old Caleb said, "I am just as vigorous to go out to battle now as I was then" (v. 11). With God's help, Caleb successfully claimed his share of the land (Numbers 14:24).

God does not forget about us as we grow older. Although our bodies age and our health may fail, God's Holy Spirit renews us inwardly each day (2 Corinthians 4:16). He makes it possible for our lives to have significance at every stage and every age.

JENNIFER BENSON SCHULDT

**With God's strength behind you and His arms beneath you,
you can face whatever lies ahead of you.**

Armed for the Fray

EPHESIANS 6:10–18

*Put on the full armor of God, so that you can take your
stand against the devil's schemes.*

EPHESIANS 6:11

Paul the apostle, a spiritual warrior, testified as he came to the end of his embattled life: "I have fought the good fight, I have finished the race, I have kept the faith" (2 Timothy 4:7).

Years earlier, that valiant soldier of Jesus Christ had pleaded with his fellow Christians to put on the armor of God that would enable them to stand firm in their conflict with the powers of darkness. He knew the vital importance of donning that armor every day. In his service for Christ, Paul had been whipped, beaten, stoned, and imprisoned, and was often hungry, thirsty, cold, and weary (2 Corinthians 11:22–28).

Strapping on the belt of truth, the breastplate of righteousness, the shoes of peace, the shield of faith, the helmet of salvation, and the sword of the Spirit (God's Word) enabled Paul to "extinguish all the flaming arrows of the evil one" (Ephesians 6:14–17). When we put on God's armor, we too are fully covered and prepared for battle.

The prince of darkness with his hosts of demonic helpers is an incredibly crafty foe. That's why we need to guard against his deceitful devices and put on the whole armor of God every day. When we do, like Paul when he was nearing the end of his days, we can be confident that we have "kept the faith."

VERNON GROUNDS

God's armor is tailor-made for you, but you must put it on.

Ex-Con in the Neighborhood

1 PETER 2:1–12

*Let your light shine before others, that they may see your good deeds
and glorify your Father in heaven.*
MATTHEW 5:16

Roddy Roderique had served seventeen years of a life sentence and was appealing for an early release before the high court in Montreal. His pastor, Charles Seidenspinner, was testifying on his behalf.

"Why should this man be released?" asked the Crown Attorney.

"Because God has come into his life and changed him, and He will hold him steady," replied the pastor.

"What do you mean 'God has come into his life?'" asked the judge. He listened thoughtfully as the pastor shared in detail how Christ transforms a life. The judge then asked a loaded question: "Suppose this man is released. Would you want him for a neighbor?" "Your Honor," said the pastor, "that would be wonderful! Some of my neighbors need to hear the same message that changed his life." Roddy was released, and today he's living for the Lord and is active in his church.

As forgiven sinners, all Christians are "ex-cons" who praise the One who has called us out of darkness (1 Peter 2:9). When our lives are characterized by honorable conduct, they are strong evidence for truth to those who might speak against us (v. 12).

Lord, may my words and actions convince people in my neighborhood of their need for Jesus.

DENNIS DEHAAN

Jesus can change the foulest sinners into the finest saints.

Better Than Your Best

COLOSSIANS 1:19–29

*To this end I strenuously contend with all the energy
Christ so powerfully works in me.*
COLOSSIANS 1:29

When John became a salesman in a well-known insurance company, his aim was to work effectively in his firm without compromising his Christian integrity. But there were those who considered him naive. In their view, one could possess job security or Christian integrity—but not both.

But John did not waver in his commitment to be a godly witness in the business world. Although he was in a job that required accurate calculations, he had a weakness when it came to simple arithmetic. This forced him to depend more on Christ in everything, which enhanced his witness.

John eventually became the company's top salesman, and God used him to win many colleagues to Christ. Later, as branch manager, John and his team became the company's largest branch worldwide—all without compromising Christian integrity.

Are you striving to live and work without compromise in a tough place? Are you doing your best, but your best is not enough? Colossians 1:29 reminds us that dependence on God's mighty power within us is what makes us effective. John, the businessman, summed it up like this: "God helps me do better than I can!"

He will do the same for you.

JOANIE YODER

**May our boast be not in what we do for Christ,
but in what Christ does for us.**

Fervent Love

1 PETER 4:7–11

Above all, love each other deeply, because love covers over a multitude of sins.
1 PETER 4:8

The Greek word for *fervent* pictures a sprinter who is straining every muscle to break the ribbon at the finish line. In other words, we must love with intensity.

Beverly Hamilton was confronted with this kind of challenge when her sister-in-law Clara appeared on her doorstep. Previously, she had ridiculed Beverly's Christian faith, and she had even tried to disrupt her marriage. She had shown no interest in her brother and his wife except when she needed financial help.

Now there she stood in shabby clothing—destitute and friendless. Beverly felt like telling Clara to leave, but she asked for God's help to love her sister-in-law. After inviting her in, Beverly outfitted her with new clothing. She fully realized that Clara might never change her ways, but she knew the Lord wanted her to love her. The Lord honored Beverly's efforts and worked a dramatic change in Clara's heart.

God calls us to love with all our strength. When we do, we'll keep on forgiving. We'll find ways to settle privately the wrongs others do against us. We'll reach out to people no matter how deeply they have fallen. We won't hold their past sins against them, but we'll help them to build a better future. That's the kind of fervent love we owe the lost around us—the kind God in Christ has shown to us.

HERB VANDER LUGT

The measure of our love is the measure of our sacrifice.

Praying in Public

MATTHEW 6:5–8

When you pray, do not be like the hypocrites, for they love to pray standing in the synagogues and on the street corners to be seen by others. Truly I tell you, they have received their reward in full.

MATTHEW 6:5

When Jesus told people to pray in secret, He didn't mean that praying in public is wrong. What He condemned are insincere prayers made only to impress people. We may all sense that subtle temptation at times.

A group of delegates from a Christian conference stopped at a busy restaurant for lunch and were seated at several different tables around the room. Just before eating, one member announced in a loud voice, "Let's pray!" Chairs shifted and heads turned. Then followed a long-winded "blessing" that did more to cool the food than warm hearts. Finally, amid snickers and grumbling, came the welcome "Amen."

Contrast that story with another scene. A history teacher at a large state university was having lunch with his family in the school cafeteria. As they began their meal, their little three-year-old cried out, "O Daddy, we forgot to pray!" "Well, honey," said the man, "would you pray for us?" "Dear Jesus," she began, "thank you for our good food and all these nice people. Amen." From nearby tables came "amens" from profs and students alike who were touched by that child's simple and sincere prayer.

May all our public praying be like that.

DENNIS DEHAAN

If we pray to catch the ear of man, we can't expect to reach the ear of God.

War, Then Peace

LUKE 23:32-43

The peace of God, which transcends all understanding,
will guard your hearts and your minds in Christ Jesus.

PHILIPPIANS 4:7

On December 7, 1941, a Japanese war plane piloted by Mitsuo Fuchida took off from the aircraft carrier *Akagi*. Fuchida led the surprise attack on the US Pacific Fleet at Pearl Harbor, Hawaii. Through the war years to follow, Fuchida continued to fly—often narrowly escaping death. At war's end, he was disillusioned and bitter.

A few years later, he heard a story that piqued his spiritual curiosity: A Christian young woman whose parents had been killed by the Japanese during the war decided to minister to Japanese prisoners. Impressed, Fuchida began reading the Bible.

As he read Jesus's words from the cross: "Father, forgive them, for they do not know what they are doing" (Luke 23:34), he understood how that woman could show kindness to her enemies. That day Fuchida gave his heart to Christ.

Becoming a lay preacher and evangelist to his fellow citizens, this former warrior demonstrated "the peace of God, which transcends all understanding" (Philippians 4:7)—a peace enjoyed by those who have trusted Christ and who "present [their] requests to God" (v. 6).

Have you found this peace? No matter what you have gone through, God makes it available to you.

DENNIS FISHER

True peace is not the absence of war; it is the presence of God.
—Loveless

What God Hates

PROVERBS 6:12–19

Let those who love the LORD hate evil, for he guards the lives of his faithful ones and delivers them from the hand of the wicked.

PSALM 97:10

God hates sin. In our Scripture reading for today, the author of Proverbs singled out seven specific transgressions that are an abomination to the Lord (it would be good to read verses 17–19 often). Sin is so horrible that when the Lord Jesus, the perfect Son of God, bore our guilt on the cross, the Father turned His back on His beloved Son. And Christ, in the blackness of that dreadful hour, cried out, "My God, my God, why have you forsaken me?" (Matthew 27:46). If sin is so terrible in the sight of God, then we must fear it, hate it, and avoid it.

In F. B. Proctor's *Treasury of Quotations* is a story told by Johann Peter Lange, a nineteenth-century German theologian and author. He said that a religious leader was viciously hated by the emperor of his day. Some of the ruler's advisors said to the monarch, "Confiscate his property, put him in irons, or have him killed." But others disagreed. They said, "You will not gain anything by all this; for in exile he would find a home with his God; . . . he kisses his chains, death opens heaven to him. There is only one way to render him unhappy; force him to sin. He fears nothing in the world but sin."

Note that last sentence: "He fears nothing in the world but sin."

But remember how God views sin. May we therefore, as lovers of Him, be haters of sin!

RICHARD DeHAAN

It is not enough for a gardener to love flowers; he must also hate weeds.

Victory Even in Death

1 CORINTHIANS 15:50–58

Therefore, my dear brothers and sisters, stand firm. Let nothing move you.
Always give yourselves fully to the work of the Lord, because you know that
your labor in the Lord is not in vain.

1 CORINTHIANS 15:58

When Harry and Nancy Goehring went to Bangladesh as missionaries, their desire was to see Bengali people become Christians. They did not know that God would use Harry's death at age thirty-two to bring at least one of those people to Jesus.

As the family and friends of the Goehrings met with Nancy and the children to comfort them, Debindra Das, a Bengali laundryman who had become a Christian, spoke with his wife Promilla about Harry's death. He said, "I was ironing the clothes in that hallway. I could see Goehring Sahib through the open door. I watched his face. I watched him die! Goehring Sahib died peacefully. This is what it is like for a Christian to die."

Promilla was impressed. Because of that simple testimony of a Christian's peaceful homegoing, she asked the Lord to save her that very night. That Bengali woman was the firstfruits of a death that had seemed so untimely.

As we do the work of the Lord, we must be "steadfast" and "immovable" (1 Corinthians 15:58 NKJV). But we must leave the results with God. If He can bring victory out of a person's death, think what He can do with a dedicated life.

DAVE BRANON

One person's salvation often depends on another's service.

It's Really True!

ROMANS 8:28–39

And we know that in all things God works for the good of those who love him, who have been called according to his purpose.

ROMANS 8:28

Often we do not know the reason for some of the adversities the Lord allows, and only heaven will reveal how the Divine purposes were accomplished through them.

William Carey and two of his missionary associates in India are examples of Christians who trusted the Lord in spite of what appeared to be a terrible setback to their labors. In March of 1812 a devastating fire swept through one of their buildings where they had been working on translating the Bible in the languages of India. They lost a large amount of newly cast type, nearly all of their Indian versions of the Bible, the Bengali dictionary, and much vital equipment. Undismayed, they went back to work. Within months they began to understand why the "disaster" had occurred. When the news of the fire reached England, many people were awakened from their spiritual lethargy. Thousands became burdened for the lost and were moved to give sacrificially for the spread of the gospel. Out of a seeming tragedy was born a new missionary zeal among God's children, and the work in India advanced as never before.

Indeed, all things do "work for the good of those who love [God]," and nothing can ever separate us from His care. Even when we may not see it immediately, believe it anyway; for it's really true!

HERB VANDER LUGT

No affliction would trouble the child of God if he only knew the Lord's blessed reason for sending it!

Unlikely Heroes

HEBREWS 11:17–31

*Faith is confidence in what we hope for and assurance
about what we do not see.*

HEBREWS 11:1

The Lord makes heroes out of very unlikely people. One such person is Angie Garber. She was born with a severe facial deformity. The surgery to correct her appearance left her deaf in one ear.

In her teens, Angie contracted polio. She survived, but after months of agonizing therapy and exercise her left leg and arm remained weak. During this difficult time her mother became ill. Angie and one of her sisters cared for their mom till she died.

Her brother George, who had been Angie's key encourager, died in an accident. And then crop failure made it necessary to sell the family farm.

Through it all, Angie kept praying that she could someday serve the Lord as a missionary-teacher. God honored her desire, and five years after her mother's death Angie began working as a teacher for a Navajo mission. She became such an effective Christian worker that two books were written about her. Angie faced incredible obstacles in her walk of faith. Yet, like the heroes of faith listed in Hebrews 11, she continued to trust God—serving the Navajo people for forty-seven years. Angie Garber, who as a newborn was not expected to live, died in 2006 at the age of ninety-four.

If you're discouraged and feel like giving up, remember, God makes spiritual heroes out of unlikely people.

HERB VANDER LUGT

Suffering can prepare ordinary Christians for extraordinary service.

Love for Children

MATTHEW 18:1–10

One day some parents brought their children to Jesus
so he could lay his hands on them and pray for them. But the disciples
scolded the parents for bothering him.

MATTHEW 19:13 NLT

Thomas Barnado entered the London Hospital medical school in 1865, dreaming of life as a medical missionary in China. Barnado soon discovered a desperate need in his own front yard—the many homeless children living and dying on the streets of London. He determined to do something about this horrendous situation. Developing homes for destitute children in London's east end, Barnado rescued some 60,000 boys and girls. Theologian John Stott said, "Today we might call him the patron saint of street kids."

Jesus said, "Let the children come to me. Don't stop them! For the Kingdom of Heaven belongs to those who are like these children" (Matthew 19:14 NLT). Imagine the surprise the crowds—and Jesus's own disciples—must have felt at this declaration. In the ancient world, children had little value and were largely relegated to the margins of life. Yet Jesus welcomed, blessed, and valued children.

James, a New Testament writer, challenged Christ-followers saying, "Pure and genuine religion in the sight of God the Father means caring for orphans . . . in their distress" (James 1:27 NLT). Today, like those first-century orphans, children of every social strata, ethnicity, and family environment are at risk due to neglect, human trafficking, abuse, drugs, and more. How can we honor the Father who loves us by showing His care for these little ones Jesus welcomes?

BILL CROWDER

Be an expression of the love of Jesus.

Carried in His Strong Arms

ISAIAH 46:1–11

*Even to your old age and gray hairs I am he, I am he who will sustain you.
I have made you and I will carry you; I will sustain you and I will rescue you.*

ISAIAH 46:4

Missionary couple Ray and Sophie de le Haye served heroically in West Africa for more than forty years. As she grew older, Sophie suffered from the loss of all motor control of her body. This once-strong servant of Christ, who had carried out a ministry of unimaginable stress, was suddenly reduced to helplessness, unable to button her clothes or lift a cup of water to her lips. But she refused to become bitter or self-pitying. In her moments of utter weakness, she would quietly remind herself, "For this you have Jesus."

Many centuries ago our heavenly Father gave a reassuring message to a burdened prophet of Israel—a message that we need today: "Listen to me, you descendants of Jacob, . . . you whom I have upheld since your birth, and have carried since you were born. Even to your old age and gray hairs I am he, I am he who will sustain you. I have made you and I will carry you; I will sustain you and I will rescue you" (Isaiah 46:3–4).

What an encouraging picture of divine grace! It calls to mind the Good Shepherd carrying a helpless lamb. Whether young or old, we can learn to let God carry us. Weak and burdened, we can lean on His everlasting arms and remind ourselves, "For this I have Jesus."

VERNON GROUNDS

You can rest in the arms of Jesus—He'll never let you down.

Touched by Calvary's Love

ISAIAH 53

*For I resolved to know nothing while I was with you except
Jesus Christ and him crucified.*
1 CORINTHIANS 2:2

When Moravian missionaries first went to Greenland, they found the people totally ignorant of the meaning of such words as *sin, righteousness,* and *justification.* So the missionaries began to educate them about various theological terms. The results were so unproductive that after a time the missionaries decided that the situation was hopeless and they might just as well leave.

Since no ship was due for some time, one of the missionaries began translating parts of the New Testament into the native tongue. Seeking to test the accuracy of his work, he read a passage to those who had been unresponsive to his ministry. The portion he chose was Christ's suffering and death on the cross.

After he finished, the chief of the tribe asked him to repeat it. The missionary read the passage again. "Why didn't you tell us about this in the first place?" inquired the leader. "Don't leave now! We'd be happy to listen to the words of a Man who suffered that much for us."

The Moravians remained and continued to tell the people about Jesus. The story of the cross had won the people's hearts.

We too have the opportunity of telling others of the love that led Christ to die for them. Let's make the cross the focus of our witness.

HENRY BOSCH

We are not saved by reciting a creed but by receiving Christ.

Fiber Man

PSALM 1

But whose delight is in the law of the LORD, and who meditates on his law day and night. That person is like a tree planted by streams of water, which yields its fruit in season and whose leaf does not wither—whatever they do prospers.

PSALM 1:2–3

Dr. Denis Burkitt (1911–1993) achieved fame for discovering the cause and cure of a disease named after him—Burkitt's lymphoma. He also received widespread acclaim for demonstrating the benefits of a fiber-rich diet, which earned him the amusing nickname "Fiber Man."

What many people don't know, however, is that Dr. Burkitt was not merely a great medical pioneer but he was also a dedicated servant of God who daily spent much time in prayer and meditation on God's Word. He observed, "I am convinced that a downgrading in priority of . . . prayer and biblical meditation is a major cause of weakness in many Christian communities. . . . Bible study demands pondering deeply on a short passage, like a cow chewing her cud. It is better to read a little and ponder a lot than to read a lot and ponder a little."

Dr. Burkitt didn't leave just a great legacy of healing; he left an example of personal holiness and closeness with the Lord. The secret was his lifelong habit of setting aside a specific time for prayer and reflection on God's Word.

Few of us will ever enjoy accomplishments like his, but by following the prescription of Psalm 1 we can attain the same spiritual health that he did.

HADDON ROBINSON

God speaks to those who take the time to listen.

By the Spirit's Power

ZECHARIAH 4:1–7

What are you, mighty mountain?
Before Zerubbabel you will become level ground.
ZECHARIAH 4:7

What do you do when there's a mountain in your way? The story of Dashrath Manjhi can inspire us. When his wife died because he was unable to get her to the hospital to receive urgent medical care, Manjhi did what seemed impossible. He spent twenty-two years chiseling a massive gap in a mountain so other villagers could get to the local hospital to receive the medical care they needed. Before he died, the government of India celebrated him for his achievement.

Rebuilding the temple must have looked impossible to Zerubbabel, one of the leaders of Israel who returned from exile. The people were discouraged, faced opposition from their enemies, and lacked resources or a big army. But God sent Zechariah to remind Zerubbabel that the task would take something more powerful than military strength, individual power, or man-made resources. It would take the Spirit's power (Zechariah 4:6). With the assurance of divine aid, Zerubbabel trusted that God would level any mountain of difficulty that stood in the way of rebuilding the temple and restoring the community (v. 7).

What do we do when there is a "mountain" before us? We have two options: rely on our own strength or trust the Spirit's power. When we trust His power, He will either level the mountain or give us the strength and endurance to climb over it.

MARVIN WILLIAMS

Human power is inadequate to accomplish God's purposes.

As Advertised

JOHN 16:25–33

"I have told you these things, so that in me you may have peace. In this world you will have trouble. But take heart! I have overcome the world."

JOHN 16:33

During a vacation, my husband and I signed up for a leisurely rafting tour down Georgia's Chattahoochee River. Dressed in sandals, a sundress, and a wide brimmed hat, I groaned when we discovered—contrary to the advertisement—that the trip included light rapids. Grateful for my life jacket, I screamed and gripped the plastic handle on the raft until we reached the muddy bank downriver. I stepped onto the shore and dumped water from my purse as my husband helped me wring out the hem of my soaked dress. We enjoyed a good laugh, even though the trip had not turned out as advertised.

Unlike the tour brochure, which clearly left out a key detail about the trip, Jesus explicitly warned His disciples that rough waters were ahead. He told them that they'd be persecuted and martyred and that He would die and be resurrected. He also guaranteed His trustworthiness, affirming that He would guide them toward undeniable triumph and everlasting hope (John 16:16–33).

Although it would be nice if life were easier when we follow Jesus, He promised to be with us. Trials won't define, limit, or destroy God's plan for us, because Jesus's resurrection has already propelled us to eternal victory.

XOCHITL DIXON

Jesus promises to be with us through the roughest waters.

Gentle Jesus

MATTHEW 18:1–10

And he said: "Truly I tell you, unless you change and become like little children, you will never enter the kingdom of heaven."

MATTHEW 18:3

Charles Wesley (1707–1788) was a Methodist evangelist who wrote more than 9,000 hymns and sacred poems. Some, like "O for a Thousand Tongues to Sing," are great, soaring hymns of praise. But his poem "Gentle Jesus, Meek and Mild," first published in 1742, is a child's quiet prayer that captures the essence of how all of us should seek the Lord in sincere, simple faith.

> *Loving Jesus, gentle Lamb,*
> *In Thy gracious hands I am;*
> *Make me, Savior, what Thou art,*
> *Live Thyself within my heart.*

When some followers of Jesus were jockeying for position in His kingdom, the Lord "called a little child to Him, and placed the child among them. And he said: 'Truly I tell you, unless you change and become like little children, you will never enter the kingdom of heaven'" (Matthew 18:2–3).

Not many children seek position or power. They want acceptance and security. They cling to adults who love and care for them. Jesus never turned children away.

The last stanza of Wesley's poem shows a childlike desire to be just like Jesus: "I shall then show forth Thy praise / Serve Thee all my happy days; / Then the world shall always see / Christ, the holy Child, in me."

DAVID MCCASLAND

Faith shines brightest in a childlike heart.

What God Can Do

2 CORINTHIANS 5:14–21

Therefore, if anyone is in Christ, the new creation has come:
The old has gone, the new is here!
2 CORINTHIANS 5:17

Some people look at the cruelty and inhumanity in our world and conclude that there cannot be a loving God. A better perspective, however, might be to think about how bad the world would be if He didn't exist.

Take, for example, the case of Iketa, a man who for years was the source of much suffering in the jungles of Ecuador. He murdered so many people that he couldn't even recall how many. And in 1956, he killed Nate Saint, an American missionary who had gone to Ecuador to work with the Huaorani people.

But then God intervened. Through the witness of the missionaries who were left behind and who refused to be frightened off, Iketa eventually became a Christian. He was on hand in the summer of 1992 when Marge Van Der Puy, Nate Saint's wife at the time of his martyrdom, visited the Huaorani and presented them with a New Testament in their language. The evil in Iketa has been conquered through the power of God in his life. His faith in Jesus Christ made him a new creation.

The evil and cruelty in our world are not evidence that God does not exist, but that people have refused to be reconciled to Him. Iketa's transformed life shows us that there is a God, and that He has power to change people.

DAVE BRANON

Christ produces a change within that breaks the chains of sin.

Faith in Action

JAMES 2:14–26

But someone will say, "You have faith; I have deeds." Show me your faith without deeds, and I will show you my faith by my deeds.

JAMES 2:18

As a friend drove to the grocery store, she noticed a woman walking along the side of the road and felt she should turn the car around and offer her a ride. When she did, she was saddened to hear that the woman didn't have money for the bus so was walking home many miles in the hot and humid weather. Not only was she making the long journey home, but she had also walked several hours that morning to arrive at work by 4 a.m.

By offering a ride, my friend put into practice in a modern setting James's instruction for Christians to live out their faith with their deeds: "Faith by itself, if it is not accompanied by action, is dead" (v. 17). He was concerned that the church take care of the widows and the orphans (James 1:27), and he also wanted them to rely not on empty words but to act on their faith with deeds of love.

We are saved by faith, not works, but we live out our faith by loving others and caring for their needs. May we, like my friend who offered the ride, keep our eyes open for those who might need our help as we walk together in this journey of life.

AMY BOUCHER PYE

We live out our faith through our good deeds.

Why We're Here

MATTHEW 5:13–16

"You are the light of the world. A town built on a hill cannot be hidden."
MATTHEW 5:14

When Mark and Alice Westlind were missionaries in Colombia, they sent out this note in a prayer letter to those who stood behind their work:

"Driving through Christmas traffic, fighting the drizzling rain, I chanced on a four-year-old little girl. She was wet and cold and shaking. Her clothes were ragged, her hair was matted, and her nose was running. She walked between the cars at the stoplight, washing headlights because she was too short to wash windshields. A few gave her coins, others honked at her to get away from their vehicles."

I admired the honesty of the Westlinds' next sentence, because I have felt the same way. "As I drove away only some fifty cents poorer, I raged at God for the injustice in the world that allowed the situation. 'God, how could you just stand by, helpless?'" The missionary concluded, "Later that evening, God came to me softly with that still small voice and responded not in like kind to my rage, but with tenderness, 'I *have* done something. I created you.'"

Jesus came as light to our sin-darkened, cruel, unfair world. As we respond with compassion and goodness to suffering people, we proclaim His life-changing power. We can't solve all the world's problems, but we can bear witness to the Light that is Jesus and bring glory to the Father (Matthew 5:16).

DAVID EGNER

Opportunities to be kind are never hard to find.

God's Special Place

LUKE 2:1–7

She gave birth to her firstborn, a son. She wrapped him in cloths and placed him in a manger, because there was no guest room available for them.

LUKE 2:7

As a young girl in the late 1920s, Grace Ditmanson Adams often traveled with her missionary parents throughout inland China. Later, she wrote about those trips and the crowded places where they stayed overnight—village inns full of people coughing, sneezing, and smoking, while babies cried and children complained. Her family put their bedrolls on board-covered trestles in a large room with everyone else.

One snowy night, they arrived at an inn to find it packed full. The innkeeper expressed his regret, then paused and said, "Follow me." He led them to a side room used to store straw and farm equipment. There they slept in a quiet place of their own.

After that, whenever Grace read that Mary "gave birth to her firstborn, a son. She wrapped him in cloths and placed him in a manger, because there was no guest room available for them" (Luke 2:7), she saw the event differently. While some described the innkeeper as an example of uncaring, sinful mankind who rejected the Savior, Grace said, "I truly believe that Almighty God used the innkeeper as the arranger for a healthier place than the crowded inn—a place of privacy."

Through eyes of faith, we see God's provision for Mary. Look for the ways He provides for you.

DAVID MCCASLAND

Those who let God provide will be satisfied.

A Real Man

MATTHEW 1:18–25

Because Joseph her husband was faithful to the law, and yet did not want to expose her to public disgrace, he had in mind to divorce her quietly.
MATTHEW 1:19

He was a young Middle-Easterner who was looking forward to the day when he and his betrothed could live as husband and wife. He was poor, but that didn't matter much, because the two of them shared a love for each other and a devotion to God. He was content to spend his days of anticipation making wood products for the people of his village.

But one day some devastating news shattered his future: his young lady was pregnant. He knew he was not the father, yet he responded gallantly. He didn't desert her. He knew she faced a prospect worse than his embarrassment—public disgrace. So he devised a plan to deal with the matter privately. Before he could take action, though, a messenger told him that this baby was not the worst news of his life; it was the best news the world had ever known. His betrothed would bear the Messiah. She was "with child of the Holy Spirit" (v. 18 NKJV). He was told to complete the marriage and to call the baby *Jesus*. Bravely, Joseph did as he was commanded.

Joseph was a "real man." He was just. He was committed to Mary. He was compassionate. He knew the Scriptures. He loved and obeyed God.

Looking for a model of a real man? Look no further than the Nazareth workshop.

DAVE BRANON

Circumstances do not make a man; they reveal what he's made of.

A Thrill of Hope

LUKE 2:11–30

*Today in the town of David a Savior has been born to you;
he is the Messiah, the Lord.*

LUKE 2:11

Reginald Fessenden had been working for years to achieve wireless radio communication. He claimed that on December 24, 1906, he became the first person to ever play music over the radio.

Fessenden held a contract with a fruit company that had installed wireless systems on roughly a dozen boats to communicate about the harvesting and marketing of bananas. That Christmas Eve, Fessenden said that he told the wireless operators on board all ships to pay attention. At 9 o'clock they heard his voice.

He reportedly pulled out his violin, playing "O Holy Night" and singing the words to the last verse as he played. Finally, he offered Christmas greetings and read from Luke 2 the story of angels announcing the birth of a Savior.

Both the shepherds in Bethlehem over two thousand years ago and the sailors on board the United Fruit Company ships in 1906 heard an unexpected, surprising message of hope on a dark night. And God still speaks that same message of hope to us today. A Savior has been born for us—Christ the Lord! (Luke 2:11). We can join the choir of angels and believers through the ages who respond with "Glory to God in the highest heaven, and on earth peace to those on whom his favor rests" (v. 14).

AMY PETERSON

Without Christ there is no hope.
—Charles Spurgeon

Are You Glad or Glum?

MATTHEW 2:1–12

When they saw the star, they were overjoyed.
MATTHEW 2:10

A little girl became ill on Christmas Day and was taken to the hospital. Lying in her bed, she heard carolers singing. She listened intently while one of the singers told how Christ had come to redeem a lost world. With childlike faith she received salvation by trusting Jesus.

Later she said to a nurse, "I know I'll have to go home as soon as I'm well, but I'll take Jesus with me. Isn't it wonderful why He was born? He came to save us." "Yes," said the nurse wearily, "that's an old story." "Oh, do you know about Jesus too? You didn't look like you do." "Why, how did I look?" she asked. "Oh, like a lot of folks—sort of glum," replied the girl. "I thought if you really understood that He came to bring us to heaven, you would be glad."

The coming of the Lord Jesus into the world nearly 2,000 years ago was a glorious event. Those who heard the good news that a Savior was born worshipped the new King with awe and wonder. Lowly shepherds returned from the manger glorifying and praising God, and later the wise men from the East were filled with exceeding joy as the guiding star led them to the Christ-child.

Once we know the saving power of the One who was born in Bethlehem, the joy of salvation should radiate from our lives. At this season of the year, we have every reason to be glad, not glum!

HENRY BOSCH

One of the best Yuletide decorations is a Christian wreathed in smiles.

Christmas Sacrifice

GALATIANS 4:1–7

When the set time had fully come, God sent his Son.
GALATIANS 4:4

O. Henry's classic tale "The Gift of the Magi" tells of Jim and Della, a young married couple who are struggling financially. As Christmas approaches they want to give special gifts to each other, but their lack of money drives them to drastic measures. Jim's prized possession is a gold watch, while Della's is her long, beautiful hair. So Jim sells his watch in order to buy combs for Della's hair, while Della sells her hair to buy a chain for Jim's watch.

The story has deservedly become beloved, for it reminds us that sacrifice is at the heart of true love, and sacrifice is love's truest measure. This idea is particularly appropriate for Christmas, because sacrifice is the heartbeat of the story of the birth of Christ. Jesus Christ was born to die, and He was born to die for us. That is why the angel told Joseph, "You are to give him the name Jesus, because he will save his people from their sins" (Matthew 1:21).

Long before Christ's birth, it had been determined that He would come to rescue us from our fallenness—which means that we can never fully appreciate the manger unless we see it in the shadow of the cross. Christmas is completely about Christ's love, seen most clearly in His sacrifice for us.

BILL CROWDER

**The essential fact of Christianity is that God
thought all humanity worth the sacrifice of His Son.**
—William Barclay

The Bond of Peace

EPHESIANS 4:1–6

Make every effort to keep the unity of the Spirit through the bond of peace.
EPHESIANS 4:3

After I confronted my friend by email over a matter on which we had differed, she didn't respond. Had I overstepped? I didn't want to worsen the situation by pestering her, but neither did I want to leave things unresolved before she went on a trip overseas. As she popped into my mind throughout the following days, I prayed for her, unsure of the way forward. Then one morning I went for a walk in our local park and saw her, pain etched on her face as she glimpsed me. "Thank you, Lord, that I can talk to her," I breathed as I approached her with a welcoming smile. We talked openly and were able to resolve matters.

Sometimes when hurt or silence intrudes on our relationships, mending them seems out of our control. But as the apostle Paul says in his letter to the church at Ephesus, we are called to work for peace and unity through God's Spirit, donning the garments of gentleness, humility, and patience as we seek God's healing in our relationships. The Lord yearns for us to be united, and through His Spirit He can bring His people together—even unexpectedly when we go walking in the park.

AMY BOUCHER PYE

God desires unity among believers.

Our Guilt Is Gone

PSALM 32:1-11

Then I acknowledged my sin to you and did not cover up my iniquity. I said, "I will confess my transgressions to the LORD." And you forgave the guilt of my sin.

PSALM 32:5

As a young girl, I invited a friend to browse with me through a gift shop near my home. She shocked me, though, by shoving a handful of colorful crayon-shaped barrettes into my pocket and yanking me out the door of the shop without paying for them. Guilt gnawed at me for a week before I approached my mom—my confession pouring out as quickly as my tears.

Grieved over my bad choice of not resisting my friend, I returned the stolen items, apologized, and vowed never to steal again. The owner told me never to come back. But because my mom forgave me and assured me that I had done my best to make things right, I slept peacefully that night.

King David also rested in forgiveness through confession (Psalm 32:1–2). He had hidden his sins against Bathsheba and Uriah (2 Samuel 11–12) until his "strength was sapped" (Psalm 32:3–4). But once David refused to "cover up" his wrongs, the Lord erased his guilt (v. 5). God protected him "from trouble" and wrapped him in "songs of deliverance" (v. 7). David rejoiced because the "LORD's unfailing love surrounds the one who trusts in him" (v. 10).

The Lord can empower us to enjoy freedom from the bondage of sin and peace through confession, as He confirms that our guilt is gone—forever.

XOCHITL DIXON

When God forgives, our guilt is gone.

We're Not Alone

GENESIS 14

He blessed Abram, saying, "Blessed be Abram by God Most High, Creator of heaven and earth."
GENESIS 14:19

Abram's nephew was in a lot of trouble. The kings of Sodom and Gomorrah, where Lot lived, had been overtaken by a group of marauding kings. They sacked Sodom, captured Lot and his household, and then fled north.

When Abram heard that his brother's son had been kidnapped, he rounded up 318 trained servants, gave chase, and rescued Lot.

What happened next is even more remarkable. Melchizedek, the king of Salem, visited Abram to congratulate him and to bless him in the name of "God Most High, Creator of heaven and earth" (Genesis 14:19).

This was unheard of. In those days, people invoked the names of Baal and other false local deities. So it was remarkable that Abram, who was just learning to trust the God of the universe, would be visited by a ruler who shared his faith in the one true God.

Sometimes we might feel that all around us are people who don't know the God of the Bible. They may speak of religion or faith, but genuine trust in the Lord of the universe seems to be the exception. That shouldn't stop us.

Abram was surrounded by people who didn't know God—yet he kept the faith. So must we, especially during those times when we feel all alone.

DAVE BRANON

When you walk with God, you'll be out of step with the world.

To Know God Is Enough

JOB 42:1–6

My ears had heard of you but now my eyes have seen you.
JOB 42:5

Job could not fully comprehend the reason for some of the trials he had to endure, yet he found peace and joy through his relationship with God. Although he went through a time of severe testing, he still affirmed, "My ears had heard of you but now my eyes have seen you." He did not claim to have a complete answer to the problem of human suffering, but the Lord had become so real to him that just knowing Him was enough.

Elisabeth Elliot made a similar discovery in a time of severe testing. When she received news that her missionary husband Jim had been martyred by tribesmen in Ecuador in January 1956, she was shaken but not to the point of complete despair. She trusted the truths of the Bible, and she was walking in daily fellowship with the Lord. She also believed that her heavenly Father had permitted this tragedy for some good purpose. The confidence she had in the all-wise God enabled her to write to a friend, saying, "Only in acceptance lies peace—not in forgetting nor in resignation nor in busyness. God's will is good and acceptable and perfect."

No matter how difficult life's circumstances prove to be, you can face the future with courage. Your heavenly Father is both loving and holy. Tell Him you trust Him because of His love for you. Then, with a new sense of His presence, you will discover that knowing Him is all you need.

HERB VANDER LUGT

Those who see God's hand in everything can best leave everything in God's hands.

The Last Word

JOHN 11:17–27

Jesus said to her, "I am the resurrection and the life. He who believes in Me, though he may die, he shall live."

JOHN 11:25 NKJV

When Walter Bouman, a retired seminary professor, learned that the cancer in his body had spread and that he had perhaps nine months to live, he pondered many things. One was comedian Johnny Carson's quip: "It is true that for several days after you die, your hair and fingernails keep on growing, but the phone calls taper off." He found that humor to be a wonderful tonic, but it was something far deeper that sustained his soul.

In Bouman's newspaper column, he wrote of his greatest source of encouragement: "The Christian good news is that Jesus of Nazareth has been raised from death, that death no longer has dominion over Him. I have bet my living, and now I am called to bet my dying, that Jesus will have the last word."

In John 11, we read what Jesus said to Martha, a close friend who was grieving the death of her brother. He said: "I am the resurrection and the life. He who believes in Me, even though he may die, he shall live. And whoever lives and believes in Me shall never die" (vv. 25–26 NKJV).

For each "today" we are given, and for the inevitable "tomorrow" that will come, we don't have to be afraid. Jesus Christ is with all who trust Him, and He will have the last word.

DAVID MCCASLAND

**Because Jesus has risen from the dead,
He has the last word in life and in death.**

OUR DAILY BREAD WRITERS

JAMES BANKS
Pastor of Peace Church in Durham, North Carolina, Dr. James Banks has written several books for Discovery House, including *Praying Together* and *Praying the Prayers of the Bible for Your Everyday Needs*. He and his wife, Cari, have two adult children.

HENRY BOSCH (1914–1995)
Henry G. Bosch was the founder of *Our Daily Bread* and one of its first writers. Throughout his life, he battled illness but turned his weaknesses into spiritual encouragement for others through his devotional writing.

DAVE BRANON
An editor with Discovery House, Dave has been involved with *Our Daily Bread* since the 1980s. He has written seventeen books, including *Beyond the Valley*, *Stand Firm*, and *Living the Psalms Life* for Discovery House.

ANNE CETAS
After becoming a Christian in her late teens, Anne was introduced to *Our Daily Bread* right away and began reading it. Now she reads it for a living as senior content editor of *Our Daily Bread*. She has also written *Our Daily Bread* articles since 2004.

POH FANG CHIA
Like Anne Cetas, Poh Fang trusted Jesus Christ as Savior as a teenager. She is an editor and a part of the Chinese editorial review committee serving in the Our Daily Bread Ministries Singapore office.

BILL CROWDER
A former pastor who is now vice president of ministry content for Our Daily Bread Ministries, Bill travels extensively as a Bible conference teacher, sharing God's truths with fellow believers in Malaysia and Singapore and other places where ODB Ministries has international offices. His published books include *Seeing the Heart of Christ* and *For This He Came: Jesus' Journey to the Cross*.

LAWRENCE DARMANI

A noted novelist and publisher in Ghana, Lawrence is editor of *Step* magazine and CEO of Step Publishers. He and his family live in Accra, Ghana. His book *Grief Child* earned him the Commonwealth Writers' Prize as best first book by a writer in Africa.

DENNIS DEHAAN (1932–2014)

When *Our Daily Bread*'s original editor Henry Bosch retired, Dennis became the second managing editor of the publication. A former pastor, he loved preaching and teaching the Word of God. Dennis went to be with the Lord in 2014.

MART DEHAAN

The former president of Our Daily Bread Ministries, Mart followed in the footsteps of his grandfather M. R. and his dad Richard in that capacity. Mart, who was associated with *Day of Discovery* as host of the program from Israel for many years, is now senior content advisor for Our Daily Bread Ministries. He can be heard daily on the radio program *Discover the Word*.

M. R. DEHAAN (1891–1965)

Dr. M. R. DeHaan founded this ministry in 1938 when his radio program went out over the air in Detroit, Michigan, and eventually Radio Bible Class was begun. He was president of the ministry in 1956 when *Our Daily Bread* was first published.

RICHARD DEHAAN (1923–2002)

Son of the founder of Our Daily Bread Ministries, Dr. M. R. DeHaan, Richard was responsible for the ministry's entrance into television. Under his leadership, *Day of Discovery* television made its debut in 1968. The program was on the air continuously until 2016.

XOCHITL DIXON

Xochitl (soh-cheel) equips and encourages readers to embrace God's grace and grow deeper in their personal relationships with Christ and others. Serving as an author, speaker, and blogger at xedixon.com, she enjoys singing, reading, motherhood, and being married to her best friend, Dr. W. Alan Dixon Sr.

DAVID EGNER

A retired Our Daily Bread Ministries editor and longtime *Our Daily Bread* writer, David was also a college professor during his working career. In fact, he was a writing instructor for both Anne Cetas and Julie Ackerman Link at Cornerstone University.

DENNIS FISHER

For many years, Dennis was senior research editor at Our Daily Bread Ministries—using his theological training to guarantee biblical accuracy. He is also an expert in C. S. Lewis studies. He and his wife, Janet, a former university professor, have retired to Northern California.

VERNON GROUNDS (1914–2010)

A longtime college president (Denver Seminary) and board member for Our Daily Bread Ministries, Vernon's life story was told in the Discovery House book *Transformed by Love*. Dr. Grounds died in 2010 at the age of 96.

TIM GUSTAFSON

Tim writes for *Our Daily Bread* and serves as an editor for Discovery Series. As the son of missionaries to Ghana, Tim has an unusual perspective on life in the West. He and his wife, Leisa, have one daughter and seven sons.

C. P. HIA

Hia Chek Phang and his wife, Lin Choo, reside in the island nation of Singapore. C. P. came to faith in Jesus Christ at the age of thirteen. During his early years as a believer, he was privileged to learn from excellent Bible teachers who instilled in him a love for God's Word. He is special assistant to the president of Our Daily Bread Ministries, and he helps with translating resources for the ministry. He and his wife have a son, daughter-in-law, grandson, and granddaughter.

CINDY HESS KASPER

A retired editor for the Our Daily Bread Ministries publication *Our Daily Journey* and other publications, Cindy began writing for *Our Daily Bread* in 2006. She and her husband, Tom, have three children and seven grandchildren.

RANDY KILGORE

Randy spent most of his 20-plus years in business as a senior human resource manager before returning to seminary. Since finishing his Master in Divinity in 2000, he has served as a writer and workplace chaplain. A collection of his devotionals appears in the Discovery House book *Made to Matter: Devotions for Working Christians*. Randy and his wife, Cheryl, and their two children live in Massachusetts.

LESLIE KOH

Born and raised in Singapore, Leslie spent more than fifteen years as a journalist in the busy newsroom of local newspaper *The Straits Times* before moving to Our Daily Bread Ministries. He's found moving from bad news to good news most rewarding, and he still believes that nothing reaches out to people better than a good, compelling story. He likes traveling, running, editing, and writing.

ALBERT LEE

Albert Lee was director of international ministries for Our Daily Bread Ministries for many years, and he lives in Singapore. Albert's passion, vision, and energy expanded the work of the ministry around the world. Albert grew up in Singapore, and took a variety of courses from Singapore Bible College, as well as served with Singapore Youth for Christ from 1971–1999. Albert appreciates art and collects paintings. He and his wife, Catherine, have two children.

JULIE ACKERMAN LINK (1950–2015)

A book editor by profession, Julie began writing for *Our Daily Bread* in 2000. Her books *Above All, Love, 100 Prayers Inspired by the Psalms*, and *Hope for All Seasons* are available through Discovery House. Julie lost her long battle with cancer in April 2015.

DAVID MCCASLAND

Living in Colorado, David enjoys the beauty of God's grandeur as displayed in the Rocky Mountains. An accomplished biographer, David has written several books, including the award-winning *Oswald Chambers: Abandoned to God* and *Eric Liddell: Pure Gold*.

KEILA OCHOA

Keila, who teaches in an international school, also assists with Media Associates International, a group that trains writers around the world to write about faith. She and her husband have two young children.

AMY PETERSON

Amy Peterson works with the Honors program at Taylor University. She has a B.A. in English Literature from Texas A&M and an M.A. in Intercultural Studies from Wheaton College. Amy taught ESL for two years in Southeast Asia before returning stateside to teach. She is the author of the book *Dangerous Territory: My Misguided Quest to Save the World*.

AMY BOUCHER PYE

Amy is a writer, editor, and speaker. The author of *Finding Myself in Britain: Our Search for Faith, Home, and True Identity*, she runs the Woman Alive book club in the UK and enjoys life with her family in their English vicarage.

HADDON ROBINSON (1931–2017)

Haddon, a renowned expert on preaching, served many years as a seminary professor. He wrote numerous books and hundreds of magazine articles. For a number of years he was a panelist on Our Daily Bread Ministries' radio program *Discover the Word*. Dr. Robinson went home to his eternal reward on July 22, 2017.

DAVID ROPER

David Roper lives in Idaho, where he takes advantage of the natural beauty of his state. He has been writing for *Our Daily Bread* since 2000, and he has published several successful books with Discovery House, including *Out of the Ordinary* and *Teach Us to Number Our Days*.

JENNIFER BENSON SCHULDT

Chicagoan Jennifer Schuldt writes from the perspective of a mom of a growing family. She has written for *Our Daily Bread* since 2010. For several years, she also penned articles for another Our Daily Bread Ministries publication: *Our Daily Journey*.

JOE STOWELL

As president of Cornerstone University, Joe stays connected to today's young adults in a leadership role. A popular speaker and a former pastor, Joe has written a number of books over the years, including *Strength for the Journey* and *Jesus Nation*.

MARION STROUD (1940–2015)

After a battle with cancer, Marion went to be with her Savior in August 2015. Marion began writing devotional articles for *Our Daily Bread* in 2014. Two of her popular books of prayers, *Dear God, It's Me and It's Urgent* and *It's Just You and Me, Lord*, were published by Discovery House.

HERB VANDER LUGT (1920–2006)

For many years, Herb was senior research editor at Our Daily Bread Ministries, responsible for checking the biblical accuracy of the literature published by the ministry. A World War II veteran, Herb spent several years as a pastor before his ODB tenure began. Herb went to be with his Lord and Savior in 2006.

PAUL VAN GORDER (1921–2009)

A writer for *Our Daily Bread* in the 1980s and 1990s, Paul was a noted pastor and Bible teacher—both in the Atlanta area where he lived and through the *Day of Discovery* TV program. Paul's earthly journey ended in 2009.

SHERIDAN VOYSEY

Sheridan Voysey is a writer, speaker, and broadcaster based in Oxford, England. Sheridan has authored several books including *Resurrection Year: Turning Broken Dreams into New Beginnings* and *Resilient: Your Invitation to a Jesus-Shaped Life*. For many years Sheridan was the host of *Open House*, a live talk show heard around Australia every Sunday night exploring life, faith, and culture.

JOANIE YODER (1934–2004)

For ten years, until her death in 2004, Joanie wrote for *Our Daily Bread*. In addition, she published the book *God Alone* with Discovery House.

MARVIN WILLIAMS

Marvin's first foray into Our Daily Bread Ministries came as a writer for *Our Daily Journey*. In 2007, he penned his first *Our Daily Bread* article. Marvin is senior teaching pastor at a church in Lansing, Michigan.

Enjoy this book? Help us get the word out!

Share a link to the book or
mention it on social media

Write a review on your blog, on a retailer site,
or on our website (dhp.org)

Pick up another copy to share with someone

Recommend this book for your
church, book club, or small group

Follow Discovery House on
social media and join the discussion

Contact us to share your thoughts:

 @discoveryhouse    @DiscoveryHouse

Discovery House
P.O. Box 3566
Grand Rapids, MI 49501 USA

Phone: 1-800-653-8333
Email: books@dhp.org
Web: dhp.org